SH 21-76

US ARMY TRAINING MANUAL

RANGER
HANDBOOK

"NOT FOR THE WEAK OR FAINTHEARTED"

2000

CIVILIAN REFERENCE EDITION – UNABRIDGED "BLACK COVER" REISSUE

MANUAL OF ARMY RANGER TRAINING, WILDERNESS OPERATIONS, MOUNTAINEERING, AND SURVIVAL

US ARMY INFANTRY TRAINING SCHOOL, RANGER TRAINING BRIGADE

Doublebit Press
Eugene. OR

Doublebit Press is an imprint of Eagle Nest Press
www.doublebitpress.com
Eugene, OR, USA

Original content under the public domain; unrestricted for civilian distribution.
Originally published in 2000 US Department of the Army, Infantry Training
School, Ranger Training Brigade

This title, along with other Doublebit Press books are available at a volume
discount for youth groups, clubs, or reading groups. Contact Doublebit Press at
info@doublebitpress.com for more information.

Military Outdoors Skills Series: Volume 5

Doublebit Press Civilian Reference Edition ISBNs
Hardcover: 978-1-64389-037-1
Paperback: 978-1-64389-038-8

First Doublebit Press Civilian Reference Edition Printing, 2019

Printed in the United States of America
when purchased at retail in the USA

The Military Outdoors Skills Series
Historic Field Manuals and Military Guides
on Outdoors Skills and Travel

Military manuals contain essential knowledge about outdoors life, thriving while in the field, and self-sufficiency. Unfortunately, many great military books, field manuals, and technical guides over the years have become less available and harder to find. These have either been rescinded by the armed forces or are otherwise out of print due to their age. This does not mean that these manuals are worthless or "out of date" – in fact, the opposite is true! It is true that the US Military frequently updates its manuals as its protocols frequently change based on the current times and combat situations that our armed services face. However, the knowledge about the outdoors over the entire history of military publications is timeless!

By publishing the **Military Outdoors Skills Series**, it is our goal at Doublebit Press to do what we can to preserve and share valuable military works that hold timeless knowledge about outdoors life, navigation, and survival. These books include official unrestricted texts such as army field manuals (the FM series), technical manuals (the TM series), and other military books from the Air Force, Navy, and texts from before 1900. Through remastered reprint editions of military handbooks and field manuals, outdoors enthusiasts, bushcrafters, hunters, scouts, campers, survivalists, nature lore experts, and military historians can preserve the time-tested skills and institutional knowledge that was learned through hard lessons and training by the U.S. Military and our expert soldiers.

Soldiers were the original campers and survivalists! Because of this, military field manuals about outdoors life contain essential knowledge about thriving in the wilds. This book is not just for soldiers!

This book is an important contribution to outdoors literature and has important historical and collector value toward preserving the American outdoors tradition. The knowledge it holds is an invaluable reference for practicing skills related to thriving in the outdoors. Its chapters thoroughly discuss some of the essential building blocks of outdoors knowledge that are fundamental but may have been forgotten as equipment gets fancier and technology gets smarter. In short, this book was chosen for Historic Edition printing because much of the basic skills and knowledge it contains could be forgotten or put to the wayside in trade for more modern conveniences and methods.

Although the editors at Doublebit Press are thrilled to have comfortable experiences in the woods and love our high-tech and light-weight equipment, we are also realizing that the basic skills taught by the old experts are more essential than ever as our culture becomes more and more hooked on digital technology. We don't want to risk forgetting the important steps, skills, or building blocks involved with thriving in the outdoors. This Civilian Reference Edition reprint represents a collection of military handbooks and field manuals that are essential contributions to the American outdoors tradition despite originating with the military. In the most basic sense, these books are the collection of experiences by the great experts of outdoors life: our countless expert soldiers who learned to thrive in the backwoods, deserts, extreme cold environments, and jungles of the world.

With technology playing a major role in everyday life, sometimes we need to take a step back in time to find those basic building blocks used for gaining mastery – the things that we have luckily not completely lost and has been recorded in books over the last two centuries. These skills aren't forgotten, they've just been shelved. *It's time to unshelve them once again and reclaim the lost knowledge of self-sufficiency.*

Based on this commitment to preserving our outdoors heritage, we have taken great pride in publishing this book as a complete original work. We hope it is worthy of both study and collection by outdoors folk in the modern era of outdoors and traditional skills life.

Unlike many other photocopy reproductions of classic books that are common on the market, this Historic Edition does not simply place poor photography of old texts on our pages and use error-prone optical scanning or computer-generated text. We want our work to speak for itself, and reflect the quality demanded by our customers who spend their hard-earned money. With this in mind, each Historic Edition book that has been chosen for publication is carefully remastered from original print books, *with the Doublebit Civilian Reference Edition printed and laid out in the exact way that it was presented at its original publication.* We provide a beautiful, memorable experience that is as true to the original text as best as possible, but with the aid of modern technology to make as beautiful a reading experience as possible for books that are typically over a century old. Military historians and outdoors enthusiasts alike are sure to appreciate the care to preserve this work!

Because of its age and because it is presented in its original form, the book may contain misspellings, inking errors, and other print blemishes that were common for the age. However, these are exactly the things that we feel give the book its character, which we preserved in this Historic Edition. During digitization, we ensured that each illustration in the text was clean and sharp with the least amount of loss from being copied and digitized as possible. Full-page plate illustrations are presented as they were found, often including the extra blank page that was often behind a plate. For the covers, we use the original cover design to give the book its original feel. We are sure you'll appreciate the fine touches and attention to detail that your Historic Edition has to offer.

For outdoors and military history enthusiasts who demand the best from their equipment, the Doublebit Press Civilian Reference Edition reprint of this military manual was made with you in mind. Both important and minor details have equally both been accounted for by our publishing staff, down to the cover, font, layout, and images. It is the goal of Doublebit Civilian Reference Edition series to preserve outdoors heritage, but also be cherished as collectible pieces, worthy of collection in any outdoorsperson's library and that can be passed to future generations.

So, without blabbering on further, we hope you enjoy your Doublebit Civilian Reference Edition. May your trails be clear!

- The Doublebit Press Editors

TABLE OF CONTENTS

CHAPTER 6 – BATTLE DRILLS

CHAPTER 7 – COMMUNICATIONS

CHAPTER 8 – ARMY AVIATION

CHAPTER 9 – WATERBORNE OPERATIONS

CHAPTER 10 – MILITARY MOUNTAINEERING

CHAPTER 11 – EVASION/SURVIVAL

CHAPTER 12 – FIRST AID

CHAPTER 13 – DEMOLITIONS

CHAPTER 14 – RANGER URBAN OPERATIONS

RANGER CREED

Recognizing that I volunteered as a Ranger, fully knowing the hazards of my chosen profession, I will always endeavor to uphold the prestige, honor, and high esprit de corps of the Rangers.

Acknowledging the fact that a Ranger is a more elite soldier who arrives at the cutting edge of battle by land, sea, or air, I accept the fact that as a Ranger my country expects me to move further, faster, and fight harder than any other soldier.

Never shall I fail my comrades I will always keep myself mentally alert, physically strong, and morally straight and I will shoulder more than my share of the task whatever it may be, one hundred percent and then some.

Gallantly will I show the world that I am a specially selected and well trained soldier. My courtesy to superior officers, neatness of dress, and care of equipment shall set the example for others to follow.

Energetically will I meet the enemies of my country. I shall defeat them on the field of battle for I am better trained and will fight with all my might. Surrender is not a Ranger word. I will never leave a fallen comrade to fall into the hands of the enemy and under no circumstances will I ever embarrass my country.

Readily will I display the intestinal fortitude required to fight on to the Ranger objective and complete the mission, though I be the lone survivor.

STANDING ORDERS ROGERS RANGERS

1. Don't forget nothing.
2. Have your musket clean as a whistle, hatchet scoured, sixty rounds powder and ball, and be ready to march at a minute's warning.
3. When you're on the march, act the way you would if you was sneaking up on a deer. See the enemy first.
4. Tell the truth about what you see and what you do. There is an army depending on us for correct information. You can lie all you please when you tell other folks about the Rangers, but don't never lie to a Ranger or officer.
5. Don't never take a chance you don't have to.
6. When we're on the march we march single file, far enough apart so one shot can't go through two men.
7. If we strike swamps, or soft ground, we spread out abreast, so it's hard to track us.
8. When we march, we keep moving till dark, so as to give the enemy the least possible chance at us.
9. When we camp, half the party stays awake while the other half sleeps.
10. If we take prisoners, we keep'em separate till we have had time to examine them, so they can't cook up a story between'em.
11. Don't ever march home the same way. Take a different route so you won't be ambushed.
12. No matter whether we travel in big parties or little ones, each party has to keep a scout 20 yards ahead, 20 yards on each flank, and 20 yards in the rear so the main body can't be surprised and wiped out.
13. Every night you'll be told where to meet if surrounded by a superior force.
14. Don't sit down to eat without posting sentries.
15. Don't sleep beyond dawn. Dawn's when the French and Indians attack.
16. Don't cross a river by a regular ford.
17. If somebody's trailing you, make a circle, come back onto your own tracks, and ambush the folks that aim to ambush you.
18. Don't stand up when the enemy's coming against you. Kneel down, lie down, hide behind a tree.
19. Let the enemy come till he's almost close enough to touch, then let him have it and jump out and finish him up with your hatchet.

MAJOR ROBERT ROGERS 1759

RANGER HISTORY

The history of the American Ranger is a long and colorful saga of courage, daring and outstanding leadership. It is a story of men whose skills in the art of fighting have seldom been surpassed. Only the highlights of their numerous exploits are told here.

Rangers primarily performed defensive missions until Benjamin Church's Company of Independent Rangers from Plymouth Colony proved successful in raiding hostile Indians during King Phillip's War in 1675. In 1756 Major Robert Rogers, a native of New Hampshire, recruited nine companies of American colonists to fight for the British during the French and Indian War. Ranger techniques and methods of operation were an inherent characteristic of the American frontiersmen; however, Major Rogers was the first to capitalize on them and incorporate them into the fighting doctrine of a permanently organized fighting force.

The method of fighting used by the first Rangers was further developed during the Revolutionary War by Colonel Daniel Morgan, who organized a unit known as "Morgan's Riflemen". According to General Burgoyne, Morgan's men were "….the most famous corps of the Continental Army, all of them crack shots."

Francis Marion, the "Swamp Fox", organized another famous Revolutionary War Ranger element known as "Marion's Partisans". Marion's Partisans, numbering anywhere from a handful to several hundred, operated both with and independent of other elements of General Washington's Army. Operating out of the Carolina swamps, they disrupted British communications and prevented the organization of loyalists to support the British cause, substantially contributing to the American victory.

The American Civil War was again the occasion for the creation of special units such as Rangers. John S. Mosby, a master of the prompt and skillful use of cavalry, was one of the most outstanding Confederate Rangers. He believed that by resorting to aggressive action he could compel his enemies to guard a hundred points. He would then attack one of the weakest points and be assured numerical superiority.

With America's entry into the Second World War, Rangers came forth to add to the pages of history. Major William O. Darby organized and activated the 1st Ranger Battalion on June19, 1942 at Carrickfergus, North Ireland. The members were all hand-picked volunteers; 50 participated in the gallant Dieppe Raid on the northern coast of France with British and Canadian commandos. The 1st, 3rd, and 4th Ranger Battalions participated with distinction in the North African, Sicilian and Italian campaigns. Darby's Ranger Battalions spearheaded the Seventh Army landing at Gela and Licata during the Sicilian invasion and played a key role in the subsequent campaign which culminated in the capture of Messina. They infiltrated German lines and mounted an attack against Cisterna, where they virtually annihilated an entire German parachute regiment during close in, night, bayonet and hand-to-hand fighting.

The 2nd and 5th Ranger Battalions participated in the D-Day landings at Omaha Beach, Normandy; it was during the bitter fighting along the beach that the Rangers gained their official motto. As the situation became critical on Omaha Beach, the division commander of the 29th Infantry Division stated that the entire force must clear the beach and advance inland. He then turned to Lieutenant Colonel Max Schneider, Commander of the 5th Ranger Battalion, and said, "Rangers, lead the way." The 5th Ranger Battalion spearheaded the breakthrough and thus enabled the allies to drive inland away from the invasion beaches.

The 6th Ranger Battalion, operating in the Pacific, conducted Ranger type missions behind enemy lines which involved reconnaissance and hard-hitting, long-range raids. They were the first American contingent to return to the Philippines, destroying key coastal installations prior to the invasion. A reinforced company from the 6th Ranger Battalion formed the rescue force which liberated American and allied prisoners of war from the Japanese prison camp at Cabanatuan.

Another Ranger-type unit was the 5307th Composite Unit (Provisional), organized and trained as a long-range penetration unit for employment behind enemy lines in Japanese occupied Burma. The unit commander was Brigadier General (later Major General) Frank D. Merrill, its 2,997 officers and men became popularly known as "Merrill's Marauders".

The men composing Merrill's Marauders were volunteers from the 5th, 154th, and 33rd Infantry Regiments and from other Infantry regiments engaged in combat in the southwest and South Pacific. These men responded to a call from then Chief of Staff, General George C. Marshall, for volunteers for a hazardous mission. These volunteers were to have a high state of physical ruggedness and stamina and were to come from jungle-trained and jungle-tested units.

Prior to their entry into the Northern Burma Campaign, Merrill's Marauders trained in India under the overall supervision of Major General Orde C. Wingate, British Army. There, they were trained from February to June 1943 in long-range penetration tactics and techniques of the type developed and first employed by General Wingate. The operations of the Marauders were closely coordinated with those of the Chinese 22nd and 38th Divisions in a drive to recover northern Burma and clear the way for the construction of Ledo Road, which was to link the Indian railhead at Ledo with the old Burma Road to China. The Marauders marched and fought through jungle and over mountains from Hukwang Valley in northwest Burma to Myitkyina and the Irrawaddy River. In 5 major and 30 minor engagements, they met and defeated the veteran soldiers of the Japanese 18th Division. Operating in the rear of the main force of the Japanese, they prepared the way for the southward advances of the Chinese by disorganizing supply lines and communications. The climax of the Marauder's operations was the capture of Myitkyina Airfield, the only all-weather strip in northern Burma. This was the final victory of "Merrill's Marauders" which was disbanded in August 1944. Remaining personnel were consolidated into the 475th Infantry Regiment which fought its last battle February 3-4,1945 at Loi-Kang Ridge, China. This Infantry Regiment would serve as the forefather of today's 75th Ranger Regiment.

Shortly after the outbreak of the Korean War in June 1950, the 8th Army Ranger Company was formed of volunteers from American units in Japan. The Company was trained in Korea and distinguished itself in combat during the drive to the Yalu River, performing task force and spearhead operations. In November 1950 during the massive Chinese intervention, this small unit, though vastly outnumbered, withstood five enemy assaults on its position.

In September 1950, a Department of the Army message called for volunteers to be trained as Airborne Rangers. In the 82nd Airborne Division, five thousand regular Army paratroopers volunteered, and from that number nine hundred men were selected to form the initial eight Airborne Ranger Companies. An additional nine companies were formed from volunteers of regular Army and National Guard Infantry Divisions. These seventeen Airborne Ranger companies were activated and trained at Fort Benning, Georgia, with most receiving additional training in the mountains of Colorado.

IN 1950 and 1951, some 700 men of the 1st, 2nd, 3rd, 4th, 5th and 8th Airborne Ranger companies fought to the front of every American Infantry Division in Korea. Attacking by land, water, and air, these six Ranger companies conducted raids, deep penetrations and ambush operations against North Korean and Chinese forces. They were the first Rangers in history to make a combat jump. After the Chinese intervention, these Rangers were the first Americans to re-cross the 38th parallel. The 2nd Airborne Ranger Company was the only African American Ranger unit in the history of the American Army. The men of the six Ranger companies who fought in Korea paid the bloody price of freedom. One in nine of this gallant brotherhood died on the battlefields of Korea.

Other Airborne Ranger companies led the way while serving with infantry divisions in the United States, Germany and Japan. Men of these companies volunteered and fought as members of line infantry units in Korea. One Ranger, Donn Porter, would be posthumously awarded the Medal of Honor. Fourteen Korean War Rangers became general officers and dozens became colonels, senior noncommissioned officers, and leaders in civilian life. They volunteered for the Army, the Airborne, the Rangers, and for combat. The first men to earn and wear the coveted Ranger Tab, these men are the original Airborne Rangers.

In October 1951, the Army Chief of Staff, General J. Lawton Collins directed, "Ranger training be extended to all combat units in the Army." The Commandant of the Infantry School was directed to establish a Ranger Department for the purpose of conducting a Ranger course of instruction. The overall objective of Ranger training was to raise the standard of training in all combat units. This program was built upon what had been learned from the Ranger Battalions of World War II and the Airborne Ranger companies of the Korean conflict.

During the Vietnam Conflict, fourteen Ranger companies consisting of highly motivated volunteers served with distinction from the Mekong Delta to the DMZ. Assigned to separate brigade, division and field force units, they conducted long-range reconnaissance and exploitation operations into enemy-held areas providing valuable combat intelligence. Initially designated at LRRP, then LRP companies, these units were later designated as C, D,E,F,G,H,I,K,L,M,N,O and P (Ranger) 75th Infantry.

Following Vietnam, recognizing the need for a highly trained and highly mobile reaction force, the Army Chief of Staff, General Abrams directed the activation of the first battalion-sized Ranger units since World War II, the 1st and 2nd Battalions (Ranger), 75th Infantry. The 1st Battalion was trained at Fort Benning, Georgia and was activated February 8, 1974 at Fort Stewart, Georgia with the 2nd Battalion being activated on October 3, 1974. The 1st Battalion is now located at Hunter Army Airfield, Georgia and the 2nd Battalion at Fort Lewis, Washington.

The farsightedness of General Abrams' decision, as well as the combat effectiveness of the Ranger battalions, was proven during the United States' invasion of the island of Grenada in October 1983 to protect American citizens there, and to restore democracy. As expected, Rangers led the way! During this operation, code named "Urgent Fury," the Ranger battalions conducted a daring, low level airborne assault (from 500 feet) to seize the airfield at Point Salines, and then continued operations for several days to eliminate pockets of resistance, and rescue American medical students.

As a result of the demonstrated effectiveness of the Ranger battalions, the Department of the Army announced in 1984, that it was increasing the strength of Ranger units to its highest level in 40 years by activating another Ranger battalion, as well as a Ranger Regimental Headquarters. These new units, the 3rd Battalion (Ranger), 75th Infantry, and Headquarters Company (Ranger) 75th Infantry, have increased the Ranger strength of the Army to over 2,000 soldiers actually assigned to Ranger units. On February 3, 1986, the 75th Infantry was re-designated the 75th Ranger Regiment.

On December 20,1989, the 75th Ranger Regiment was once again called upon to demonstrate its effectiveness in combat. For the first time since its reorganization in 1984, the Regimental Headquarters and all three Ranger battalions were deployed on Operation "Just Cause" in Panama. During this operation, the 75th Ranger Regiment spearheaded the assault into Panama by conducting airborne assaults onto Torrijos/Tocumen Airport and Rio Hato Airfield to facilitate the restoration of democracy in Panama, and protect the lives of American citizens. Between December 20, 1989 and January 7, 1990, numerous follow-on missions were performed in Panama by the Regiment.

Early in 1991, elements of the 75th Ranger Regiment deployed to Saudi Arabia in support of Operation Desert Storm.

In August 1993 elements of the 75th Ranger Regiment deployed to Somalia in support of Operation Restore Hope, and returned November 1993.

The performance of these Rangers significantly contributed to the overall success of these operations and upheld the Ranger tradition of the past. As in the past, the Regiment stands ready to execute its mission to conduct special operations in support of the United States' policies and objectives.

Ranger Medal Of Honor Recipients

Millett, Lewis L. Sr	Captain	Feb 7 1951	Co. E 2/27th Infantry
* Porter, Donn F.	Sergeant	Sept 7 1952	Co. G 2/14th Infantry
Mize, Ola L.	Sergeant	June 10-11 1953	Co. K 3/15th Infantry
Dolby, David C.	Staff Sergeant	May 21 1966	Co. B 1/8th (ABN) Calvary
Foley, Robert F.	Captain	Nov 5 1966	Co. A 2/27th Infantry
Zabitosky, Fred M.	Staff Sergeant	Feb 19 1968	5th Special Forces
Bucha, Paul W.	Captain	May 16-19 1968	Co. D 3/187 Infantry
* Rabel, Laszlo	Staff Sergeant	Nov 13 1968	74th Infantry (LRRP)
Howard, Robert L.	Sergeant First Class	Dec 30 1968	5th Special Forces
* Law, Robert D.	Specialist 4	Feb 22 1969	Co. I 75th Infantry (Ranger)
Kerrey, J. Robert	Lieutenant	Mar 14 1969	Seal Team 1
* Doane, Stephen H.	1st Lieutenant	Mar 25 1969	Co. B 1/5th Infantry
* Pruden, Robert J.	Staff Sergeant	Nov 22 1969	Co. G 75th Infantry (Ranger)
Littrell, Gary L.	Sergeant First Class	April 4-8 1970	Advisory Team 21 (Ranger)
* Lucas, Andre C.	Lt Colonel	Jul 1-23 1970	HHC 2/506 Infantry
* Gordon, Gary I.	Master Sergeant	Oct 3 1993	Task Force Ranger
* Shughart, Randall D.	Sergeant First Class	Oct 3 1993	Task Force Ranger

*posthumously

HISTORY OF THE RANGER DEPARTMENT / RANGER TRAINING BRIGADE

The Ranger Course was conceived during the Korean War and was known as the Ranger Training Command. On 10 October 1951, the Ranger Training Command was inactivated and became the Ranger Department, a branch of the Infantry School at Fort Benning, Georgia. Its purpose was, and still is, to develop combat skills of selected officers and enlisted men by requiring them to perform effectively as small unit leaders in a realistic tactical environment, under mental and physical stress approaching that found in actual combat. Emphasis is placed on the development of individual combat skills and abilities through the application of the principles of leadership while further developing military skills in the planning and conduct of dismounted infantry, airborne, airmobile, and amphibious independent squad and platoon-size operations. Graduates return to their units to pass on these skills.

From 1954 to the early 1970's, the Army's goal, though seldom achieved, was to have one Ranger qualified NCO per infantry platoon and one officer per company. In an effort to better achieve this goal, in 1954 the Army required all combat arms officers to become Ranger/ Airborne qualified.

The Ranger course has changed little since its inception. Until recently, it was an eight-week course divided into three phases. The course is now 61 days in duration and divided into three phases as follows:

BENNING PHASE (4th Ranger Training Battalion) – Designed to develop the military skills, physical and mental endurance, stamina, and confidence a small-unit combat leader must have to successfully accomplish a mission. It also teaches the Ranger student to properly maintain himself, his subordinates, and his equipment under difficult field conditions.

MOUNTAIN PHASE (5th Ranger Training Battalion) – The Ranger student gains proficiency in the fundamentals, principles and techniques of employing small combat units in a mountainous environment. He develops his ability to lead squad-sized units and to exercise control through planning, preparation, and execution phases of all types of combat operations, including ambushes and raids, plus environmental and survival techniques.

FLORIDA PHASE (6th Ranger Training Battalion) – Emphasis during this phase is to continue the development of combat leaders, capable of operating effectively under conditions of extreme mental and physical stress. The training further develops the student's ability to plan and lead small units on independent and coordinated airborne, air assault, amphibious, small boat, and dismounted combat operations in a mid-intensity combat environment against a well-trained, sophisticated enemy.

On 2 December 1987, on York Field, Fort Benning, Georgia, the Ranger Department, in accordance with permanent orders number 214-26, became the Ranger Training Brigade with an effective date of 1 November 1987.

After 40 years and 23 Directors and Commanders, the Ranger Course is still dedicated to producing the finest trained soldier in the world...the United States Army Ranger!

CHAPTER ONE
PRINCIPLES OF LEADERSHIP

1-1. GENERAL. Leadership is the most essential element of combat power. Leadership provides purpose, direction, and motivation in combat. The leader determines the degree to which maneuver, firepower, and protection are maximized, ensures these elements are effectively balanced, and decides how to bring them to bear against the enemy.

a. **PRINCIPLES OF LEADERSHIP.**

(1) **BE -**
   (a) Technically and tactically proficient: Can accomplish all tasks to standard that are required to accomplish the wartime mission.
   (b) Possess professional character traits: Courage, Commitment, Candor, Competence and Integrity.

(2) **KNOW -**
   (a) Four major factors of leadership and how they affect each other: The Led, The Leader, The Situation, and Communications.
   (b) Yourself and seek self-improvement: Strengths and weaknesses of your character, knowledge, and skills. Continually develop your strengths and work on overcoming your weaknesses.
   (c) Your soldiers and lookout for their well-being. Train them for the rigors of combat, take care of their physical/safety needs, and discipline/reward them.

(3) **DO -**
   (a) **SEEK RESPONSIBILITY and TAKE RESPONSIBILITY FOR YOUR ACTIONS:** Leaders must exercise initiative, be resourceful, and take advantage of opportunities on the battlefield that will lead to victory. Accept just criticism and take corrective actions for mistakes.
   (b) **MAKE SOUND AND TIMELY DECISIONS:** Rapidly assess the situation and make sound decisions. Gather essential information, announce decisions in time for soldiers to react, and consider short/long-term effects of your decision.
   (c) **SET THE EXAMPLE:** Be a role model for your soldiers. Set high, but attainable standards, be willing to do what you require of your soldiers, and share dangers and hardships with your soldiers.
   (d) **KEEP YOUR SUBORDINATES INFORMED:** Keeping your subordinates informed helps them make decisions and execute plans within your intent, encourage initiative, improve teamwork, and enhance morale.
   (e) **DEVELOP A SENSE OF RESPONSIBILITY IN SUBORDINATES:** Teach, challenge, and develop subordinates. Delegation indicates you trust your subordinates and will make them want even more responsibility.
   (f) **ENSURE THE TASK IS UNDERSTOOD, SUPERVISED, AND ACCOMPLISHED:** Soldiers need to now what you expect from them: What you want done, what the standard is, and when you want it.

(g) **BUILD THE TEAM:** Train and cross train your soldiers until they are confident in the team's technical/tactical abilities. Develop a team spirit that motivates them to go willingly and confidently into combat.

(h) **EMPLOY YOUR UNIT IN ACCORDANCE WITH ITS CAPABILITIES:** Know the capabilities and limitations of your unit. As a leader you are responsible to recognize both of these factors and employ your patrol accordingly.

1-2. DUTIES AND RESPONSIBILITIES. To complete all assigned tasks, every soldier in the patrol must do his job. Each soldier must accomplish his specific duties and responsibilities and be a part of the team.

a. **PLATOON LEADER (PL):** Responsible for what the patrol does or fails to do. This includes tactical employment, training, administration, personnel management, and logistics. He does this by planning, making timely decisions, issuing orders, assigning tasks, and supervising patrol activities. He must know his men and how to employ the patrol's weapons. He is responsible for positioning and employing all assigned or attached crew-served weapons and employment of supporting weapons. The platoon leader:

(1) Establishes time schedule using backwards planning. Consider time for execution, movement to the objective, and the planning and preparation phase of the operation.

(2) Takes the initiative to accomplish the mission in the absence of orders. Keeps higher informed by using periodic situation reports (SITREP).

(3) Plans with the help of the Platoon Sergeant (PSG), Squad leaders, and other key personnel (Team Leaders, FO, attachment leaders).

(4) Stays abreast of the situation through coordination with adjacent patrols and higher HQ, supervise, issue FRAGOs, and accomplish the mission.

(5) If needed to perform the mission, requests more support for his patrol from higher headquarters.

(6) Directs and assists the Platoon Sergeant in planning and coordinating the patrol's CSS effort and casualty evacuation (CASEVAC) plan.

(7) During planning, receives on-hand status reports from the Platoon Sergeant, and squad leaders.

(8) Reviews patrol requirements based on the tactical plan.

(9) Checks security, corrects unsatisfactory actions, and spot checks.

(10) During execution, positions himself where he can influence the most critical task for mission accomplishment; usually with the main effort.

(11) Commands through his squad leaders using the intent of the two levels higher commanders.

(12) Conducts rehearsals.

b. **PLATOON SERGEANT (PSG):** Senior NCO in the patrol and second in succession of command. Helps and advises the patrol leader, and leads the patrol in the patrol leader's absence. Supervises the patrol's administration, logistics, and maintenance. Prepares and issues paragraph 4 of the patrol OPORD.

(1) **Duties of the Platoon Sergeant**:
 (a) Organizes and controls the patrol CP IAW the unit SOP, patrol leader's guidance, and METT-TC factors.
 (b) Receives squad leader's requests for rations, water, and ammunition. Work with the company first sergeant or XO to request resupply. Directs the routing of supplies and mail.
 (c) Directs the patrol medic and patrol aid-litter teams in moving casualties to the rear.
 (d) Maintains patrol personnel status, consolidate and forward the patrol's casualty reports (DA Forms 1155 and 1156), and receive and orient replacements.
 (e) Monitors the morale, discipline, and health of patrol members.
 (f) Supervises task-organized elements of patrol:
 (g) Quartering parties.
 (h) Security forces during withdrawals.
 (i) Support elements during raids or attacks.
 (j) Security patrols during night attacks.
 (k) Coordinates and supervises company-directed patrol resupply operations.
 (l) Ensures that supplies are distributed IAW the patrol leader's guidance and direction.
 (m) Ensures that ammunition, supplies, and loads are properly and evenly distributed (a critical task during consolidation and reorganization).
 (n) Ensures the casualty evacuation plan is complete and executed properly.
 (o) Ensures that the patrol adheres to the Platoon Leader's time schedule.
 (p) The following checklist outlines the Platoon Sergeant's duties and responsibilities during specific actions:
(2) **Actions of the Platoon Sergeant during movement and halts**:
 (a) Takes action necessary to facilitate movement.
 (b) Supervises rear security during movement.
 (c) Supervises, establishes, and maintains security during halts.
 (d) Knows unit location.
 (e) Performs additional tasks as required by the patrol leader and assists in every way possible. Focuses on security and control of patrol.
(3) **Actions by Platoon Sergeant at Danger Areas**:
 (a) Directs positioning of near-side security (usually conducted by the trail squad or team).
 (b) Maintains accountability of personnel.
(4) **Actions by Platoon Sergeant on the Objective Area**:
 (a) Assists with ORP occupation.
 (b) Supervises, establishes, and maintains security at the ORP.
 (c) Supervises the final preparation of weapons and equipment in the ORP per patrol leader's guidance.
 (d) Assists the patrol leader in control and security.

(e) Supervises the reorganization and redistribution of ammo and equipment. Ensures accountability and status of personnel is maintained, to include WIAs and KIAs.

(f) Performs additional tasks assigned by the patrol leader and reports status to Platoon Leader.

(5) **Action by the Platoon Sergeant in the Patrol Base:**

(a) Assists in patrol base occupation.

(b) Assists in establishing and adjusting perimeter.

(c) Enforces security in the patrol base.

(d) Keeps movement and noise to a minimum.

(e) Supervises and enforces camouflage.

(f) Assigns sectors of fire.

(g) Ensures designated personnel remain alert and equipment is maintained in a high state of readiness.

(h) Requisitions supplies, water, ammo and supervises their distribution.

(i) Supervises the priority of work and ensures its accomplishment.

    1. Security plan. Ensures crew served weapons tied in according to platoon sector sketch.

    2. Maintenance plan.

    3. Hygiene plan.

    4. Messing plan.

    5. Water plan.

    6. Rest plan.

(j) Performs additional tasks assigned by the patrol leader and assists him in every way possible.

c. **SQUAD LEADER (SL).** Responsible for what the squad does or fails to do. He is a tactical leader that leads by example.

(1) **Duties of the Squad Leader:**

(a) Controls the maneuver of his squad and its rate and distribution of fire.

(b) Manages the logistical and administrative needs of his squad. Requests and issues ammunition, water, rations, and special equipment.

(c) Maintains equipment accountability.

(d) Completes casualty feeder reports and review the casualty reports completed by squad members.

(e) Directs the maintenance of the squad's weapons and equipment.

(f) Inspects the condition of soldiers' weapons, clothing and equipment.

(g) Keeps the Platoon Leader/Platoon Sergeant informed on status of squad.

(h) Submits ACE report to Platoon Sergeant.

(2) **Actions by Squad Leader throughout the mission:**

(a) Obtains status report from team leaders and submits reports to PL/PSG.

(b) Makes a recommendation to the PL/PSG when problems are observed.

(c) Ensures tasks are accomplished by delegating tasks to team leaders by establishing a priority of tasks in accordance with orders received from the PL.

(d) Uses initiative in the absence of orders.

(e) Follows the PL's plan and makes recommendations.

(3) **Actions by Squad Leader during movement and halts:**

(a) Rotates heavy equipment and difficult duties.

(b) Ensures PL is notified when rest halts and water replenishment are required.

(c) Maintains proper movement techniques while monitoring route, pace, and azimuth.

(d) Prevents breaks in contact.

(e) Ensures subordinate leaders are disseminating information, assigning sectors of fire, and checks personnel.

(4) **Action by Squad Leader in the objective area:**

(a) Ensures special equipment has been prepared for actions at the objective.

(b) Maintains security and control during conduct of the assault.

(c) Obtains status reports from team leaders and ensures ammunition is redistributed and reports status to PL.

(5) **Actions by Squad Leader in the patrol base:.**

(a) Ensures patrol base is occupied according to the plan.

(b) Ensures that his sector of the patrol base is covered by interlocking fires; makes final adjustments, if necessary.

(c) LP/OP's sent out in front of assigned sector. (METT-TC Dependent).

(d) Ensures priorities of work are being accomplished and reports accomplished priorities to the PL/PSG.

(e) Adheres to time schedule.

(f) Ensures personnel know the alert and evacuation plan the locations of key leaders, OPs and the location of the alternate patrol base.

d. **WEAPONS SQUAD LEADER (When designated).** Responsible for all that the weapons squad does or fails to do. His duties are the same as the squad leader. Additionally, he controls the machine guns and MAWs in support of the patrol's mission. He advises the PL on employment of his squad.

(1) Supervises machine gun teams to ensure they follow priority of work.

(2) Inspects machine gun teams for correct range cards, fighting positions, and understanding of fire plan.

(3) Supervises maintenance of machine guns (done correctly, deficiencies corrected, reported and does not violate security plan).

(4) Assists PL in planning.

(5) Positions machine guns not attached to squads according to patrol SOP at halts and danger areas.

(6) Rotates loads. Machine gunners normally get tired first.

(7) Submits ACE report to PSG.

(8) Designates targets for each gun.

(9) Gives additional fire commands to achieve maximum effectiveness of
  firepower:
    (a) Shifting fires.
    (b) Corrects windage or elevation to increase accuracy.
    (c) Alternates firing guns.
    (d) Prevents lulls in fire.
(10) Knows location of assault elements, security elements and prevents
  fratricide.
(11) Reports to higher.
e. **TEAM LEADER (TL)**. Controls the movement of his fire team and the rate
  and placement of fire by leading from the front and using the proper
  commands and signals. Maintains accountability of his men, weapons and
  equipment. Ensures his soldiers maintain unit standards in all areas. The
  following checklist outlines specific duties and responsibilities of team leaders
  during mission planning and execution. The Team Leader leads by example.
  (1) **Actions Taken by Team leader During Planning and Preparation:**
    (a) Warning Order.
      (1) Assists in control of the squad.
      (2) Monitors squad during issue of the order.
    (b) OPORD Preparation.
      (1) Posts changes to time schedule.
      (2) Posts/Updates team duties on warning order board.
      (3) Prepares ammo and supply lists.
      (4) Turns in and picks up supply requests.
      (5) Distributes ammo and special equipment.
      (6) Performs all tasks given by the SL special instructions paragraph.
    (c) Operation Order.
      (1) Monitors squad during issue of the order.
      (2) Assists SL during rehearsals.
  (2) **Actions taken by Team Leader during a Movement and at Halts**:
    (a) Takes actions necessary to facilitate movement.
      (1) Enforces rear security during movement.
      (2) Supervises, establishes, and maintains security at all times.
      (3) Performs additional tasks as required by the SL and assists him in
        every way possible, particularly control and security.
  (3) **Action taken by Team Leader in the ORP:**
    (a) Assists in the occupation of the ORP.
    (b) Assists in the supervision, establishment and maintenance of security.
    (c) Supervises the final preparation of men, weapons, and equipment in
      the ORP as per the squad leader guidance.
    (d) Assists in control of personnel departing and entering the ORP.
    (e) Reorganizes perimeter after recon party departs.
    (f) Maintains commo with higher headquarters.
    (g) Upon return of recon party, assists in the reorganization of personnel
      and redistribution of ammo and equipment; ensures accountability of
      all personnel and equipment are maintained.

(h) Disseminates PIR to his team.

(i) Performs additional tasks assigned by the SL.

(4) **Actions taken by Team Leader in the Patrol Base:**

(a) Inspects the perimeter to ensure team has interlocking sectors of fire; prepares team sector sketch.

(b) Enforces the priority of work and ensures it is properly accomplished.

(c) Performs additional tasks assigned by the SL and assist him in every way possible.

(5) **Actions taken by Team Leader during Link Up:**

(a) Assists in the preparation of men and equipment.

(b) Ensures all personnel are knowledgeable of their tasks and the operation.

f. **MEDIC.** Assists the PSG in directing aid and litter teams; monitors the health and hygiene of the platoon.

(1) Treats casualties and assists in their evacuation under the control of the PSG.

(2) Aids the PL/PSG in field hygiene matters, personally checks the health and physical condition of platoon members.

(3) Requests Class VIII (medical) supplies through the PSG.

(4) Provides technical expertise and supervision of combat lifesavers.

(5) Ensures casualty feeder reports are correct and attached to each evacuated casualty.

(6) Carries out other tasks assigned by the PL/PSG.

g. **RADIOTELEPHONE OPERATOR (RTO).** Responsible for establishing and maintaining communications with higher headquarters and within the patrol. The RTO also serves as an enroute recorder and keeps a detailed patrol log. The patrol RTO must know the use and care of the radio to include:

(1) Waterproofing and presetting frequencies.

(2) Use of the SOI.

(3) How to construct and erect field-expedient antennas.

1-3. ASSUMPTION OF COMMAND. Any platoon/squad member may have to take command of his element in an emergency - all members must be prepared to do so.

a. During an assumption of command, situation permitting, the following tasks are accomplished applying METT-TC. Tasks are not necessarily accomplished in the following order:

(1) Informs the unit's subordinate leaders of the command and notifies higher headquarters.

(2) Checks security.

(3) Checks crew served weapons.

(4) Pinpoints location.

(5) Coordinates and checks equipment.

(6) Checks personnel status.

(7) Issues FRAGO (if required).

(8) Reorganizes as needed maintaining unit integrity when possible.

(9) Maintains noise and light discipline.
(10) If done in a patrol base, continues patrol base activities, especially security.
(11) Makes reconnaissance (at a minimum, a map recon).
(12) Finalizes plan.
(13) Executes the mission.

This page intentionally left blank for notes.

CHAPTER TWO
OPERATIONS

This chapter provides techniques and procedures used by infantry platoons and squads. These techniques are used throughout the planning and execution phases of platoon and squad tactical operations.

COMMAND AND CONTROL

This section discusses troop-leading procedures, combat orders, and techniques for preparing a platoon to fight. These topics pertain to all combat operations. Their application requires time. With more time, leaders can plan and prepare in depth. With less time, they must rely on previously rehearsed actions, battle drills, and standing operating procedures (SOPs).

2-1. TROOP LEADING PROCEDURES

- Troop leading is the process a leader goes through to prepare his unit to accomplish a tactical mission.
- Begins when he is alerted for a mission or receives a change or a new mission.
- The troop-leading procedures comprise the steps listed below. Steps 3 through 8 may not follow a rigid sequence. Many of the steps may be accomplished concurrently.

1. Receive the mission.	5. Reconnoiter.
2. Issue a warning order.	6. Complete the plan.
3. Make a tentative plan.	7. Issue the complete order.
4. Initiate Movement	8. Supervise.

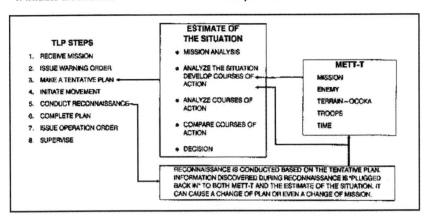

Figure 2-1. Tools of the tactician relationship

a. **STEP 1. Receive the Mission.** The leader may receive the mission in a warning order, an operation order (OPORD), or a fragmentary order (FRAGO).
- The leader should use no more than one third of the available time for his own planning and for issuing his operation order.
- The remaining two thirds is for subordinates to plan and prepare for the operation.
- Leaders should also consider other factors such as available daylight and travel time to and from orders and rehearsals.

b. **STEP 2. Issue a Warning Order.** The leader provides initial instructions in a warning order. The warning order contains enough information to begin preparation as soon as possible.
- The warning order mirrors the five-paragraph OPORD format.
- The following information may be included in a warning order.
- The mission or nature of the operation. (mission statement)
- Time and place for issuance of the operation (coordinating instructions)
- Who is participating in the operation? (coordinating instructions)
- Time of the operation. (timeline)

c. **STEP 3. Make a Tentative Plan.** The leader develops an estimate of the situation to use as the basis for his tentative plan. The estimate has five steps.
(1) Conduct a detailed mission analysis.
   (a) **The Higher Commanders' Concept and intent two levels up.** This information is found in paragraph 1b for two levels up and in paragraphs 2 and 3 for one higher.
   (b) **The Unit's Tasks.** Tasks that are clearly stated in the order (Specified Tasks) or tasks that become apparent as the OPORD is analyzed (Implied Tasks). Examples of specified tasks are:
   - Retain hill 545 to prevent envelopment of B Co.
   - Provide one squad to the 81-mm platoon to carry ammo.
   - Establish an OP VIC GL124325 NLT 301500 NOV 89.
   Examples of implied tasks are:
   - Provide security during movement.
   - Conduct resupply operations.
   - Coordinate with adjacent units.
   (c) **The Unit's Limitations.** The leader next determines all control measures or instructions in the OPORD that restrict his freedom of action; these are called limitations. In every operation, there are some limitations on the unit. The following are some examples of common limitations:
   - Graphic control measures.
   - Cross the LD at 100030 OCT 94.
   - MOPP4 in effect.
   - ADA weapons status, tight; warning status, yellow.
   (d) **Mission-Essential Task(s).** After reviewing all the above factors, the leader identifies his mission-essential task(s). Failure to accomplish a mission-

essential task results in the unit's failure to accomplish its primary purpose for that operation. The mission essential task should be found in the maneuver paragraph.

(e) **The Restated Mission Statement.** The restated mission statement becomes the focus for the remainder of the estimate process. This is a clear, concise statement of the mission essential task(s) to be accomplished by the unit and the purpose to be achieved. The mission statement will state **WHO**, **WHAT** (the task), **WHEN** (the critical time), **WHERE** (usually a grid coordinate), and **WHY** (the purpose the unit must achieve). Some examples of restated missions follow:

- (WHO) 1st Platoon attacks (WHAT) to seize (WHERE) HILL 482 VIC NB 457371 (OBJ BLUE) (WHEN) NLT 090500Z Dec 92 L 482 (OBJ BLUE) (WHY) to enable the company's main effort to destroy enemy command bunker.
- (WHO) 1st Platoon, C Company defends (WHAT) to destroy from (WHERE) AB163456 to AB163486 to AB123486 to AB123456 (WHEN) NLT 281530Z Oct 97 (WHY) to prevent enemy forces from enveloping B Company, 1-66 infantry (L) from the south.

(2) Analyze the situation and develop a course of action. Each COA must be:
   (a) Feasible: It accomplishes the mission and supports the commander's concept.
   (b) Reasonable: The unit remains an effective force after completing the mission.
   (c) Distinguishable: It is not just a minor variation of another COA.

(3) Upon developing a COA, the unit leader will assign C2 headquarters, complete generic task organization assigning all organic and attached elements, and prepare COA statement and sketch.

(4) With the restated mission from step one to provide focus the leader continues the estimate process using the remaining factors of METT-TC:
   (a) What is known about the **ENEMY?**
   (b) **Composition.** This is an analysis of the forces and weapons that the enemy can bring to bear. Determine what weapons systems they have available, and what additional weapons and units are supporting him.
   (c) **Disposition.** The enemy's disposition is how he is arrayed on the terrain, such as in defensive positions, in an assembly area, or moving in march formation.
   (d) **Strength.** Percentage strength.
   (e) **Recent Activities.** Identify recent and significant enemy activities that may indicate future intentions.
   (f) **Reinforcement Capabilities.** Determine positions for reserves and estimated time to counterattack or reinforce.
   (g) **Possible Courses of Actions.** Determine the enemy's possible COAS. Analyzing these COAs may ensure that the friendly unit is not surprised during execution.

(5) How will **TERRAIN** and weather affect the operation? Analyze terrain using OCOKA.

    (a) **Obstacles.** Identify the existing and reinforcing obstacles and hindering terrain that will affect mobility.

    (b) **Cover and concealment.** The analysis of cover and concealment is often inseparable from the fields of fires and observation. Weapon positions must have both to be effective and to be survivable. Infantry units are capable of improving poor cover and concealment by digging in and camouflaging their positions. When moving, the terrain is used to provide cover and concealment.

    (c) **Observation and fields of fire.** Determine locations that provide the best observation and fields of fire along the approaches, near the objective, or on key terrain. The analysis of fields of fire is mainly concerned with the ability to cover the terrain with direct fire.

    (d) **Avenues of approach.** Avenues of approach are developed next and identified one level down. Aerial and subterranean avenues must also be considered.

        (1) Offensive considerations:

- How can these avenues support my movement?
- What are the advantages/disadvantages of each? (Consider enemy, speed, cover, and concealment.)
- What are the likely enemy counterattack routes?

        (2) Defensive considerations:

- How can the enemy use these approaches?
- Which avenue is most dangerous? Least? (Prioritize each approach.)
- Which avenues would support a counterattack?

    (e) **Key Terrain.** Key terrain is any location or area that the seizure, retention, or control of affords a marked advantage to either combatant. Using the map and information already gathered, look for key terrain that dominates avenues of approach or the objective area. Next, look for decisive terrain that if held or controlled will have an extraordinary impact on the mission.

        (1) What **TROOPS** are available?

        (2) How much **TIME** is available?

        (3) How do **CIVILIANS** on the Battlefield effect the operation?

(6) **Analyze courses of action** (Wargame). This analysis is conducted by war-gaming the friendly courses of action against the enemy's most probable courses of action.

(7) **Compare courses of action.** The leader compares the COAs and selects the one that is most likely to accomplish the assigned mission. He considers the advantages and disadvantages for each COA. He also considers how the critical events impact on COAs.

(8) **Make a decision.** The leader selects the COA that he believes has the best chance of accomplishing the mission.

d. **STEP 4. Start Necessary Movement.** The unit may need to begin movement while the leader is still planning or forward reconnoitering. This step could occur at any time during the troop-leading procedure.

e. **STEP 5. Reconnoiter.** If time allows, the leader makes a personal reconnaissance. When time does not allow, the leader must make a map reconnaissance. Sometimes the leader must rely on others (for example, scouts) to conduct the reconnaissance.

f. **STEP 6. Complete the Plan.** The leader completes his plan based on the reconnaissance and any changes in the situation.

g. **STEP 7. Issue the Complete Order.** Platoon and squad leaders normally issue oral operations orders to aid subordinates in understanding the concept for the mission. If possible, leaders should issue the order with one or both of the following aides:
(1) Within sight of the objective or on the defensive terrain
(2) On a terrain model or sketch. Leaders may require subordinates to repeat all of part of the order or demonstrate on the model or sketch their understanding of the operation. They should also quiz their soldiers to ensure that all soldiers understand the mission.

h. **STEP 8. Supervise.** The leader supervises the unit's preparation for combat by conducting rehearsals and inspections.
1. The leader uses rehearsals to--
   - Practice essential tasks (improve performance).
   - Reveal weaknesses or problems in the plan.
   - Coordinate the actions of subordinate elements.
   - Improve soldier understanding of the concept of the operation (foster confidence in soldiers).
2. Rehearsals include the practice of having squad leaders brief their planned actions in execution sequence to the platoon leader.
3. The leader should conduct rehearsals on terrain that resembles the actual ground, and in similar light conditions.
4. The platoon may begin rehearsals of battle drills and other SOP items before the receipt of the operation order. Once the order has been issued, it can rehearse mission specific tasks. Some important tasks to rehearse include--
   - Actions on the objective.
   - Assaulting a trench, bunker, or building.
   - Actions at the assault position.
   - Breaching obstacles (mine and wire).
   - Using special weapons or demolitions.
   - Actions on unexpected enemy contact.
5. Rehearsal Types
   (a) **Backbrief**
   - Key leaders brief actions required during operation.

- Patrol leader controls
- Briefed sequentially
- Best to conduct the rehearsal two times:
  (1) immediately following FRAGO (Confirmation Brief)
  (2) after subordinates develop own plan
(b) **Reduced Force**
  - Conducted when time is key constraint
  - Conducted when security must be maintained
  - Key leaders normally attend
  - Mock-ups, sand tables, and small scale replicas used
(c) **Full Force**
  - Most effective type
  - First executed in daylight and open terrain
  - Secondly conduct in same conditions as operation
  - All soldiers participate
  - May use force on force

6. **Rehearsal Techniques**
   (a) Force on Force
   (b) Map
   - limited value
   - limited number of attendees
   (c) Radio
   - cannot mass leaders
   - confirms communications
   (d) Sand table/terrain model
   - key leaders
   - includes all control measures
   (e) Rock drill
   - similar to sand table/terrain model
   - subordinates are actually moving themselves

7. **Inspections.** Squad leaders should conduct initial inspections shortly after receipt of the warning order. The platoon sergeant spot checks throughout the unit's preparation for combat. The platoon leader and platoon sergeant make a final inspection. They should inspect:
   (a) Weapons and ammunition.
   (b) Uniforms and equipment.
   (c) Mission-essential equipment.
   (d) Soldier's understanding of the mission and their specific responsibilities.
   (e) Communications.
   (f) Rations and water.
   (g) Camouflage.
   (h) Deficiencies noted during earlier inspections.

2-2. COMBAT INTELLIGENCE. Gathering information is one of the most important aspects of conducting patrolling operations. The following details what information to collect and how to report it.

a. Reporting. All information must be quickly, completely, and accurately reported. Use the SALUTE report format for reporting and recording information.

> SIZE – Seven Enemy Soldier
> ACTIVITY – Traveling SW
> LOCATION – GL123456
> UNIT/UNIFORM – OD uniforms with red six-point star on left shoulder
> TIME – 210200JAN99
> EQUIPMENT – Carrying one machine gun and one rocket launcher

b. Field Sketching. When reporting information include a sketch, if possible. Limit the detail of the sketch to aspects of military importance such as targets, objectives, obstacles, sector limits, or troop dispositions and locations. The symbols used should be the standard Army symbols IAW FM 101-5-1. Notes should be used to explain the drawing, but they should not clutter the sketch. Personnel/weapons and/or equipment should not be used on the sketch, as it is a part of the "SALUTE" report.

b. Captured Documents. Documents are collected by the leader and turned in when he makes his reports. The documents should be marked as to time and place of capture.

c. Prisoners. If prisoners are captured during a patrolling operation, they should be treated IAW the Geneva Convention and handled by the 5-S rule:
   (1) Search
   (2) Silence
   (3) Segregate
   (4) Safeguard
   (5) Speed to Rear

d. Debriefing. Immediately upon return from a mission, the unit will be debriefed using the standard NATO report format.

2-3. WARNING ORDER. Warning orders give subordinates advance notice of operations that are to come. This gives them time to prepare. The order should be brief, but complete. A WARNING ORDER DOES NOT AUTHORIZE EXECUTION UNLESS SPECIFICALLY STATED. A sample annotated WARNORD format follows:

WARNING ORDER _____
(Number)

References: Refer to higher headquarters' OPORD, and identify map sheet for operation.

Time Zone Used throughout the Order: (Optional)

Task Organization: (Optional) (See paragraph 1c.)

1. SITUATION
a. Enemy forces. Include significant changes in enemy composition dispositions and courses of action. Information not available for inclusion in the initial WARNO can be included in subsequent warning orders.
b. Friendly forces. (Optional) Only address if essential to the WARNO.
(1) Higher commander's mission.
(2) Higher commander's intent.
c. Attachments and detachments. Initial task organization, only address major unit changes.

2. MISSION. Concise statement of the task and purpose (who, what, when, where, and why). If not all information is known, state which parts of the mission statement are tentative.

3. EXECUTION
Intent:
a. Concept of operation. Provide as much information as available. The concept should describe the employment of maneuver elements.
b. Tasks to maneuver units. Provide information on tasks to subordinate units for execution, movement to initiate, reconnaissance to initiate, or security to emplace. Identify special teams within squad and platoon.
c. Tasks to combat support units. See paragraph 3b.
d. Coordinating instructions. Include any information available at the time of the issuance of the WARNO. Include the following:
- Uniform and Equipment Common to All (changes in SOP e.g., drop rucks, drop or pick up helmets).
- Time line.
- CCIR.
- Risk guidance.
- Deception guidance.
- Specific priorities, in order of completion.

- Guidance on orders and rehearsals.
- Orders group meeting (attendees, location, and time).
- Earliest movement time and degree of notice.

4. SERVICE SUPPORT (Optional) Include any known logistics preparation for the operation.
a. Special equipment. Identifying requirements, and coordinating transfer to using units.
b. Transportation. Identifying requirements, and coordinating for pre-position of assets.

5. COMMAND AND SIGNAL (Optional)
a. Command. State the chain of command if different from unit SOP.
b. Signal. Identify current SOI edition, and pre-position signal assets to support operation.

This space intentionally left blank for notes.

This page intentionally left blank for notes.

2-4. OPERATIONS ORDER. An Operations Order (OPORD) is a directive issued by a leader to his subordinates in order to effect the coordinated execution of a specific operation. A five-paragraph format (shown below) is used to organize the briefing, to ensure completeness, and to help subordinate leaders understand and follow the order. Use a terrain model or sketch along with a map to explain the order. When possible, such as in the defense, give the order while observing the objective. The platoon/squad leader briefs his OPROD orally off notes that follow the five-paragraph format. A sample OPORD format follows:

OPERATION ORDER _____ (code name)
                        (Number)

Plans and orders normally contain a code name and are numbered consecutively within a calendar year.

References: The heading of the plan or order includes a list of maps, charts, datum, or other related documents the unit will need to understand the plan or order. The user does not need to reference the SOP, but may refer to it in the body of the plan or order. The user references a map using the map series number (and country or geographic area, if required), sheet number and name, edition, and scale, if required. Datum is the mathematical model of the earth used to calculate the coordinate on any map. Different nations use different datum for printing coordinates on their maps. The datum is usually referenced in the marginal information of each map.

Time Zone Used Throughout the Order: The time zone used throughout the order (including annexes and appendixes) is the time zone applicable to the operation. Operations across several time zones use ZULU time.

Task Organization: Describe the allocation of forces to support the commander's concept. Task organization may be shown in one of two places: preceding paragraph one, or in an annex, if the task organization is long and complicated.

1. Weather and Light Data and General Forecast:

High	Moonrise	Sunrise
Low	Moonset	Sunset
Wind Speed	Moonphase	BMNT
Wind Direction	% Illumination	EENT

2. Terrain: OCOKA

NOTE: Describe the effects on enemy and friendly forces for lines (1) and (2).

1. SITUATION

a. Enemy forces. The enemy situation in higher headquarters' OPORD (paragraph 1.a.) is the basis for this, but the leader refines this to provide the detail required by his subordinates.

1. Include the enemy's composition, disposition, strength
2. Recent activities
3. Known/suspected locations and capabilities
4. Describe the enemy's most likely and most dangerous course of action

b. Friendly forces. This information is in paragraph 1b, 2 and 3 of higher headquarters' OPORD.

1. Include the mission, the commander's intent, and concept of operations for headquarters one and two levels up.
2. Locations of units to the left, right, front, and rear. State those units' task and purpose and how those units will influence your unit, particularly adjacent unit patrols.

c. Attachments and detachments. Do not repeat information already listed under Task Organization. Try to put all information in the Task Organization. However, when not in the Task Organization, list units that are attached or detached to the headquarters that issues the order. State when attachment or detachment is to be effective if different from when the OPORD is effective (such as on order, on commitment of the reserve). Use the term "remains attached" when units will be or have been attached for some time.

2. MISSION. State the mission derived during the planning process. There are no subparagraphs in a mission statement. Include the 5 W's: Who, What (**task**), Where, When, and Why (**purpose**).

3. EXECUTION

a. Concept of the Operations. The concept of operations may be a single paragraph, may be divided into two or more subparagraphs or, if unusually lengthy, may be prepared as a separate annex. The concept of operations should be based on the COA statement from the decision-making process and will designate the main effort. The concept statement should be concise and understandable and describe, in general terms, how the unit will accomplish its mission from start to finish.
The concept describes—

- The employment of major maneuver elements in a scheme of maneuver.
- A plan of fire support or "scheme of fires" supporting the maneuver with fires.
- The integration of other major elements or systems within the operation. These include, for example, reconnaissance and security elements, intelligence assets, engineer assets, and air defense.
- Any be-prepared missions.

1. **Maneuver.** The maneuver paragraph addresses, in detail, the mechanics of the operations. Specifically address all subordinate units and attachments by name, giving each its mission in the form of a **task** and **purpose**. The main effort must be designated and all other subordinates' missions must relate to the main effort.

Actions on the objective will comprise the majority of this paragraph and therefore could address the plan for actions on the objective, engagement/disengagement criteria, an alternate plan in the event of compromise or unplanned movement of enemy forces, and a withdrawal plan.

2. **Fires.** Clarify scheme of fires to support the overall concept. This paragraph should state which maneuver unit is the main effort and has priority of fires, to include stating purpose of, priorities for, allocation of, and restrictions for fire support. A target list worksheet and overlay are referenced here, if applicable. Specific targets are discussed and pointed out on the terrain model (see chapter 3, Fire Support).

b. Tasks to maneuver units. Clearly state the missions or tasks for each maneuver unit that reports directly to the headquarters issuing the order. List units in the same sequence as in the task organization, including reserves. Use a separate subparagraph for each maneuver unit. Only state tasks that are necessary for comprehension, clarity, and emphasis. Place tactical tasks that affect two or more units in subparagraph 3d. Platoon leaders task their subordinate squads. Those squads may be tasked to provide any of the following special teams: reconnaissance and security, assault, support, aid and litter, EPW and search, clearing, and demolitions. Detailed instructions may also be given to platoon sergeant, RTO's, compassman, and paceman.

c. Tasks to combat support units. Use these subparagraphs only as necessary. List CS units in subparagraphs in the same order as they appear in the task organization. Use CS subparagraphs to list only those specific tasks that CS units must accomplish and that are not specified or implied elsewhere. Include organization for combat, if not clear from task organization.

d. Coordinating instructions. *List only instructions applicable to two or more units and not routinely covered in unit SOPs.* This is always the last subparagraph in paragraph 3. Complex instructions should be referred to in an annex. Subparagraph d(1)-d(5) below are mandatory.
    (1) Time Schedule (rehearsals, backbriefs, inspections and movement).
    (2) Commander's critical information requirements (CCIR)
        (a) Priority intelligence requirements (PIR) – Intelligence required by the commander needed for planning and decision making.
        (b) Essential elements of friendly information (EEFI). – Critical aspects of friendly operations that, if known by the enemy, would compromise, lead to failure, or limit success of the operation.
        (c) Friendly force information requirements (FFIR). – Information the commander needs about friendly forces available for the operation. May include personnel status, ammunition status, and leadership capabilities.
    (3) Risk reduction control measures. These are measures unique to this operation and not included in unit SOPs and can include mission-oriented protective posture, operational exposure guidance, vehicle recognition signals, and fratricide prevention measures.
    (4) Rules of engagement (ROE).

(5) Environmental considerations.
(6) Force Protection
(7) Movement Plan. Use terrain model and/or sketch. State azimuths, directions, and grid coordinates.
    a. Order of Movement, formation, and movement technique
    b. Actions at halts (long and short).
    c. Routes.
    d. Departure and Re-entry of friendly lines.
    e. Rally points and actions at rally points (plan must include IRP, ORP, PF, and RRP and all other planned rally points to include grid location and terrain reference).
    f. Actions at danger areas (general plan for unknown linear, small open areas and large open areas; specific plan for all known danger areas that unit will encounter along the route.

4. SERVICE SUPPORT Address service support in the areas shown below as needed to clarify the service support concept. Subparagraphs can include:
    a. General: Reference the SOP's that govern the sustainment operations of the unit. Provide current and proposed company trains locations, casualty, and damaged equipment collection points and routes.
    b. Materiel and Services.
        (1) Supply
            a. Class I – Rations Plan
            b. Class V – Ammunition
            c. Class VII – Major end items (weapons)
            d. Class VIII – Medical
            e. Class IX – Repair parts
            f. Distribution Methods
        (2) Transportation
        (3) Services (Laundry and showers)
        (4) Maintenance (weapons and equipment)
            a. Medical evacuation and hospitalization. Method of evacuating dead and wounded, friendly and enemy personnel. Include priorities and location of CCP.
            b. Personnel support. Method of handling EPW's and designation of the EPW collection point.

5. COMMAND AND SIGNAL
This paragraph states where command and control facilities and key leaders are located during the operation.
    a. Command.
        (1) Location of the higher unit commander and CP.
        (2) Location of key personnel and CP during each phase of the operation.
        (3) Succession of Command.
        (4) Adjustments to the patrol SOP.
    b. Signal.

(1) SOI index in effect.
(2) Methods of communication in priority.
(3) Pyrotechnics and signals, to include arm and hand signals.
(4) Code words.
(5) Challenge and password (used when behind friendly lines).
(6) Number Combination (used when forward of friendly lines).
(7) Running Password.
(8) Recognition signals (near/far and day/night).
c. Special Instructions to RTOs.

6. ISSUE ANNEXES.
7. GIVE TIME HACK.
8. ASK FOR QUESTIONS.

This space intentionally left blank for notes.

This page intentionally left blank for notes.

2-5. FRAGMENTARY ORDERS (FRAGO). A FRAGO is an abbreviated form of an operations order, usually issued on a day-to-day basis that eliminates the need for restating information contained in a basic operations order. It is issued after an OPORD to change or modify that order or to execute a branch or sequel to that order. The following is an annotated sample FRAGO:

FRAGMENTARY ORDER_____
                                                                (number)
Time Zone referenced throughout order:

Task Organization:

Weather and Light Data
    High: BMNT: Moonrise:
    Low: Sunrise: Moonset:
    Wind Speed: Sunset: % Illum:
    Wind Direction: EENT:
    Forecast:
Terrain (changes that will effect operation in new area of operations)
    Obstacles:
    Avenues of approach:
    Key Terrain:
    Observation/Fields of fire:
    Cover and concealment:

1. SITUATION (brief changes from base OPORD specific to this day's operation)
    a. Enemy Situation
        (1) Composition, disposition and strength
        (2) Capabilities
        (3) Recent activities
        (4) Most likely COA
    b. Friendly Situation
        (1) Higher mission
        (2) Adjacent patrols task/purpose
        (3) Adjacent patrol objective/route (if known)

2. MISSION (who, what (task), when, where, why (purpose)—from higher HQ maneuver paragraph)

3. EXECUTION
    a. Concept of the operation (explain how platoon will accomplish mission in general terms. Identify mission essential task, designate the main effort and how the supporting efforts support the main effort)

(1) Maneuver (assign task/purpose for squads/elements and discuss actions on the objective in detail from the ORP to dissemination) (Use a sketch or terrain model to brief)

(2) Fires (in support of today's mission, portions that do not change not briefed)
   (a) Purpose
   (b) Priority of fires (PL normally retains at platoon-level)
   (c) Allocation
   (d) Restrictions on fires
   (e) Fires planned during movement
   (f) Fires planned on objective

b. Tasks to maneuver units (list tasks that apply to the squads unique to each squad)

c. Coordinating Instructions:

(1) Timeline
   (a) Hit time:
   (b) ORP time:
   (c) Movement time from PB:
   (d) Final inspection:
   (e) Platoon rehearsal:
   (f) Squad rehearsal:
   (g) FRAGO complete:

(2) Movement plan (Use a sketch to brief)
   (a) Route (primary and alternate)
   (b) OOM
   (c) Formations
   (d) Movement technique

(3) PIR (specific to this mission)

(4) Rehearsal plan

(5) Patrol Base plan (if not IAW SOP)
   (a) Teams
   (b) Occupation plan
   (c) Operations plan (Security plan, alert plan, Black and Gold)
   (d) Priorities of work

(6) Air assault plan (provided w/higher FRAGO, if applicable)
   (a) Number/type/ACL aircraft
   (b) PZ grid/DOL/PZ posture time
   (c) Load time/lift time/flight time
   (d) # of lifts and composition
   (e) Air checkpoints enroute
   (f) LZ grid/DOL/LZ time
   (g) Actions after getting off aircraft
   (h) Actions on contact on LZ

(7) Link-up plan (if applicable)
   (a) Time of link-up
   (b) Location of link-up site
   (c) Stationary element

      (d) Moving element
      (e) Rally points
      (f) Actions at link-up point
      (g) Near/far recognition signals (day and night)

4. SERVICE SUPPORT (Only cover changes from base order that apply for today's mission)
a. Material and services
    (1) Any changes in classes of supply
    (2) Resupply plan
    (3) Water resupply plan
    (4) Aerial resupply plan (if applicable)
    (5) Truck plan
    (6) Maintenance issues specific to plan
b. Medical evacuation plan specific to mission
    (1) CCP point and markings
    (2) Aid and litter duties (if not SOP)

5. COMMAND AND SIGNAL
  a. Command
    (1) Location of Company CP
    (2) Location of PL
    (3) Location of key leaders
    (4) Succession of command
  b. Signal
    (1) Location of radios
      (a) During movement
      (b) During actions on the objective
    (2) SOI in effect
      (a) Bn command freq: Co CP callsign:
      (b) Bn MEDEVAC freq: PL callsign:
      (c) Retrans freq: PSG callsign:
      (d) Company freq: 1 SL callsign:
      (e) Platoon freq: 2 SL callsign:
                               3 SL callsign:
                               WSL callsign:
    (3) Pyro signals in use
    (4) Running password/number combination
    (5) OPSKEDs in effect

The Field FRAGO is intended to take no more then 40 minutes to issue, with 30 minutes as the target. The proposed planning guide is as follows:
      Paragraph 1 and 2 – 5 minutes
      Paragraph 3 – 20/30 minutes
      Paragraph 4 and 5 – 5 minutes

The FRAGO should focus on actions on the objective. The PL may use subordinates to prepare para 1, 4, 5 and routes and fires for the FRAGO. It is acceptable for subordinates to brief the portions of the FRAGO they prepare.

Use of sketches and a terrain model are critical to allow rapid understanding of the operation/FRAGO.

Rehearsals are critical as elements of the constrained planning model. The FRAGO used in conjunction with effective rehearsals reduces preparation time and allows the PL more time for movement and recon.

SPECIAL CONSIDERATIONS FOR PLANNING IN A FIELD ENVIRONMENT.
Planning in a field environment will necessarily reduce the amount of time leaders have for in-depth mission planning. The Troop Leading Procedures were specifically designed to provide leaders a framework for mission planning and orders production in a time-constrained environment.

This space intentionally left blank for notes.

This page intentionally left blank for notes.

2-6. OPERATION ORDER ANNEXES. Operation order annexes are necessary to complete the plan and to provide greater clarity and understanding during complex or critical aspects of the operation. Information issued in annex form include the: aerial re-supply, truck movement, air assault, patrol base, small boat, link up, and stream crossing annexes. Annexes are prepared only if the subject is not addressed thoroughly enough in the OPORD; brevity remains the standard. Annexes are always issued after the operation order.

a. AIR MOVEMENT ANNEX.
1. Situation.
    a. Enemy situation
        (1) Enemy air capability
        (2) Enemy ADA capability
        (3) Include in Weather: % Illum, Illum angle, NVG Window, Ceiling and Visibility.
    b. Friendly situation
        (1) Unit(s) supporting operation
        (2) Friendly ADA status
2. Mission.
3. Execution.
    a. Concept of operation
    b. Sub-unit missions
    c. Coordinating instructions
    (1) PZ
        (a) Name/Number
        (b) Coordinates
        (c) Load Time
        (d) Takeoff Time
        (e) Markings
        (f) Control
        (g) Landing Formation
        (h) Approach/Departure Direction
        (i) Alternate PZ Name/Number
        (j) Penetration Points
        (k) Extraction Points
    (2) LZ
        (a) Name/Number
        (b) Coordinates
        (c) H-Hour
        (d) Markings
        (e) Control
        (f) Landing Formation/Direction
        (g) Alt LZ Name/Number
        (h) Deception Plan
        (i) Extraction LZ

(3) Laager Site
    (a) Communications
    (b) Security Force
(4) Flight Routes and Alternates
(5) Abort Criteria
(6) Down Aircraft/Crew (Designated Area of Recovery (DAR)
(7) Special Instructions
(8) Cross-FLOT Considerations
(9) Aircraft Speed
(10) Aircraft Altitude
(11) Aircraft Crank Time
(12) Rehearsal Schedule/Plan
(13) Actions on Enemy Contact (Enroute and on the Ground)

4. Service Support.
    a. Forward Area Refuel/Rearm Points
    b. Class I, III, and V (specific)
5. Command and Signal.
    a. Command.
    b. Signal.
       (1) Air/ground call signs and frequencies.
       (2) Air/ground emergency code.
       (3) Passwords/Number Combinations
       (4) Fire Net/Quick Fire Net
       (5) Time Zone
       (6) Time Hack

b. AERIAL RESUPPLY ANNEX.
1. Situation.
    a. Enemy Forces (Include Weather)
    b. Friendly Forces
    c. Attachments and Detachments
2. Mission.
3. Execution.
    a. Concept of operation
       (1) Maneuver
       (2) Fires
    b. Tasks to Combat Units
       (1) Command and Control
       (2) Security
       (3) Marking
       (4) Recovery/Transport
    c. Tasks to Combat Support Units
    d. Coordinating Instructions
       (1) Flight Route
          (a) General

        (b) Checkpoints

        (c) Communication checkpoint (CCP)

           - Marking of CCP

           - Report time

        (d) Heading from CCP

    (2) Landing/Drop Zone

        (a) Location.

           - Primary

           - Alternate

        (b) Marking

           - Near

           - Far

    (3) Drop Information.

        (a) Date/time of resupply (and alternates)

        (b) Code letter at DZ/LZ

        (c) Length of DZ in seconds or dimensions of LZ

        (d) Procedures for turning off DZ/LZ

        (e) Formation, altitude, and air speed.

           - Enroute

           - At DZ/LZ

    (4) Actions on enemy contact during resupply

    (5) Abort Criteria: Enroute and at DZ/LZ

    (6) Actions at DZ/LZ

        - Rehearsals

4. Service Support.

5. Command and Signal.

  a. Command.

    (1) Location of patrol leader

    (2) Location of assistant patrol leader

    (3) Location of members not involved in resupply

  b. Signal.

    (1) Air to ground call-signs and frequencies (primary and alternate).

    (2) Long range visual signals

    (3) Short range visual signals

    (4) Emergency procedures and signals

    (5) Air drop communication procedures

    (6) Code Words

c. PATROL BASE ANNEX.

1. Situation

  a. Enemy Forces

  b. Friendly Forces

  c. Attachments and Detachments

2. Mission.

3. Execution.

  a. Concept of Operation.

(1) Maneuver
(2) Fires
b. Tasks to Combat Units
    (1) Teams
        - Security
        - Recon
        - Surveillance
        - LP/OPs
    (2) Individuals
c. Tasks to Combat Support Units
d. Coordinating instructions
    (1) Occupation plan
    (2) Operations plan
        - Security Plan
        - Alert Plan
        - Priority of work
        - Evacuation plan
        - Alternate patrol base(used when primary is unsuitable or compromised).
4. Service Support.
a. Water plan
b. Maintenance plan
c. Hygiene plan
d. Messing plan
e. Rest plan
5. Command and signal.
a. Command
    (1) Location of patrol leader
    (2) Location of assistant patrol leader
    (3) Location of patrol CP
b. Signal
    (1) Call signs and frequencies
    (2) Code words
    (3) Emergency signals

d. SMALL BOAT ANNEX.

1. Situation.
a. Enemy forces
    (1) Weather
        (a) Tide
        (b) Surf
        (c) Wind
    (2) Terrain
        (a) River width
        (b) River depth and water temperature

    (c) Current

    (d) Vegetation

   (3) Identification, location, activity and strength.

  b. Friendly forces (Unit furnishing support)

  c. Attachments and detachments

  d. Organization for movement

2. Mission.

3. Execution.

  a. Concept of operation

   (1) Maneuver

   (2) Fires

  b. Tasks to Combat Units

   (1) Security

   (2) Tie-down teams

    (a) Load equipment

    (b) Secure equipment

   (3) Designation of coxswains and boat commanders

   (4) Selection of navigator(s) and observer(s)

  c. Coordinating instructions

   (1) Formations and order of movement

   (2) Route and alternate route

   (3) Method of navigation

   (4) Actions on enemy contact

   (5) Rally points

   (6) Embarkation plan

   (7) Debarkation plan

   (8) Rehearsals

   (9) Time schedule

4. Service Support.

  a. Ration plan

  b. Arms and ammunition

  c. Uniform and equipment

   (1) Method of distribution of paddles and life jackets

   (2) Disposition of boat, paddles and life jackets upon debarkation.

5. Command and Signal.

  a. Command

   (1) Location of patrol leader

   (2) Location of assistant patrol leader

  b. Signal

   (1) Signals used between and in boats

   (2) Code words

e. STREAM CROSSING ANNEX.

1. Situation.

  a. Enemy forces

(1) Weather
(2) Terrain
 (a) River width
 (b) River depth and water temperature
 (c) Current
 (d) Vegetation
 (e) Obstacles
(3) Enemy location, identification, activity.
 b. Friendly forces
 c. Attachments and detachments
2. Mission.
3. Execution.
 a. Concept of operation
  (1) Maneuver
  (2) Fires
 b. Tasks to Combat Units
  (1) Elements
  (2) Teams
  (3) Individuals
 c. Tasks to Combat Support Units
 d. Coordinating Instructions
  (1) Crossing procedure/techniques
  (2) Security
  (3) Order of crossing
  (4) Actions on enemy contact
  (5) Alternate plan
  (6) Rallying points
  (7) Rehearsal plan
  (8) Time schedule
4. Service Support.
5. Command and Signal.
 a. Command
  (1) Location of patrol leader
  (2) Location of assistant patrol leader
  (3) Location of CP
 b. Signal
  (1) Emergency signals
  (2) Signals

f. LINK UP ANNEX.

1. Situation.
 a. Enemy Forces
 b. Friendly forces
 c. Attachments and Detachments
2. Mission.

3. Execution.
    a. Concept of operation
       (1) Maneuver
       (2) Fires
    b. Tasks to Combat Units
       (1) Security Teams
       (2) Surveillance Teams
       (3) Link-Up element
    c. Tasks to Combat Support Units
    d. Coordinating instructions
       (1) Time of link up
       (2) Location of link up site (primary and alternate)
       (3) Rally points
       (4) Actions upon enemy contact
       (5) Actions at the link up site
       (6) Actions following link up
       (7) Rehearsals
       (8) Restrictive Fire Lines
       (9) Time Schedule
4. Service Support.
5. Command and Signal.
    a. Command
       (1) Location of patrol leader and assistant patrol leader
       (2) Location of patrol headquarters
    b. Signal
       (1) Call signs and frequencies
       (2) Spares and code words
         (a) Far recognition signal
         (b) Near recognition signal
         (c) Link up complete
       (3) Posting authentication (verbal)
       (4) Brevity codes (spares)
       (5) Emergency signals
       (6) Abort criteria and signals

g. TRUCK ANNEX.

1. Situation.
    a. Enemy Forces
    b. Friendly Forces
    c. Attachments and Detachments
2. Mission.
3. Execution.
    a. Concept of operation
       (1) Maneuver
       (2) Fires

b. Tasks to Combat Units
  c. Tasks to Combat Support Units
  d. Coordinating Instructions
     (1) Time of departure and return
     (2) Loading plan and order of movement
     (3) Route (primary and alternate)
     (4) Air Guards
     (5) Actions on enemy contact (vehicle ambush) during movement, loading, and downloading
     (6) Actions at the de-trucking point
     (7) Rehearsals
     (8) Vehicle speed, separation, and recovery plan
     (9) Broken vehicle instructions
4. Service Support.
5. Command and Signal.
   a. Command- Location of PL and PSG
   b. Signal
      (1) Radio call signs and frequencies
      (2) Code words

2-7. COORDINATION CHECKLISTS. The following checklists are items that a platoon/squad leader must check when planning for a combat operation. In some cases, he will coordinate directly with the appropriate staff section, in most cases this information will be provided by the company commander or platoon leader. The platoon/squad leader, to keep him from overlooking anything that may be vital to his mission, may carry copies of these checklists.

a. **INTELLIGENCE.** In this coordination, the leader is informed of any changes in the situation as given in the operation order of mission briefing. He must keep himself constantly updated to ensure the plan is sound
   (1) Identification of enemy unit
   (2) Weather and light data
   (3) Terrain update
      (a) Aerial photos
      (b) Trails and obstacles not on map
   (4) Known or suspected enemy locations
   (5) Weapons
   (6) Probable course of action
   (7) Recent enemy activities
   (8) Reaction time of reaction forces
   (9) Civilians on the battlefield
  (10) Update to CCIR

b. **OPERATIONS.** This coordination occurs with the platoon leader/company commander so that the platoon/squad leader can confirm his mission and operational plan, receive any last-minute changes to his mission or plan, and to update his subordinates or issue a FRAGO, if required.

    (1) Mission backbrief
    (2) Identification of friendly units
    (3) Changes in the friendly situation
    (4) Route selection, LZ/PZ/DZ selection
    (5) Link up procedures
    (6) Transportation/Movement plan
    (7) Resupply (in conjunction with S4)
    (8) Signal Plan
    (9) Departure and re-entry of forward units
    (10) Special equipment requirements
    (11) Adjacent units operating in the area of operations
    (12) Rehearsal areas
    (13) Method of insertion/extraction

c. **FIRE SUPPORT.** The platoon/squad leader will normally coordinate the following with the platoon Forward Observer (FO).

    (1) Mission backbrief
    (2) Identification of supporting unit
    (3) Mission and objective
    (4) Route to and from the objective (include alternate routes)
    (5) Time of departure and expected time of return
    (6) Unit target list (from fire plan)
    (7) Type of available support (artillery, mortar, naval gunfire and aerial support to include Army, Navy and Air Force) and their location.
    (8) Ammunition available (to include different fuses)
    (9) Priority of fires
    (10) Control measures
        (a) Checkpoints
        (b) Boundaries
        (c) Phase lines
        (d) Fire support coordination measures
        (e) Priority targets (target list)
        (f) RFA
        (g) RFL
        (h) No fire areas
        (i) Pre-coordinated authentication
    (11) Communication (include primary and alternate means, emergency signals and code words)

d. **COORDINATION WITH FORWARD UNIT.** A platoon/squad that requires foot movement through a friendly forward unit must coordinate with that unit's commander for a safe and orderly passage. If no time and place has been designated for coordination with the forward unit, the platoon/squad leader should set a time and place when he coordinates with the S3. He must talk with someone

2-30

at the forward unit who has the authority to commit that unit in assisting the platoon/squad during departure. Coordination entails a two-way exchange of information.

(1) Identification (yourself and your unit)

(2) Size of platoon/squad

(3) Time(s) and place(s) of departure and return, location(s) of departure point(s), IRP and detrucking points

(4) General area of operations

(5) Information on terrain and vegetation

(6) Know or suspected enemy positions or obstacles

(7) Possible enemy ambush sites

(8) Latest enemy activity

(9) Detailed information on friendly positions (e.g., crew-served weapons, FPF)

(10) Fire and barrier plan

(11) Support the unit can furnish. How long and what can they do?

    (a) Fire Support

    (b) Litter teams

    (c) Navigational signals and aids

    (d) Guides

    (e) Communications

    (f) Reaction units

    (g) Other

(12) Call signs and frequencies

(13) Pyrotechnic plan

(14) Challenge and password, running password, number combination forward of FFU

(15) Emergency signals and code words

(16) If the unit is relieved, pass the information to the relieving unit

(17) Recognition signals

e. **ADJACENT UNIT COORDINATION.** Immediately after the operation order of mission briefing, the platoon/squad leader should check with other platoon/squad leaders who will be operating in the same areas. If the leader is not aware of any other units operating is his area, he should check with the S3 during the operations coordination. The S3 can help arrange this coordination if necessary. The platoon/squad leaders should exchange the following information with other units operating in the same area.

(1) Identification of the unit

(2) Mission and size of unit

(3) Planned times and points of departure and re-entry

(4) Route(s)

(5) Fire support and control measures

(6) Frequencies and call signs

(7) Challenge and password, running password, number combination

(8) Pyrotechnic plan

(9) Any information that the unit may have about the enemy

(10) Recognition signals

f. **REHEARSAL AREA COORDINATION.** This coordination is conducted with the platoon leader/company commander to facilitate the unit's safe, efficient and effective use of rehearsal area prior to its mission.
   (1) Identification your unit
   (2) Mission
   (3) Terrain similar to objective site
   (4) Security of the area
   (5) Availability of aggressors
   (6) Use of blanks, pyrotechnics and ammunition
   (7) Mock-ups available
   (8) Time the area is available (preferably when light conditions approximate light conditions of patrol)
   (9) Transportation
   (10) Coordination with other units using area

g. **ARMY AVIATION COORDINATION.** This coordination is conducted with the platoon leader/company commander and/or S3 Air to facilitate the time, detailed and effective use of aviation assets as they apply to your tactical mission.
1. Situation.
   a. Enemy situation
      (1) Enemy air capability
      (2) Enemy ADA capability
      (3) Include in Weather: % Illum, Illum angle, NVG Window, Ceiling and Visibility.
   b. Friendly situation
      (1) Unit(s) supporting operation, Axis of movement/corridor/routes
      (2) Friendly ADA status
2. Mission.
3. Execution.
   a. Concept of the Operation: Overview of what requesting unit want to accomplish with the air assault/air movement.
   b. Tasks to Combat Units.
      1. Infantry
      2. Attack aviation
   c. Task to combat support units
      1. Artillery
      2. Aviation (lift)
   d. Coordinating Instructions
      PZ Operations
      1. Direction of landing
      2. Time of landing/flight direction
      3. Location of PZ/Alternate PZ
      4. Loading procedures
      5. Marking of PZ (panel, smoke, SM, lights)

6. Flight route planned (SP, ACP, RP)
7. Formations: PZ, enroute, LZ
8. Codewords: PZ secure (prior to landing), PZ clear (lead bird and last bird) -
   alternate PZ (at PZ, enroute, LZ), names of PZ/alt PZ
9. TAC air/artillery
10. Number of pax per bird and for entire lift
11. Equipment carried by individuals
12. Marking of key leaders
13. Abort criteria (PZ, enroute, LZ)
LZ Operations
1. Direction of landing
2. False insertion plans
3. Time of landing (LZ time)
4. Location of LZ and Alternate LZ
5. Marking of LZ (panel, smoke, SM, lights)
6. Formation of landing
7. Code words, LZ name, alternate LZ name
8. TAC air/artillery preparation, fire support coordination
9. Secure LZ or not?

4. Service and Support
   a. Number of aircraft per lift and number of lifts
   b. Refuel/rearm during mission or not?
   c. Special equipment/aircraft configuration for weapons carried by unit personnel
   d. Bump plan

5. Command and Signal
   a. Frequencies, call signs and codewords
   b. Locations of air missions commander, ground tactical commander and air assault
      task force commander

h. **VEHICULAR MOVEMENT COORDINATION.** This is coordinated with the
   supporting unit through the platoon sergeant/first sergeant to facilitate the effective,
   detailed, and efficient use of vehicular support and/or assets.
   a. Identification of the unit
   b. Supporting unit identification
   c. Number and type of vehicles and tactical preparation
   d. Entrucking point
   e. Departure/loading time
   f. Preparation of vehicles for movement
      1. Driver responsibilities
      2. Platoon/squad responsibilities
      3. Special supplies/equipment required
   g. Availability of vehicles for preparation/rehearsals/inspection (time and location)
   h. Routes
      1. Primary
      2. Alternate
      3. Checkpoints

    i. Detrucking points
       1. Primary
       2. Alternate
    j. March internal/speed
    k. Communications (frequencies, call signs, codes)
    l. Emergency procedures and signals

This space intentionally left blank for notes.

2-8 DOCTRINAL TERMS. Doctrinal terms used in intents, mission statements, and concepts of operations:

1. Tactical task: A clearly defined, measurable activity accomplished by individuals and organizations. Tasks are specific activities that contribute to the accomplishment of encompassing missions or other requirements. A task should be definable, measurable, and decisive (achieve the purpose).

Enemy	Terrain	Friendly
Attack by fire	Clear	Breach
Block	Occupy	Cover
Bypass	Reconnoiter	Disengage
Canalize	Retain	Exfiltrate
Contain	Secure	Follow and support
Defeat	Seize	Guard
Delay		Infiltrate
Demonstrate		Retire
Destroy		Screen
Feint		Support by fire

Fix		Withdraw
Interdict		
Isolate		
Neutralize		
Penetrate		
Pursue		
Recon		
Rupture		
Suppress		

2. Purpose (in order to): The desired or intended result of the tactical operation stated in terms related to the enemy or the desired situation. The *why* of the mission statement. The most important component of the mission statement.

Allow	Divert	Prevent
Cause	Enable	Protect
Create	Envelop	Support
Deceive	Influence	Surprise
Deny	Open	

3. Operations: "A military action or the carrying out of a military action to gain the objectives of any battle or campaign." Types of operations include –

Attack	Counterattack	Defend
Movement to contact	Retrograde	Mobility
Countermobility	Survivability	River
Crossing	Breakout	Security
Exploitation		
Deception		

This space intentionally left blank for notes.

This page intentionally left blank for notes.

CHAPTER THREE
FIRE SUPPORT

3-1. FIRE SUPPORT.

(a) Planning is the continual process of selecting targets on which fires are prearranged to support a phase of the commander's plan.

  (1) Principles:

    (a) Consider what the commander wants to do.

    (b) Plan early and continuously.

    (c) Exploit all available targeting assets.

    (d) Use all available lethal and non-lethal fire support means.

    (e) Use the lowest echelon able to furnish effective support.

    (f) Observe all fires.

    (g) Use the most effective fire support asset available.

    (h) Provide adequate fire support.

    (i) Avoid unnecessary duplication.

    (j) Provide for safety of friendly forces and installations.

    (k) Provide for flexibility.

    (l) Furnish the type of fire support requested.

    (m) Consider the airspace.

    (n) Provide rapid and effective coordination.

    (o) Keep all fire support informed.

(b) Fire support tasks:

  (1) All operations:

    (a) Locate targets.

    (b) Integrate all available assets.

    (c) Destroy, neutralize, or suppress all enemy direct and indirect fire systems.

    (d) Provide illumination and smoke.

    (e) Provide fires in support of JA/ATT and SEAD missions.

    (f) Deliver scatterable mines.

    (g) Prepare for future operations.

    (h) Provide positive clearance of fires.

  (2) Offensive operations:

    (a) Support the movement to contact, chance contact.

    (b) Soften enemy defenses before the attack by arranging short, violent preparations, where required.

    (c) Provide support during the attack by attacking high payoff targets.

    (d) Plan for deep and flanking fires.

    (e) Plan fires during consolidation.

    (f) Provide counterfires.

(c) Capabilities:

FIELD ARTILLERY

WEAPON	MAX RANGE(m)	MIN RANGE(m)	MAX RATE Rds per Min	Burst Radius	SUSTAINED RATE Rds per Min
105mm Howitzer M102, Towed	11,500 14,500(RAP)	0	10 for 3 min	35 m	3
105mm Howitzer M119, Towed	14,000m	0	6 for 2 min	35 m	3 Rds for 30 min, then 1 rd per min
155mm Howitzer M198, Towed	18,100 30,000(RAP)	0	4 for 3 min 2 for 30 min	50 m	1 rd per min Temp Dependent
155mm Howitzer M109A2/A3 SP	18,100 23,500(RAP)	0	4 for 3 min	50 m	1 for 60 min 0.5
203mm Howitzer M110A2, SP	22,900 30,000 (RAP)	0	1.5 for 3 min	80 m	0.5

MORTARS

WEAPON	MUNITION AVAILABLE	MAX RANGE(m)	MIN RANGE(m)	MAX RATE Rds per Min	Burst Radius	SUSTAINED RATE Rds per Min
60mm	HE,WP,ILLUM	3500 (HE)	70 (HE)	30 for 4 min	30 m	20
81mm	HE,WP,ILLUM	5600 (HE)	70 (HE)	25 for 2 min	38 m	8
107mm	HE,WP,ILLUM	6840 (HE)	770 (HE)	18 for 1 min 9 for 5 min	40 m	3
120mm	HE,SMK,ILLUM	7,200 (HE)	180 (HE)	15 for 1 min	60 m	5

NAVAL GUN				
WEAPON	FULL CHARGE	REDUCED CHARGE	MAX RATE Rds per Min	SUSTAINED RATE Rds per Min
5 in / 38	15,904	8,114	20	15
5 in / 54	23,133	12,215	35	20
16 in / 50	36,188	22,951	2	1

NOTE: The term **DANGER CLOSE** is included in the Method of Engagement portion of the call for fire when the target is within 600 meters of any friendly troops for both mortars and field artillery. When adjusting naval gun fire the term DANGER CLOSE is announced when the target is located within 750 meters when using 5 inch or smaller naval guns. For naval guns larger than 5 inch, DANGER CLOSE is announced when the target is within 1000 meters.

The creeping method of adjustment is used exclusively during DANGER CLOSE missions. The FO should make range changes by creeping the rounds to the target using corrections of no more than 100 meters.

(d) Target Overlay. A complete fire support overlay must include:
    (1) Unit and official capacity of person making overlay.
    (2) Date the overlay was prepared.
    (3) Map Sheet Number.
    (4) Effective Period of Overlay (DTG).
    (5) Priority target.
    (6) ORP Location.
    (7) Call signs and frequencies. (PRI/ALT)
    (8) Routes - Primary/Alternate.
    (9) Phase Lines/Checkpoints used by the patrol.
    (10) Spares.
    (11) Index marks to position overlay on map.
    (12) Objective.
    (13) Target Symbols.
    (14) Description, location and remarks column, complete.

(e) Sterile Overlay must include:
    (1) Index marks to position overlay on map.
    (2) Target Symbols.

(f) Target Overlay Symbols:
   (1) Point Target:

                                                        Less than 200 meters
                                                        in length and width.

ALT   TARGET
                TYPE

    (2) Linear Target:

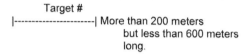

Target #

More than 200 meters
but less than 600 meters
long.

    (3) Circular Target:

Undisclosed area
and desired radius.

3-2. CLOSE AIR SUPPORT (CAS). There are two types of close air support requests, planned and immediate. Planned requests are processed by the Army chain to Corps for approval. Immediate requests are initiated at any level and processed by the battalion S-3 FSO, and Air Liaison Officer.

a. Format for requesting immediate CAS:
   (1) Observer identification.
   (2) Warning Order (Request Close Air)
   (3) Target location (Grid).
   (4) Target description. (Description must include, as a minimum: type and number of targets, activity or movement; point or area targets, include desired results on target and time on target.
   (5) Location of Friendly Forces
   (6) NAV Details (Elevation).
   (7) Threats - ADA, Small Arms, etc.
   (8) Hazards - Friendly Aircraft in Area.
   (9) Wind Direction.

b. Close Air Support Capabilities:

CLOSE AIR SUPPORT RESOURCES		
AIRCRAFT	SERVICE	CHARACTERISTICS
A-4 *	N/MC	Sub-sonic; typical load 4000 lbs, maximum load 9000 lbs.
A-7 *	AF Res/NG/N	Very accurate delivery; sub-sonic; typical load 8000 lbs, max load 15,000 lbs.
A-10 *	AF	Specialized CAS aircraft; sub-sonic; typical load 6000 lbs, max load 16,000 lbs; 30mm gun.
F-16 *	AF	A multi-role aircraft; complements the F-4 and F-15 in an air-to-air role. Most accurate ground delivery system in the inventory; supersonic; typical load 6000 lbs, max load 10,600 lbs.
F-18 *	N/MC	A multi-role fighter scheduled to replace the F-4. A wide variety of air-to-surface weapons. Typical load 7000 lbs, max load 17,000 lbs, 20mm gun mounted in the nose; air-to-air missiles.
AC-130	AF/R	A specialized CAS/RACO aircraft propeller driven. Two models: A model is equipped with two 40mm guns, two 20mm guns and two 7.62mm miniguns. The H model is similar, except no 7.62mm miniguns and one of the 40mm guns is replaced with a 105mm Howitzer. Both models have advanced sensors and target acquisition system including forward looking infrared radar (FLIR) and low light TV. Weapons employment accuracy is outstanding. This aircraft is vulnerable to enemy air defense systems and must operate in a low threat environment.

NOTE: * Denotes aircraft with FM capability.

3-3. ELEMENTS AND SEQUENCE OF CALL FOR FIRE.

a. Observer's Identification - Call Signs.

b. Warning Order:
    (1) Type of mission:
        (a) Adjust fire
        (b) Fire for effect
        (c) Suppress
        (d) Immediate suppression

(2) Size of element to fire for effect - When the observer does not specify what size element to fire, the battalion FDC will decide.

(3) Method of target location:
   (a) Polar Plot
   (b) Shift from a known point (give point TRP)
   (c) Grid

(4) Location of Target:
   (a) Grid Coordinate - 6 digit. 8 digit if greater accuracy is required.
   (b) Shift from a Known Point:
      (1) Send OT direction:
      - Mils (nearest 10).
      - Degrees.
      - Cardinal Direction.
      - Send lateral shift(Right/Left)(Nearest 10m)
      - Send range shift (Add/Drop) (Nearest 100m)
      - Send vertical shift (Up/Down) Use only if it exceeds 35 meters. (Nearest 5m)
   (c) Polar Plot:
      (1) Send direction. (Nearest 10 mils)
      - Send distance. (Nearest 100m)
      - Send vertical shift. (Nearest 5m)

(5) Description of Target:
   (a) Type.
   (b) Activity.
   (c) Number.
   (d) Degree of protection.
   (e) Size and shape. (Length/Width or Radius)

(6) Method of Engagement:
   (a) Type of Adjustment - When the observer does not request a specific type of fire control adjustment, area fire issued.
      (1) Area fire - moving target.
      (2) Precision fire - point target.

(7) Danger Close - When friendly troops are within:
   (a) 600m for mortars.
   (b) 600m for artillery.
   (c) 750m for naval guns 5 inches or smaller.
   (d) 1000m for naval guns over 5 inches.
   (e) 2000m for 16 inch naval guns (ICM or controlled variable time).

(8) Mark - Used to orient observer or to indicate targets.

(9) Trajectory:
    (a) Low angle. (Standard)
    (b) High angle. (Mortars or if requested)

(10) Ammunition - HE quick will be used unless specified by the observer.
    (a) Projectile. (HE, ILLUM, ICM, SMOKE, etc.)
    (b) Fuse. (Quick, Time, etc.)
    (c) Volume of Fire. (Observer may request the number of rounds to be fired.)

(11) Distribution:
    (a) 100m sheaf. (Standard)
    (b) Converged sheaf. (Used for small hard targets.)
    (c) Special sheaf. (Any length, width and attitude)
    (d) Open sheaf. (Separate bursts)
    (e) Parallel sheaf. (Linear target)

(12) Method of Fire and Control:
    (a) Method of Fire - Specific guns and a specific interval between rounds. Normally adjust fire, one gun is used with a 5-second interval between rounds.
    (b) Method of Control:
        (1) "At My Command" - "Fire". Remains in effect until observer announces "Cancel at my Command."
        (2) "Cannot Observe". Observer can't see the target.
        (3) "Time on Target". Observer tells FDC when he wants the rounds to impact.
        (4) Continuous Illumination. Calculated by the FDC otherwise observer indicates interval between rounds in seconds.
        (5) Coordinated Illumination. Observer may order the interval between ILLUM and HE shells.
        (6) "Cease Loading" to indicate the suspension of loading rounds.
        (7) "Check Firing". Immediate halt.
        (8) "Continuous Fire". Load and fire as fast as possible.
        (9) "Repeat". Fire another round(s) with or without adjustments.

(13) Authentication. Challenge and reply.

(14) Message to Observer:
    (a) Battery(ies) to fire for effect.
    (b) Adjusting battery.
    (c) Changes to the initial call for fire.
    (d) Number of rounds (per tube) to be fired for effect.
    (e) Target numbers.
    (f) Additional information:
        (1) Time of flight. Moving target mission.

(2) Probable error in range. 38 meters or greater (normal mission).
(3) Angle T. 500 mils or greater.

c. Correction of Errors. When FDC has made an error when reading back he fire support data, the observer announces "CORRECTION" and transmits the correct data in its entirety.

Examples of Call for Fire Transmissions:

GRID MISSION

OBSERVER
F24, this is J42, ADJUST
    FIRE, OVER.
GRID WM180513, DIRECTION
    0530, OVER.
Infantry platoon dug in, OVER

SHOT OUT

SPLASH OUT
End of mission, 15 casualties,
    Platoon dispersed, OVER.

FIRING UNIT
J42, this is F24, AJUST
    FIRE, OUT.
GRID WM180513, DIRECTION
    0530, OUT.
Infantry platoon dug in, OUT
    SHOT OVER

    SPLASH, OVER

End of mission, 15 casualties,
    Platoon dispersed, OUT.

SHIFT FROM KNOWN POINT

OBSERVER
J42, this is F24, ADJUST
    FIRE, SHIFT AB1001, OUT.
DIRECTION 2420, RIGHT
    400, ADD 400, OUT.
5 T72 Tanks at POL site,
    OVER
I AUTHENTICATE Tango
    OVER.
SHOT OUT
SPLASH OUT
End of mission, 2 tanks
destroyed, 3 in woodline,
OVER

FIRING UNIT
J42, this is F24, ADJUST
    FIRE, SHIFT AB1001, OUT.
DIRECTION 2420, RIGHT
    400, ADD 400, OUT.
5 T72 Tanks at POL site,
    AUTHENTICATE Juliet
November, OVER.
        SHOT, OVER.
    SPLASH, OVER.

    End of mission, 2 tanks
destroyed, 3 in
woodline, OUT.

CHAPTER FOUR
MOVEMENT

4-1. GENERAL. To survive on the battlefield, stealth, dispersion, and security must be enforced in all tactical movements. The leader must be skilled in all movement techniques.

a. Definition of Formations. Formations are arrangements of elements and soldiers in relation to each other. Squads use formations for control based on a METT-TC analysis. Leaders are where they can best control formations. This allows the fire team leader to lead by example, "Follow me and do as I do." All soldiers in the team must be able to see their leader (see figure 4-1).

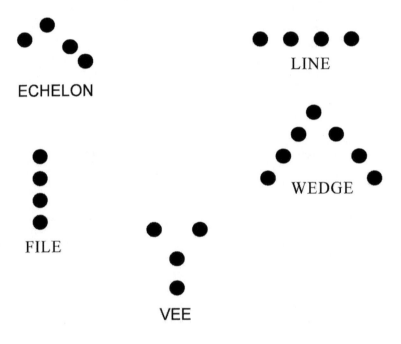

Figure 4-1: FORMATIONS

b. Techniques. A movement technique is the manner a unit uses to traverse terrain. There are three movement techniques: traveling, traveling overwatch, and bounding overwatch. The selection of a movement technique is based on the likelihood of enemy contact and the need for speed. Factors to consider for each technique are control, dispersion, speed, and security. Movement techniques are not fixed formations. They refer to the distances between soldiers, teams, and squads that vary based on mission, enemy, terrain, visibility, and any other factor that affects control. Soldiers must be able to see his fire team leaders. The platoon leader should be able to see his lead squad leader. Leaders control movement with arm-and-hand signals and use radios only when needed.

c. Standards.
   (1) Unit moves on designated route or arrives at specified location IAW OPORD maintaining accountability of all assigned/attached personnel.
   (2) Unit uses movement formation and technique ordered by the leader based on METT-TC.
   (3) Leaders remain oriented (within 200m) and follow planned route unless METT-TC dictates otherwise.
   (4) Unit will maintain 360 degree security and a 100% alert during movement.
   (5) Unit maintains 360 degree security and a minimum of 75% security during halts.
   (6) If contact with the enemy is made, it is made with the smallest element possible.
   (7) Control measures are used during movement (head counts, rally points, phase lines, etc.).

d. Fundamentals.
   (1) Have men who can navigate. Preparations are worthless if the objective cannot be found in time, or if the patrol is compromised because it is run into during movement. Plan to use at least two compass and pace men per patrol. NOTE: The element point man must not be tasked to perform compass or pace duties. The point man's sole responsibility is forward security for the element.
   (2) Avoid Detection: Patrols must use stealth, and use the cover and concealment of the terrain to its maximum advantage. Whenever possible, move during limited visibility in order to maximize technological advantages gained by night vision devices and to hinder the enemy's ability to detect the patrol. Exploit the enemy's weaknesses, and attempt to time movements to coincide with other operations that are distracting the enemy.
   (3) Maintain Constant Security: The patrol must use both active and passive security measures constantly. Give men or subunits responsibility for security enroute, at danger areas, at patrol bases, and most importantly in the objective area.
   (4) Plan for Use of Support Fires: Plan for fire support, (artillery, tactical air, attack helicopter, naval gunfire) even if you think it may not be needed during movement.
   (5) The enemy situation determines which of the three movement techniques will be used. When contact is not likely: TRAVELING; when possible: TRAVELING OVERWATCH; expected: BOUNDING OVERWATCH. Squads/platoons will usually move with traveling overwatch.

(6) In open terrain, keep men widely dispersed. When enemy contact is possible, have one fire team well forward and overwatch with the other fire team. Assign duties for the movement.

(7) Fire teams maintain visual contact, but the distance between them is such that the entire patrol does not become engaged if contact is made. Fire teams can spread their formations as necessary to gain better observation to the flanks. Although widely spaced, men retain their relative position in their wedge and follow their team leader. Only in extreme situations should the file be used.

(8) The lead squad must secure the front along with assuming responsibility for navigation. For a long movement, the PL may rotate the lead squad's responsibilities. The fire team/squad in the rear is charged with rear security.

(9) Vary movement techniques to meet the changing situation.

(10) With the exception of fire team leaders, leadership moves inside their formation where they can maintain the best control.

e. Movement techniques.

(1) The traveling is used when enemy contact is not likely but speed is necessary.

(2) The traveling overwatch is used when enemy contact is possible.

(3) The bounding overwatch is used when enemy contact is likely, or when crossing a danger area.

f. Traveling. In the traveling technique, the distance between individuals is about 10 meters with 20 meters between squads. It has the following characteristics:

(1) More control than traveling overwatch but less than bounding overwatch.

(2) Minimum dispersion.

(3) Maximum speed.

(4) Minimum security.

g. Traveling Overwatch. The traveling overwatch technique is the basic movement technique.

(1) The distance between individuals is about 20 meters, between teams about 50 meters

(2) In platoon traveling overwatch, the lead squad must be far enough ahead of the rest of the platoon to detect or engage any enemy before the enemy observes or fires on the main body. However, it must be close enough to be supported by the platoon's small arm's fires. This is normally between 50 to 100 meters, depending on terrain, vegetation, and light and weather conditions.

(3) In a column formation, only the lead squad should use the traveling overwatch; however, if greater dispersion is desired, all squads may use it.

(4) In other formations, all squads use traveling overwatch unless the platoon leader specifies not to.

(5) Traveling overwatch has the following characteristics:
- Good control
- Good dispersion
- Good speed
- Good security forward

h. Bounding Overwatch (Figure 4-1).
   (1) In the bounding overwatch technique, the distance between men remains
       approximately 20 meters. The distance between teams and squads varies.
   (2) The squad or platoon has a bounding element and an overwatch element. The
       bounding element moves while the overwatch element occupies an overwatch
       position that can cover the route of the bounding element by fire. Each bound is
       within supporting range of the overwatch element.

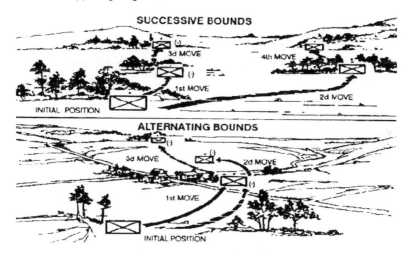

Figure 4-1. Squad Bounding Overwatch

   (3) The length of a bound depends on the terrain, visibility, and control.
   (4) Before a bound, the leader gives the following instructions to his subordinates:
       • Direction of the enemy if known
       • Position of overwatch elements
       • Next overwatch position
       • Route of the bounding element
       • What to do after the bounding element reaches the next position
       • How the elements receive follow-on orders
   (5) The characteristics of bounding overwatch are:
       • Maximum control
       • Maximum dispersion
       • Minimum speed
       • Maximum security

i. Platoon Bounding Overwatch (Figure 4-2).
  (1) Method One. When platoons use bounding overwatch, one squad bounds and one squad overwatches; the third squad awaits orders. Forward observers stay with the overwatching squad to call for fire. Platoon leaders normally stay with the overwatching squad who use machine guns and attached weapons to support the bounding squad.
  (2) Method Two. Another way is to have one squad use bounding overwatch and have the other two squads use traveling or traveling overwatch technique

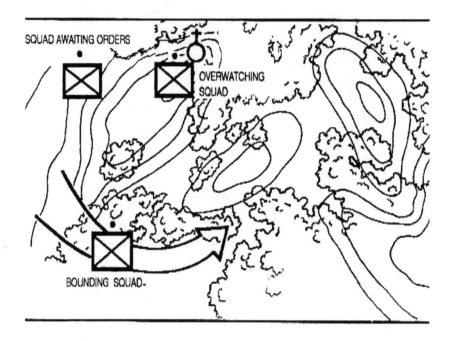

SQUAD AWAITING ORDERS

OVERWATCHING SQUAD

BOUNDING SQUAD.

Figure 4-2. Platoon Bounding Overwatch

  (3) Movement Considerations. When deciding where to move the bounding element, consider:
    • Where the enemy is likely to be
    • The mission
    • The routes to the next overwatch position
    • The weapons ranges of the overwatching unit

- The responsiveness of the rest of the unit
- The fields of fire at the next overwatch position

4-2. TACTICAL MARCHES. Platoons conduct two types of marches with the company: foot marches and motor (road) marches.

a. Purpose/General. A successful foot march is when troops arrive at their destination at the prescribed time, physically able to execute their tactical mission. Keep in mind that a Ranger moves faster, further, and fights harder than any other soldier.

b. Standard.
   (1) The unit crosses the start point and release point at the time specified in the order.
   (2) The unit follows the prescribed route, rate of march, and interval without deviation unless required otherwise by enemy action or higher headquarters action.

c. Fundamentals.
   (1) Effective control
   (2) Detailed Planning

d. Considerations.
   (1) METT-TC
   - Mission- Task and Purpose
   - Enemy- Intentions, Capabilities, and Course of Action
   - Terrain and Weather- Road Condition/Trafficability, and visibility
   - Troops/Equipment- Condition of soldiers and their load, number and types of weapons and radios.
   - Time- Start time, release time, rate of march, time available
   - Civilians- Movement through populated areas, refugees, OPSEC
   - Task Organization.
   - Headquarters- Command and Control
   - Security- Advance and trail teams
   - Main Body- Two remaining line squads and weapons squad
   - Command and Control
   - Control measures.
   (2) Start point and release point (given by higher)
      (a) Check Points- report to higher, utilize to remain oriented
      (b) Rally or rendezvous points- utilized if elements become separated
         - Location of Leaders- Where they can best control their elements
         - Commo Plan- Location of radios, frequencies, call signs, and OPSKEDs
         - Movement Techniques-
            (1) 3-5 meters day
            (2) 1-3 meters night

(3) March Order. May be issued as an OPORD, FRAGO, or Annex to either (must use operational overlay or strip map)
(4) Formations and order of movement
(5) Route of march- Assembly area, start point, release point, rally points, check points, break/halt points
(6) Start point time, release point time, and rate of march
(7) March interval for squads, teams and individuals
(8) Actions on enemy contact—air and ground
(9) Actions at halts
(10) Fires— detailed plan of fire support for the march
(11) Water supply plan

e. Duties and Responsibilities
(1) Platoon Leader:
- Before- Issue Warning Order, FRAGO, inspect, and supervise
- During- Makes SP time, ensures interval is maintained, maintains security, checks condition of men, enforces water discipline and field sanitation.
- After the March- Ensures men are prepared to accomplish their mission, supervises SLs, and ensures medical coverage is provided to men as needed
(2) Platoon Sergeant:
- Before- Assists PL, makes recommendations, and enforces uniform and packing lists
- During- Controls stragglers, assist platoon leader in maintaining proper interval and security
- At Halts- Enforces security, ensures welfare of men, enforces field sanitation
- After March- Coordinates for water, rations, and medical supplies. Recovers casualties
(3) Squad Leaders
- Before- Provides detailed instruction to TLs, inspects boots and socks for serviceability and proper fit, adjustment of equipment, full canteens, and equal distribution of loads.
- During- Controls squad, maintains proper interval between men and equipment, enforces security, and remains oriented.
- At Halts- Ensures security is maintained, provided men for water resupply as detailed. Physically checks the men in his squad, ensures they drink water, and change socks as necessary. Rotates heavy equipment.
- After March- Occupies squad sector of assembly area, conducts foot inspection and report condition of men to PL, prepares men for accomplishment of the mission.
(4) Security Squad:
- Lead Team- Point element for platoon, recon route to SP, call in check points, provide early warning, and maintain rate of march
- Move 10-20 meters in front of main body
(5) Medic:

- Assists platoon leadership in the assessment and treatment of march casualties. Advise the chain of command on the evacuation and transportation requirements of casualties

(6) Individual:

- Maintains interval, follows TLs examples, relays hand and arm signals, and remains alert during movement and at halts.

4-3. MOVEMENT DURING LIMITED VISIBILITY CONDITIONS. At night or when visibility is poor, a platoon must be able to function the same as during the day. It must be able to control, navigate maintain security, move and stalk at night or during limited visibility.

a. Control. When visibility is poor, the following methods aid in control.
  (1) Use of night vision devices
  (2) Leaders move closer to the front
  (3) Platoon reduces speed
  (4) Use of luminescent tape on equipment
  (5) Reduce intervals between men and elements
  (6) Headcounts conducted regularly

b. Navigation. To assist in navigation during limited visibility, leaders may use the following techniques:
  (1) Terrain association
  (2) Dead reckoning
  (3) Resection
  (4) Paralleling specific terrain features (handrail)
  (5) Guides or marked routes
  (6) GSR to guide units to link-ups
  (7) Navigation computers

c. Security. For stealth and security in night movements squads and platoons—
  (1) Enforce strict noise and light discipline
  (2) Use radio-listening silence
  (3) Use of camouflage
  (4) Use of terrain to avoid detection by enemy surveillance or night vision devices
  (5) Make frequent listening halts (SLLS)
  (6) Mask the sounds of movement with artillery fires

d. Rally Points. Actions to be taken at rally points must be planned in detail. The plan must provide for continuation as long as there is a good chance to accomplish the mission. Some form of communications must be left in the rally point to inform stragglers of how many men linked up and the direction they took. There are two techniques for actions at rally points:
  (1) Men available: The assembled members will wait until a set number of men arrive and then go on with the mission under the senior man present. This plan

is good for a reconnaissance patrol when two or three men may be able to accomplish the mission.

(2) Time Available: The assembled members wait for a set period of time, after which the senior man present will decide whether to continue the mission, based on troops and equipment present. This may be the plan when a minimum number of men, or certain items of equipment, or both, are needed to accomplish the mission.

e. Actions at halts. During halts, security must be posted and all approaches into the sector will be covered with key weapons.

4-4. DANGER AREAS. A danger area is any place on a unit's route where the leader's estimate process tells him his unit may be exposed to enemy observation or fire. Some examples of danger areas are open areas, roads and trails, native villages, enemy positions, and obstacles such as minefields, streams, and wire obstacles. Avoid danger areas whenever possible. If they must be passed or crossed, use great caution.

a. Standards:
    (1) The unit prevents the enemy from surprising the main body.
    (2) The unit moves all personnel and equipment across the danger area.
    (3) The unit prevents decisive engagement by the enemy

b. Fundamentals:
    (1) Designate near and far side rally points
    (2) Secure near side, left and right flank, and rear security
    (3) Recon and secure the far side
    (4) Cross the danger area
    (5) Plan for fires (when possible)

c. Technique for crossing danger areas:
    (1) Linear Danger Area (LDA) for a squad:
      STEP 1: The alpha team leader (ATL) observes the linear danger area and sends the hand and arm signal to the SL who determines to bound across.
      STEP 2: SL directs the ATL to move his team across the LDA far enough to fit the remainder of the squad on the far side of the LDA. Bravo team moves to the LDA to the right or left to provide an overwatch position prior to A team crossing.
      STEP 3: SL receives the hand and arm signal that it is safe to move the rest of the squad across (B team is still providing overwatch).
      STEP 4: SL moves himself, RTO and B team across the LDA. (A team provides overwatch for squad missions.)
      STEP 5: A team on azimuth at SLs command or hand and arm signal.

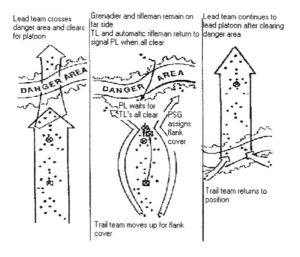

Figure 4-3. Linear Danger Area

(2) LDA crossing for a platoon:

    (a) The lead squad halts the platoon, and signals danger area.

    (b) The platoon leader moves forward to the lead squad to confirm the danger area and decides if current location is a suitable crossing site.

    (c) The platoon leader confirms danger area/crossing site and establishes near and far side rally points.

    (d) On the platoon leader's signal, the A team of the lead squad establishes an overwatch position to the left of the crossing site. Prior to crossing, the compassman with the lead two squads confirm azimuth and pace data.

    (e) B team of the lead squad establishes an overwatch position to the right of the crossing site.

    (f) Once overwatch positions are established, the platoon leader gives the second squad in movement the signal to bound across by fire team.

    (g) Once across, the squad is now lead in movement and continues on azimuth.

    (h) One stop, look, listen and smell (SLLS) is conducted, squad leader signals platoon leader all clear.

        (1) Day time—hand and arm signal (e.g. thumbs up)

        (2) Night time—Clandestine signal (e.g. IR, red lens)

    (i) Platoon leader receives all clear and crosses with RTO, FO, WSL, and 2 gun teams.

    (j) Once across, PL signals the 3rd squad in movement to cross at their location.

(k) PSG with medic and one gun team crosses after 2nd squad is across (sterilizing central crossing site).

(l) PSG signals security squad to cross at their location.

> **Note 1**: Platoon leader will plan for fires at all known LDA crossing sites.
> **Note 2**: Squads in overwatch 2nd and 3rd will sterilize where they cross.

Sequence—
- A and B teams of lead squad occupy overwatch positions
- Second squad crosses, and continues on azimuth
- PL crosses with RTO, FO, WSL, and 2 gun teams
- Third squad crosses in movement, link-up with 1st squad
- PSG crosses with medic and gun team
- Security squad crosses, link-up with 2nd squad
- With the new order of movement (formerly 2nd squad in movement now leading and the former 1st squad in movement in trail) the platoon continues movement on azimuth.

(3) Danger Area (Small/Open)

(a) The lead squad halts the platoon and signals danger area.

(b) The PL moves forward to the lead squad to confirm the danger area.

(c) The platoon leader confirms danger area and establishes near and far side rally points.

(d) The PL designates lead squad to bypass danger area using the detour-bypass method.

(e) Upon signal to move, lead squad offsets compass 90 degrees left or

(f) right as designated and moves in that direction. Paceman stops pace count and starts new pace count.

(g) After moving set distance (as instructed by PL). Lead squad assumes original azimuth, pace man original pace.

(h) After passing by the open area, the lead squad once again stops and again offset compass 90 degrees left or right and paceman starts pace once again.

(4) Danger Areas (series): A series of danger areas is two or more danger areas within an area that can be either observed or covered by fire.

- Double linear danger area (use linear danger area technique and cross as one LDA)
- Linear/small open danger area (use by-pass/contour technique. Figure 4-4)
- Linear/large open danger area (use platoon wedge in crossing)

Note: A series of danger areas is crossed using the technique which provides the most security.

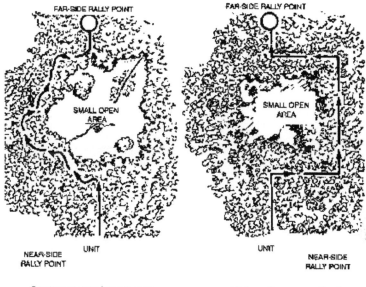

Contour around open area   Detour Bypass method

Figure 4-4. Small Open Area

(5) Danger Area (Large).
    (a) Lead squad halts the platoon, and signals danger area.
    (b) The platoon leader moves forward with RTO and FO and to confirm danger area.
    (c) The platoon leader confirms danger area and establishes near and far side rally points.
    (d) PL designates direction of movement.
    (e) PL may designate change of formation as necessary.

Note 1. Prior to the point man stepping into the danger area. The PL and FO will plan for fires.
Note 2. If far side of danger area is less than 250 meters- PL establishes overwatch, and designates lead squad to clear woodline on far side.

This page intentionally left blank for notes.

CHAPTER FIVE
PATROLLING

Patrols are missions to gather information or to conduct combat operations. Infantry platoons and squads primarily conduct two types of patrols: reconnaissance, and combat. This chapter describes the principles of patrolling, planning considerations used in preparation for patrols, conduct of patrols, supporting tasks, establishment of and actions in a patrol base, and movement to contact.

5-1. PRINCIPLES OF PATROLLING. All patrols are governed by five principles.

a. **Planning**. Quickly make a simple plan and effectively communicate it to the lowest level. A great plan that takes forever to complete and is poorly disseminated isn't a great plan. Plan and prepare to a realistic standard, and rehearse everything.
b. **Reconnaissance**. Your responsibility as a Ranger leader is to confirm what you think you know, and to find out what you don't.
c. **Security**. Preserve your force as a whole, and your recon assets in particular. Every Ranger and every rifle counts; anyone could be the difference between victory and defeat.
d. **Control**. Clear concept of the operation and commander's intent, coupled with disciplined communications, to bring every man and weapon you have available to overwhelm your enemy at the decisive point.
e. **Common Sense**. Do what you're supposed to do, without someone having to tell you, despite your own personal discomfort or fear.

5-2. PATROL PLANNING CONSIDERATIONS.
This paragraph provides the planning considerations common to most patrols. It discusses task organization, initial planning and coordination, completion of the plan, and contingency planning.

a. **Task Organization**. A patrol is a mission, not an organization. To accomplish the patrolling mission, a platoon or squad must perform specific tasks; for example, secure itself, cross danger areas, recon the patrol objective, breach, support, or assault. As with other missions, the leader tasks elements of his unit in accordance with his estimate of the situation, identifying those tasks his unit must perform and designating which elements of his unit will perform which tasks. Where possible, in assigning tasks, the leader should maintain squad and fire team integrity. The chain of command continues to lead its elements during a patrol. In this chapter, the terms "element" and "team" refer to the squads, fire teams, or buddy teams that perform the tasks as described. Squads and fire teams may perform more than one task in an assigned sequence; others may perform only one task. The leader must plan carefully to ensure that he has identified and assigned all required tasks in the most efficient way. Elements and teams for platoons conducting patrols include the following:
(1) Elements common to all patrols.

(a) Headquarters Element. The headquarters consists of the platoon leader (PL), RTO, platoon seargeant (PSG), FO and FO RTO. It may consist of any attachments that the PL decides that he or the PSG must control directly.

(b) Aid and Litter Team. Aid and litter teams are responsible for buddy aid and evacuating casualties.

(c) Enemy Prisoner of War (EPW) Team. EPW teams are responsible for controlling enemy prisoners IAW the five S's and the leader's guidance.

(d) Surveillance Team. The surveillance team keeps watch on the objective from the time that the leader's reconnaissance ends until the unit deploys for actions on the objective. They then rejoin their parent element.

(e) Enroute Recorder. The enroute recorder records all information collected during the mission.

(f) Compass Man. The compass man assists in navigation by ensuring the patrol remains on course at all times. Instructions to the compass man must include initial and subsequent azimuths. As a technique, the compass man should preset his compass on the initial azimuth before the unit moves out, especially if the move will be during limited visibility conditions. The platoon or squad leader should also designate an alternate compass man.

(g) Point/Pace Man. As required, the PL designates a point man and a pace man for the patrol. The pace man aids in navigation by keeping an accurate count of distance traveled. The point man selects the actual route through the terrain, guided by the compass man or team leader. In addition the point man also provides frontal security.

(2) Common elements of Combat Patrols.

(a) Assault Element. The assault element seizes and secures the objective and protects special teams as they complete their assigned actions on the objective.

(b) Security Element. The security element provides security at danger areas, secures the ORP, isolates the objective, and supports the withdrawal of the rest of the platoon once actions on the objective are complete. The security element may have separate security teams, each with an assigned task or sequence of tasks.

(c) Support Element. The support element provides direct and indirect fire support for the unit.

(d) Demolition Team. Demolition teams are responsible for preparing and detonating the charges to destroy designated equipment, vehicles, or facilities on the objective.

(e) Search Team. The assault element may provide two-man (buddy teams) or four-man (fire team) search teams to search bunkers, buildings, or tunnels on the objective. These teams will search the objective or kill zone for casualties, documents, or equipment. EPW Teams may double as Search Teams.

(f) Breach Element. The breach team conducts initial breaches as required in order to allow the patrol to enter an objective. This is typically done IAW

METT-TC and the steps outlined in the "Conduct an initial breach of a mined wire obstacle" battle drill in Chapter 6.

(3) Elements common to Reconnaissance patrols.
    (a) Reconnaissance Team. Reconnaissance teams reconnoiter the objective area once the security teams are in position. Normally these are two-man teams (buddy teams) to reduce the possibility of detection.
    (b) Reconnaissance and Security Teams. R&S teams are normally used in a zone reconnaissance, but may be useful in any situation when it is impractical to separate the responsibilities for reconnaissance and security.
    (c) Security Element. When the responsibilities of reconnaissance and security are separate, the security element provides security at danger areas, secures the ORP, isolates the objective, and supports the withdrawal of the rest of the platoon once the recon is complete. The security element may have separate security teams, each with an assigned task or sequence of tasks.

b. **Initial Planning and Coordination**. Leaders plan and prepare for patrols using the troop-leading procedures and the estimate of the situation, as described in Chapter 2. Through an Estimate of the Situation, leaders identify required actions on the objective (mission analysis) and plan backward to departure from friendly lines and forward to reentry of friendly lines. Because patrolling units act independently, move beyond the direct-fire support of the parent unit, and operate forward of friendly units, coordination must be thorough and detailed. Coordination is continuous throughout planning and preparation. PLs use checklists to preclude omitting any items vital to the accomplishment of the mission.
(1) Coordination with Higher Headquarters. Includes Intelligence, Operations, and Fire Support Coordination IAW Chapter 2-7, Coordination Checklists. This initial coordination is an integral part of Step 3 of Troop-Leading Procedures, Make a Tentative Plan.
(2) Coordination with Forward Units. The leader coordinates with the unit through which his platoon or squad will conduct its forward and rearward passage of lines, IAW Chapter 2-7, Coordination Checklists.
(3) Coordination with Adjacent Units. The leader also coordinates his unit's patrol activities with the leaders of other units that will be patrolling in adjacent areas at the same time, IAW Chapter 2-7, Coordination Checklists.

c. **Complete the Plan**. As the PL completes his plan he considers the following:
(1) Essential and supporting tasks. The PL ensures that he has assigned all essential tasks to be performed on the objective, at rally points, at danger areas, at security or surveillance locations, along the route(s), and at passage lanes. These make up the maneuver and tasks to subordinate units sub-paragraphs of the Execution paragraph.
(2) Key travel and execution times. The leader estimates time requirements for movement to the objective, leaders reconnaissance of the objective, establishment of security and surveillance, completion of all assigned tasks on the objective, and passage through friendly lines. Some planning factors are-

- Movement: Average of 1 KM/HR in Woodland Terrain;
- Leader's Recon: NLT 1 ½ HR;
- Establishment of Security and Surveillance: ½ HR;
- Passage through FFU: NLT ½ HR.

(3) Primary and alternate routes. The leader selects primary and alternate routes to and from the objective. The return routes should differ from the routes to the objective. The PL may delegate route selection to a subordinate, but is ultimately responsible for the routes selected.

(4) Signals. The leader should consider the use of special signals. These include hand-and-arm signals, flares, voice, whistles, radios, and infrared equipment. All signals must be rehearsed so that all soldiers know their meaning.

(5) Challenge and password forward of friendly lines. The challenge and password from the unit's SOI must not be used beyond the FLOT.

   (a) Odd-number system. The leader specifies an odd number. The challenge can be any number less than the specified number. The password will be the number that must be added to it to equal the specified number. (Example: the number is 7; the challenge is 3, and the password is 4)

   (b) Running Password. SOIs may also designate a running password. This code word alerts a unit that friendly soldiers are approaching in a less than organized manner and possibly under pressure. This may also be used to get soldiers quickly through a compromised passage of friendly lines. The number of soldiers approaching ("Ranger five") follows the running password.

(6) Location of leaders. The PL considers where he and the PSG and other key leaders are located for each phase of the patrol mission. The PL positions himself where he can best control the actions of the patrol. The PSG is normally with the following elements for each type of patrol:

- On an ambush, he normally controls the support element.
- On a raid, he normally controls the CCP.
- On an area reconnaissance, he normally stays in the ORP.
- On a zone reconnaissance, he normally moves with the reconnaissance element that establishes the link-up point.

(7) Actions on enemy contact. Unless required by the mission, the unit avoids enemy contact. The leader's plan must address actions on chance contact at each phase of the patrol mission. The unit's ability to continue will depend on how early contact is made, whether the platoon is able to break contact successfully (so that its subsequent direction of movement is undetected), and whether the unit receives any casualties as a result of the contact. The plan must address the handling of seriously wounded soldiers and KIAs. The plan must also address the handling of prisoners who are captured as a result of chance contact and are not part of the planned mission.

(8) Contingency Plans. The leader leaves his unit for many reasons throughout the planning, coordination, preparation, and execution of his patrol mission. Each time the leader departs the patrol main body, he must issue a five-point contingency plan to the leader left in charge of the unit. The contingency plan is described by the acronym GOTWA, and includes:

- G: Where the leader is GOING.

- O: OTHERS he is taking with him.
- T: TIME he plans to be gone.
- W: WHAT to do if the leader does not return in time.
- A: The unit's and the leader's ACTIONS on chance contact while the leader is gone.

(9) Rally points. The leader considers the use and location of rally points. A rally point is a place designated by the leader where the unit moves to reassemble and reorganize if it becomes dispersed. Soldiers must know which rally point to move to at each phase of the patrol mission should they become separated from the unit. They must also know what actions are required there and how long they are to wait at each rally point before moving to another.

(a) Criteria. Rally points must be:
- Easy to find;
- Have no recent signs of enemy activity.
- Have cover and concealment;
- Be away from natural lines of drift and high speed avenues of approach.
- Be defendable for short periods of time.

(b) Types of rally points. The most common types of rally points are initial, en route, objective, reentry, and near-and-far-side rally points.

(10) Actions at the ORP. Actions at the ORP typically include:
- Leaders Recon of the Objective.
- Conduct SLLS and pinpoint location.
- Issuing a FRAGO, if needed.
- Making final preparations before continuing operations; for example, recamouflaging, preparing demolitions, lining up rucksacks for quick recover. Preparing EPW bindings, first aid kits, litters, and inspecting weapons.
- Accounting for soldiers and equipment after actions at the objective are complete.
- Reestablishing the chain of command after actions at the objective are complete.
- Disseminating information from reconnaissance, if contact was not made.

(11) Leader's Reconnaissance of the Objective. The plan must include a leader's reconnaissance of the objective once the platoon or squad establishes the ORP. Before departing the leader must issue a 5 point contingency plan. During his reconnaissance, the leader pinpoints the objective, selects reconnaissance, security, support, and assault positions for his elements, and adjusts his plan based on his observation of the objective. Each type of patrol requires different tasks during the leader's reconnaissance. The platoon leader will bring different elements with him. (These are discussed separately under each type of patrol). The leader must plan time to return to the ORP, complete his plan, disseminate information, issue orders and instructions, and allow his squads to make any additional preparations.

(12) Actions on the Objective. Each type of patrol requires different actions on the objective. Actions on the objective are discussed under each type of patrol.

5-3. TYPES OF PATROLS.
The two types of patrols covered in this section are reconnaissance (recon) patrols and combat patrols. Combat patrols are further divided into raids and ambushes. A third type of patrol, the tracking patrol, is not covered in this section, but can be found in FM 7-8. This section will cover each of these types of patrols in terms of fundamentals and planning considerations, task standards, and execution (actions on the objective).

a. **RECONNAISSANCE PATROLS.** Recon patrols provide timely and accurate information on the enemy and terrain. They confirm the leader's plan before it is executed. Units on reconnaissance operations collect specific information [Priority Intelligence Requirements (PIR)] or general information [Information Requirements (IR)] based on the instructions from their higher commander. The two types of recon patrols discussed here are area and zone. This section discusses the fundamentals of reconnaissance, task standards for the two most common types of recon, and actions on the objective for those types of recon.

(1) Fundamentals of Reconnaissance. In order to have a successful area reconnaissance, the platoon leader must apply the fundamentals of the reconnaissance to his plan during the conduct of the operation.

(a) Gain all Required Information: The parent unit tells the patrol leader (PL) what information is required. This is in the form of the IR (Intelligence Requirements) and PIR (Priority Intelligence Requirements). The platoon's mission is then tailored to what information is required. During the entire patrol, members must continuously gain and exchange all information gathered, but cannot consider the mission accomplished unless all PIR has been gathered.

(b) Avoid Detection by the Enemy: A patrol must not let the enemy know that it is in the objective area. If the enemy knows he is being observed, he may move, change his plans, or increase his security measures. Methods of avoiding detection are:

(1) Minimize movement in the objective area (Area Recon).

(2) Move no closer to the enemy than necessary.

(3) If possible use long range surveillance devices or night observation devices.

(4) Camouflage, stealth, noise and light discipline.

(5) Minimize radio traffic.

(c) Employ security measures: A patrol must be able to break contact and return to the friendly unit with what information is gathered. If necessary, break contact and continue the mission. Security elements are emplaced so that they can overwatch the reconnaissance elements and suppress the enemy so the reconnaissance element can break contact.

(d) Task Organization: When the platoon leader receives the order, he analyzes his mission to ensure he understands what must be done. Then he task organizes his platoon to best accomplish the mission IAW METT-TC. Recons are typically squad-sized missions.

(2) Task Standards.
    (a) Area Recon. The area recon patrol collects all available information on PIR and other intelligence requirements specified in the order for the area. The patrol completes the recon and reports all information by the time specified in the order. The patrol is not compromised.
    (b) Zone Recon. The zone recon patrol determines all PIR and other intelligence requirements specified in the order for its assigned zone. The patrol reconnoiters without detection by the enemy. The patrol completes the recon and reports all information by the time specified in the order.

(3) Actions on the Objective (Area Recon)(Figure 5-1).
    (a) The element occupies the ORP as discussed in the section on occupation of the ORP. RTO calls in spare for occupation of ORP. The leader confirms his location on map while subordinate leaders make necessary perimeter adjustments.
    (b) The PL organizes the platoon in one of two ways: separate recon and security elements, or combined recon and security elements.
    (c) The PL takes subordinates leaders and key personnel on a leader's recon to confirm the objective and plan.
        (1) Issues a 5 point contingency plan before departure.
        (2) Establishes a suitable release point. That is out of sight and sound distance from the objective (if possible), but (at a minimum) definitely out of sight of the objective, and should also possess good rally point characteristics.
        (3) Allows all personnel to become familiar with the release point and surrounding area.
        (4) Identifies (pinpoints) the objective and emplaces surveillance. The surveillance team is positioned with one man facing the objective, and one facing back in the direction of the release point.
        (5) Takes subordinate leaders forward to pinpoint the objective, establish a limit of advance, and choose vantage points.
        (6) Maintains commo with the platoon throughout the leader's recon.
        (7) Designates a surveillance team to keep the objective under surveillance. Issues a contingency plan to the senior man remaining with the surveillance team.
    (d) The PSG maintains security and supervises priorities of work in the ORP.
        (1) Reestablishes security at the ORP.
        (2) Disseminates the PLs contingency plan.
        (3) Oversees preparation of recon personnel (Personnel recamouflaged, NODs and Binos prepared, Weapons on safe with a round in the chamber).
    (e) The PL and his recon party return to the ORP.
        (1) Confirms the plan or issues a FRAGO.

(2) Allows subordinate leaders time to disseminate the plan.
(f) The patrol conducts the recon by long-range observation and surveillance if possible.
  (1) R&S elements move to observation points that offer cover and concealment, and that are outside of small-arms range and range of local security measures.
  (2) Establishes a series of OPs if information cannot be gathered from one location.
  (3) Gathers all PIR using the acronym SALUTE.
(g) If necessary, the patrol conducts its recon by short-range observation and surveillance.
  (1) Moves to an OP near the objective.
  (2) Passes close enough to the objective to gain information.
  (3) Gathers all PIR using the acronym SALUTE.
(h) R&S teams move using a technique such as the cloverleaf method to move to successive OP's. In this method, R&S teams avoid paralleling the objective site, maintain extreme stealth, do not cross the limit of advance, and Maximize the use of available cover and concealment.
(i) During the conduct of the recon, each R&S team will return to the release point when any of the following occurs:
  (1) They have gathered all their PIR.
  (2) They have reached the limit of advance.
  (3) The allocated time to conduct the recon has elapsed.
  (4) Contact has been made.
(j) At the release point, the leader will analyze what information has been gathered and determine if he has met the PIR requirements.
(k) If the leader determines that he has not gathered sufficient information to meet the PIR requirements, or if the information he and the subordinate leader gathered differs drastically, he may have to send R&S teams back up to the objective site. Before doing this, he will issue new five-point contingency plans all around and may even have to return to the ORP to alert the PSG of the change.
(l) The R&S element returns undetected to the ORP by the specified time.
  (1) Disseminates information to all patrol members through key leaders at the ORP, or moves to a position at least one terrain feature or one kilometer away to disseminate. To disseminate, the leader has the RTO prepare three sketches of the objective site based on his (the leader's) sketch and provides the copies to the subordinate leaders to assist in dissemination.
  (2) Reports any information requirements and/or any information requiring immediate attention to higher headquarters, and departs for the designated area.
(m) If contact is made:
  (1) Moving to the release point: the recon element will attempt to break contact and return to the ORP, secure rucksacks, and quickly move out of the area. Once they have moved a safe distance away, the leader will inform higher HQ of the situation and take further instructions from them.

(2) While emplacing surveillance: These individuals will withdraw through the release point to the ORP and follow the same procedures as above.

(3) While conducting the recon: All personnel will fire a full magazine on to the objective site. Surveillance will fire a LAW on the biggest weapon on the objective. All elements will pull off the objective and move to the release point. The senior man will quickly account for all personnel and return to the ORP. Once in the ORP, the procedures as outlined in (1) above will be followed.

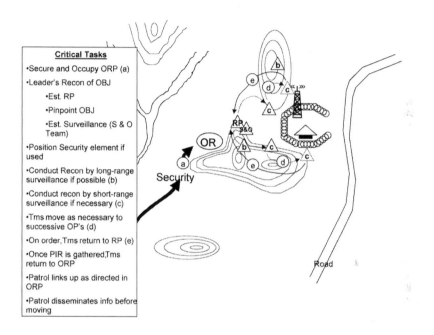

Critical Tasks
- Secure and Occupy ORP (a)
- Leader's Recon of OBJ
  - Est. RP
  - Pinpoint OBJ
  - Est. Surveillance (S & O Team)
- Position Security element if used
- Conduct Recon by long-range surveillance if possible (b)
- Conduct recon by short-range surveillance if necessary (c)
- Tms move as necessary to successive OP's (d)
- On order, Tms return to RP (e)
- Once PIR is gathered,Tms return to ORP
- Patrol links up as directed in ORP
- Patrol disseminates info before moving

Figure 5-1. Actions on the Objective -- Area Recon

(4) Actions on the Objective (Zone Recon)(Figures 5-2, 5-3, 5-4).

(a) The element occupies the initial ORP as discussed in the section occupation of the ORP. RTO calls in spare for occupation of ORP. The leader confirms his location on map while subordinate leaders make necessary perimeter adjustments.

(b) The recon team leaders organize their recon elements.

(1) Designate security and recon elements.

(2) Assign responsibilities (point man, pace man, enroute recorder, and rear security), if not already assigned.
(3) Designates easily recognizable rally points.
(4) Ensure local security at all halts.
(c) The patrol recons the zone.
    (1) Moves tactically to the ORP's.
    (2) Occupies designated ORP's.
    (3) Follows the method designated by the PL:
        a. Fan Method. Utilizes a series of ORP's. The patrol establishes security at the first ORP. Each recon element moves from the ORP along a different fan-shaped route that overlaps with others to ensure recon of the entire area. The leader typically maintains a reserve at the ORP. When all recon elements have returned to the ORP, the PL collects and disseminates all information before moving to the next ORP.
        b. Converging Routes Method. The PL selects routes from the ORP through the zone to a link-up point at the far side of the zone from the ORP. Each recon element moves and recons along a specified route, and all elements converge at one time and place to link-up.
        c. Box Method. The PL sends his recon elements from the first ORP along routes that form a box. He sends other elements along routes through the area within the box. All teams link-up at the far side of the box from the ORP.
(d) The recon teams perform reconnaissance.
    (1) During movement the squad will gather all PIR specified by the order.
    (2) Recon team leaders will ensure sketches are drawn of all enemy hardsites, roads, and trails.
    (3) When the squad arrives at new rendezvous point or ORP, the recon team leaders report to the PL with all information gathered.
    (4) Return to the ORP, or link up at the rendezvous point on time.
(e) The PL continues to control the recon elements.
    (1) PL moves with the recon element that establishes the link-up point.
    (2) PL changes recon methods as required.
    (3) PL designates times for the elements to return to the ORP or to link-up.
    (4) PL collects all information and disseminates it to the entire patrol. PL will brief all key subordinate leaders on information gathered by other squads, establishing one consolidated sketch if possible, and allow team leaders time to brief their teams.
    (5) PL and PSG account for all personnel.
(f) The patrol continues the recon until all designated areas have been reconned, and returns undetected to friendly lines.

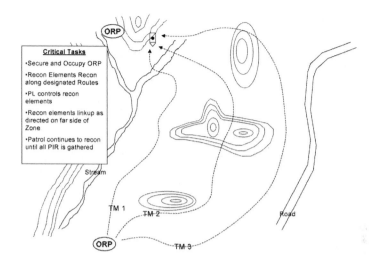

Figure 5-2. Actions on the Objective -- Zone Recon, Box Method.

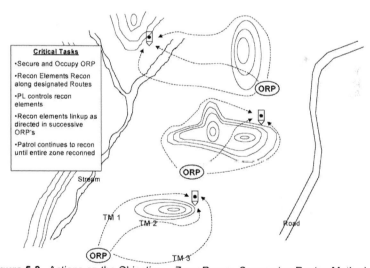

Figure 5-3. Actions on the Objective -- Zone Recon, Converging Routes Method

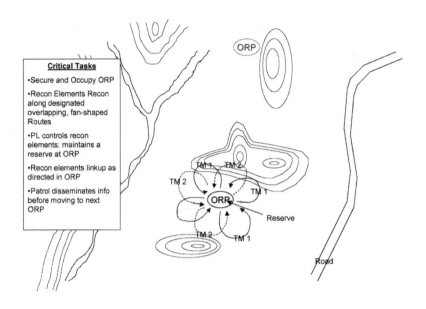

Critical Tasks

•Secure and Occupy ORP

•Recon Elements Recon along designated overlapping, fan-shaped Routes

•PL controls recon elements; maintains a reserve at ORP

•Recon elements linkup as directed in ORP

•Patrol disseminates info before moving to next ORP

Figure 5-4. Actions on the Objective -- Zone Recon, Fan Method

This space intentionally left blank for notes.

b. COMBAT PATROLS. Units conduct combat patrols to destroy or capture enemy soldiers or equipment; destroy installations, facilities, or key points; or harass enemy forces. Combat patrols also provide security for larger units. The two types of combat patrol missions are ambush and raid. This section describes overall combat patrol planning considerations, task considerations for each type of combat patrol, and finally actions on the objective for each type.

(1) **Planning Considerations** (General). In planning a combat patrol, the PL considers the following:

  (a) **Tasks to Subordinate Units**. Normally the platoon headquarters element controls the patrol on a combat patrol mission. The PL makes every attempt to maintain squad and fire team integrity as he assigns tasks to subordinates units.

    (1) The PL must consider the requirements for assaulting the objective, supporting the assault by fire, and security of the entire unit throughout the mission.

      a. For the assault on the objective, the PL considers the required actions on the objective, the size of the objective, and the known or presumed strength and disposition of the enemy on and near the objective.

      b. The PL considers the weapons available, and the type and volume of fires required to provide fire support for the assault on the objective.

      c. The PL considers the requirement to secure the platoon at points along the route, at danger areas, at the ORP, along enemy avenues of approach into the objective, and elsewhere during the mission.

      d. The PL will also designate engagement/disengagement criteria.

    (2) The PL assigns additional tasks to his squads for demolition, search of EPWs, guarding of EPWs, treatment and evacuation (litter teams) of friendly casualties, and other tasks required for successful completion of patrol mission (if not already in the SOP).

    (3) The PL determines who will control any attachments of skilled personnel or special equipment.

  (b) **Leader's Reconnaissance of the Objective**. In a combat patrol, the PL has additional considerations for the conduct of his reconnaissance of the objective from the ORP.

    (1) Composition of the leader's reconnaissance party. The platoon leader will normally bring the following personnel.

      • Squad Leaders to include the Weapons Squad Leader.

      • Surveillance team.

      • Forward Observer.

      • Security Element (dependent on time available).

    (2) Conduct of the leader's reconnaissance. In a combat patrol the PL considers the following additional actions in the conduct of the leader's reconnaissance of the objective.

      a. The PL designates a release point approximately half way between the ORP and this objective. The PL posts the surveillance team. Squads and fire teams separate at the release point and move to their assigned positions.

b. The PL confirms the location of the objective or kill zone. He notes the terrain and identifies where he can place mines or claymores to cover dead space. Any change to his plan is issued to the squad leaders (while overlooking the objective if possible).

c. If the objective is the kill zone for an ambush, the leader's reconnaissance party should not cross the objective; to do so will leave tracks that may compromise the mission.

d. The PL confirms the suitability of the assault and support positions and routes from them back to the ORP.

e. The PL issues a five-point contingency plan before returning to the ORP.

(2) **Task Standards**.

(a) **Hasty Ambush**. The platoon moves quickly to concealed positions. The ambush is not initiated until the majority of the enemy is in the kill zone. The unit does not become decisively engaged. The platoon surprises the enemy. The patrol captures, kills, or forces the withdrawal of the enemy within the kill zone. On order, the patrol withdraws all personnel and equipment in the kill zone from observation and direct fire. The unit does not become decisively engaged by follow-on elements. The platoon continues follow-on operations.

(b) **Deliberate (Point/Area) Ambush**. The ambush is emplaced NLT the time specified in the order. The patrol surprises the enemy and engages the enemy main body. The patrol kills or captures all enemy in the kill zone and destroys equipment based on the commander's intent. The patrol withdraws all personnel and equipment from the objective, on order, within the time specified in the order. The patrol obtains all available PIR from the ambush and continues follow-on operations.

(c) **Perform Raid**. The patrol initiates the raid NLT the time specified in the order, surprises the enemy, assaults the objective, and accomplishes its assigned mission within the commander's intent. The patrol does not become decisively engaged. The patrol obtains all available PIR from the raid objective and continues follow-on operations.

(3) **Planning Considerations (Ambush)**. An ambush is a surprise attack from a concealed position on a moving or temporarily halted target. Ambushes are classified by category--hasty or deliberate; type--point or area; and formation--linear or L-shaped. The leader uses a combination of category, type, and formation in developing his ambush plan. The key planning considerations include:

- Cover the entire kill zone by fire.
- METT-TC
- Use existing or reinforcing obstacles (Claymores and other mines) to keep the enemy in the kill zone.
- Security teams are typically equipped with hand held AT weapons (AT-4 or LAW) and claymores.
- Protect the assault and support elements with mines, claymores, or explosives.
- Use security elements or teams to isolate the kill zone.

- Assault into the kill zone to search dead and wounded, assemble prisoners, and collect equipment. (The assault element must be able to move quickly through its own protective obstacles.)
- Time the actions of all elements of the platoon to preclude loss of surprise.
- When the ambush must be manned for a long time, use only one squad to conduct the entire ambush and determining movement time of rotating squads from the ORP to the ambush site.

(a) Categories

    (1) Hasty ambush. A unit conducts a hasty ambush when it makes visual contact with an enemy force and has time to establish an ambush without being detected. The actions for a hasty ambush must be well rehearsed so that soldiers know what to do on the leader's signal. They must also know what action to take if the unit is detected before it is ready to initiate the ambush.

    (2) Deliberate ambush. A deliberate ambush is conducted against a specific target at a predetermined location. The leader requires the following detailed information in planning a deliberate ambush: size and composition of the targeted enemy, and weapons and equipment available to the enemy.

(b) Types

    (2) Point ambush. In a point ambush, soldiers deploy to attack an enemy in a single kill zone.

    (3) Area ambush. In an area, soldiers deploy in two or more related point ambushes.

(c) Formations(Figure 5-5)

    (1) Linear. In an ambush using a linear formation, the assault and support elements deploy parallel to the enemy's route. This positions both elements on the long axis of the kill zone and subjects the enemy to flanking fire. This formation can be used in close terrain that restricts the enemy's ability to maneuver against the platoon, or in open terrain provided a means of keeping the enemy in the kill zone can be effected.

    (2) L-Shaped. In an L-shaped ambush the assault element forms the long leg parallel to the enemy's direction of movement along the kill zone. The support element forms the short leg at one end of and at right angles to the assault element. This provides both flanking (long leg) and enfilading fires (short leg) against the enemy. The L-shaped ambush can be used at a sharp bend in a trail, road, or stream. It should not be used where the short leg would have to cross a straight road or trail.

Linear Ambush Formation

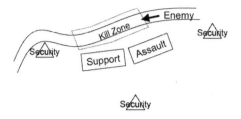

L-Shaped Ambush Formation

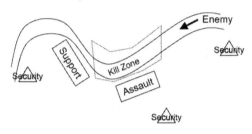

Figure 5-5. Ambush Formations

(4) **Planning Considerations (Raid).** A raid is a combat operation to attack a position or installation followed by a planning withdrawal. Squads do not conduct raids. The sequence of platoon actions for a raid is similar to those for an ambush. Additionally, the assault element of the platoon may have to conduct a breach of an obstacle. It may have additional tasks to perform on the objective; for example, demolition of fixed facilities. Fundamentals of the raid include:
- Surprise and speed. Infiltrate and surprise the enemy without being detected.
- Coordinated fires. Seal off the objective with well-synchronized direct and indirect fires.
- Violence of action. Overwhelm the enemy with fire and maneuver.
- Planned withdrawal. Withdraw from the objective in an organized manner, maintaining security.

(5) **Actions on the Objective (Deliberate Ambush) Figure 5-6.**
   (a) The PL prepares the patrol for the ambush in the ORP.
   (b) The PL prepares to conduct a leader's recon.
      (1) Designates the members of the leader's recon party (typically includes squad leaders, surveillance team, RTO/FO, and possibly the security element.
      (2) Issues a contingency plan to the PSG.
   (c) The PL conducts his leader's recon.
      (1) Ensures the leader's recon party moves undetected.
      (2) Confirms the objective location and suitability for the ambush.
      (3) Selects a kill zone.
      (4) Posts a surveillance team at the site and issues a contingency plan.
      (5) Confirms suitability of assault and support positions and routes from them to the ORP.
   (d) The PL adjusts his plan based on info from the recon.
      (1) Assigns positions.
      (2) Designates withdrawal routes.
      (3) Designates necessary control measures.
   (e) The PL confirms the ambush formation.
   (f) The security team(s) occupy first, securing the flanks of the ambush site, and providing early warning. The security element must be in position before the support and assault elements move forward of the release point. A security team remains in the ORP if the patrol plans to return to the ORP after actions on the objective.
   (g) Support element leader assigns sectors of fire.
      (1) Emplaces mines and obstacles as designated.
      (2) Identifies sectors of fire and emplaces limiting stakes to prevent friendly fires from hitting other elements.
      (3) Overwatches the movement of the assault element into position.
   (h) Once the support element is in position, or on the PLs order, the assault element departs the ORP and moves into position. Actions of the assault element should include:
      (1) Identify individual sectors of fire as assigned by the PL. Emplace aiming stakes.
      (2) Emplace claymores and other protective devices.
      (3) Emplace claymores, mines, or other explosives in dead space within the kill zone.
      (4) Camouflage positions.
      (5) Move weapon selector switches to FIRE.
   (i) The security element spots the enemy and notifies the PL, reporting the direction of movement, size of the target, and any special weapons or equipment carried. The security element must also keep the platoon leader informed if any enemy forces are following the lead force.
   (j) The PL alerts other elements, and determines if the enemy force is too large, or if his ambush can engage successfully.
   (k) The PL initiates the ambush using the highest casualty-producing device. He may use a command-detonated claymore. He must also plan backup method for

initiating the ambush should the primary means fail. This should also be a casualty-producing device such as his individual weapon. This information must be passed out to all soldiers and practiced during rehearsals.

(l) The PL ensures that the assault and support elements deliver fire with the heaviest, most accurate volume possible. The patrol must have a means of engaging the enemy in the kill zone during period of limited visibility if it becomes necessary to initiate the ambush under this situation. Use of tracers must be weighed against how it might help the enemy to identify friendly positions. The platoon leader may use handheld or indirect illumination flares to illuminate the kill zone.

(m) The PL gives the signal to lift or shift fires if the target is to be assaulted. The PL directs lift or shift prior to any assault.

(n) The assault element assaults before the remaining enemy can react.
    (1) Kills or captures enemy in the kill zone.
    (2) Uses individual movement techniques or bounds by fire teams to move.
    (3) Establishes security for special teams along a designated limit of advance (LOA) and gives ACE reports to higher.

(o) The PL directs special teams (EPW search, aid and litter, demo) to accomplish their assigned task once the assault element has established its LOA.
    (1) Once the kill zone has been cleared collect and secure all EPWs and move them out of the kill zone before searching bodies. Establish a location for EPWs and enemy wounded who will not be taken out that provides them cover, yet allows them to be found easily by their units.
    (2) Search from one side to the other and mark bodies that have been searched to ensure the area is thoroughly covered. Search all dead enemy personnel using two-man search techniques. [As the search team approaches a dead enemy soldier, one man guards while the other man searches. First, he kicks the enemy weapon away. Second, he rolls the body over (if on the stomach) by lying on top and when given the go ahead by the guard (who is positioned at the enemy's head), the searcher rolls the body over on him. This is done for protection in case the enemy soldier has a grenade with the pin pulled underneath him. The searchers then conduct a systematic search of the dead soldier from head to toe removing all papers and anything new (different type rank, shoulder boards, different unit patch, pistol, weapon, or NVD). They note if the enemy has a fresh or shabby haircut and the condition of his uniform and boots. They take note of the radio frequency, SOI, and maps. Once the body has been thoroughly searched, the search team will continue in this manner until all enemy personnel in and near the kill zone have been searched.]
    (3) Identify, collect, and prepare all equipment to be carried back or destroyed.
    (4) The demolition team prepares dual-primed explosives (C4 with two M60 fuse lighters and time fuse) or incendiary grenades and awaits the signal to initiate. This is normally the last action performed before the unit departs the objective and may signal the security elements to return to the ORP.
    (5) Evacuate and treat friendly wounded first, then enemy wounded, time permitting.

(6) Actions on the objective with stationary assault line; all actions are the same with the exception of the search teams. They must work in 3 men teams in order to provide security within the teams to the far side of the kill zone while the search is being conducted. All KIAs should be dragged to the near side of the kill zone prior to the search.

(p) If a flank security team makes contact, it fights as long as possible without becoming decisively engaged. It uses a prearranged signal to let the platoon leader know it is breaking contact. The platoon leader may direct a portion of the support element to assist the security team in breaking contact.

(q) The platoon leader directs the unit's withdrawal from the ambush site:

- Elements normally withdraw in the reverse order that they established their positions.
- The elements may return to the RP or directly to the ORP, depending on the distance between elements.
- The security element of the ORP must be alert to assist the platoon's return to the ORP. It maintains security for the ORP while the rest of the platoon prepares to leave.

(r) The PL and PSG direct actions at the ORP, to include accountability of personnel and equipment and recovery of rucksacks and other equipment left at the ORP during the ambush.

(s) The platoon leader disseminates information, or moves the platoon to a safe location (no less than one kilometer or one terrain feature away from the objective) and disseminates information.

(t) As required, the PL and FO execute indirect fires to cover the platoon's withdrawal.

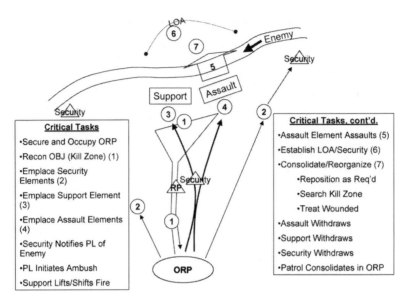

Figure 5-6. Actions on the Objective -- Deliberate Ambush

(6) **Actions on the Objective (Hasty Ambush) Figure 5-7.**

    (a) Using visual signals, any soldier alerts the unit that an enemy force is in sight. The soldier continues to monitor the location and activities of the enemy force until his team or squad leader relieves him, and gives the enemy location and direction of movement.

    (b) The platoon or squad halts and remains motionless.

    (c) The PL gives the signal to conduct a hasty ambush, taking care not to alert the enemy of the patrol's presence.

    (d) The leader determines the best nearby location for a hasty ambush. He uses arm-and-hand signals to direct the unit members to covered and concealed positions.

    (e) The leader designates the location and extent of the kill zone.

    (f) Teams and squads move silently to covered and concealed positions, ensuring positions are undetected and have good observation and fields of fire into the kill zone.

    (g) Security elements move out to cover each flank and the rear of the unit. The leader directs the security elements to move a given distance, set up, and rejoin the unit on order or, after the ambush (the sound of firing ceases). At squad level, the two outside buddy teams normally provide flank security as well as fires into the kill zone. At platoon level, fire teams make up the security elements.

(h) The PL assigns sectors of fire and issues any other commands necessary (control measures, etc.).
(i) The PL initiates the ambush, using the greatest casualty-producing weapon available, when the largest percentage of enemy is in the kill zone.
  (1) Controls the rate and distribution of fire.
  (2) Employs indirect fire to support the ambush.
  (3) Orders cease-fire.
(h) The PL designates personnel to conduct a hasty search of enemy personnel and process enemy prisoners and equipment.
(i) The PL orders the platoon to withdraw from the ambush site along a covered and concealed route.
(j) The PL gains accountability, reorganizes as necessary, disseminates information, reports the situation, and continues the mission as directed.

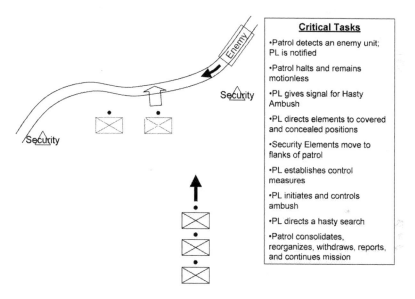

Critical Tasks

•Patrol detects an enemy unit; PL is notified

•Patrol halts and remains motionless

•PL gives signal for Hasty Ambush

•PL directs elements to covered and concealed positions

•Security Elements move to flanks of patrol

•PL establishes control measures

•PL initiates and controls ambush

•PL directs a hasty search

•Patrol consolidates, reorganizes, withdraws, reports, and continues mission

Figure 5-7. Actions on the Objective -- Hasty Ambush

(7) **Actions on the Objective (Raid) Figure 5-8.**
  (a) The patrol moves to and occupies the ORP IAW the patrol SOP. The patrol prepares for the leader's recon.
  (b) The PL, squad leaders, and selected personnel conduct a leader's recon.
    (1) PL leaves a contingency plan with the PSG.

(2) PL establishes the RP, pinpoints the objective, observes the objective, and verifies and updates intelligence information.

(3) Leader's recon verifies location of and routes to security, support, and

(4) assault positions.

(5) Leader's recon conducts the recon without compromising the patrol.

(6) Leader's recon normally recons support first, then assault.

(7) PL leaves a surveillance team to observe the objective.

(8) If the security teams were brought forward on the leader's reconnaissance, the security leader can begin moving security into position while the platoon leader and the remainder of the leaders reconnaissance party move back to the ORP.

(c) The PL updates his plan and issues instructions to his squad leaders.

(1) Assigns positions and withdrawal routes to all elements.

(2) Designates control measures on the objective (element objectives, lanes, limits of advance, and assault line).

(3) Allows SLs time to disseminate information, and confirm that their elements are ready.

(d) Security elements occupy designated positions, moving undetected into positions that provide early warning and can seal off the objective from outside support or reinforcement.

(e) The support element leader moves the support element to designated positions. The support element leader ensures his element can place well-aimed fire on the objective.

(f) The PL moves with the assault element into the assault position. The assault position is normally the last covered and concealed position before reaching the objective. As it passes through the assault position the platoon deploys into its assault formation; that is, its squads and fire teams deploy to place the bulk of their firepower to the front as they assault the objective.

(1) Makes contact with the surveillance team to confirm any enemy activity on the objective.

(2) Ensures that the assault position is close enough for immediate assault if the assault element is detected early.

(3) Moves into position undetected, and establish local security and fire control measures.

(g) Element leaders inform the PL when their elements are in position and ready.

(h) The PL directs the support element to fire.

(i) Upon gaining fire superiority, the PL directs the assault element to move towards the objective.

(1) Assault element holds fire until engaged, or until ready to penetrate the objective.

(2) PL signals the support element to lift or shift fires. The support element lifts or shifts fires as directed, shifting fire to the flanks of targets or areas as directed in the FRAGO.

(j) The assault element attacks and secures the objective. The assault element may be required to breech a wire obstacle. As the platoon or its assault element moves onto the objective, it must increase the volume and accuracy of fires.

Squad leaders assign specific targets or objectives for their fire teams. Only when these direct fires keep the enemy suppressed can the rest of the unit maneuver. As the assault element gets closer to the enemy, there is more emphasis on suppression and less on maneuver. Ultimately, all but one fire team may be suppressing to allow that one fire team to break into the enemy position. Throughout the assault, soldiers use proper individual movement techniques, and fire teams retain their basic shallow wedge formation. The platoon does not get "on-line" to sweep across the objective.

(1) Assault element assaults all the way through the objective to the designated LOA.

(2) Assault element leaders establish local security along the LOA, and consolidate and reorganize as necessary, providing ACE reports to the PL and PSG. The platoon establishes security, mans key weapons, provides first aid and prepares wounded soldiers for MEDEVAC, redistributes ammunition and supplies, relocates selected weapons to alternate positions if leaders believe that the enemy may have pinpointed them during the attack, adjusts other positions to maintain mutual support and squad and team leader provide ammunition, casualty, and equipment (ACE) reports to the platoon leader. The PL/PSG reorganize the patrol based on the contact.

   (a) On order, special teams accomplish all assigned tasks under the supervision of the PL, who positions himself where required to maintain control of the patrol.

   (b) Special Team Leaders report to PL when assigned tasks are complete.

(k) On order or signal of the PL, the assault element withdraws from the objective. Using prearranged signals the assault line begins an organized withdrawal from the objective site maintaining control and security as the withdrawal is conducted. The assault element will bound back in the vicinity of the original assault line and will begin a single file withdrawal through the APLs choke point. It is critical for all men to move through the choke point to maintain an accurate count. Once the assault element is a safe distance from the objective and the headcount is confirmed, the platoon can withdraw the support element. If the support element were a part of the assault line they will withdraw together and the security would be given the signal to withdraw. Once the support is a safe distance off the objective they will notify the platoon leader and the platoon leader will contact the security element and give them the signal to withdraw. All security teams will link-up at the release point and notify the platoon leader prior to moving to the ORP. As personnel return to the ORP, they immediately secure their equipment and establish 360-degree security. Once the security element returns, the platoon will move out of the objective area as soon as possible, normally within 2 – 3 minutes.

(1) Prior to withdrawal, demo team activates demo devices and charges.

(2) Support element or designated personnel within the assault element maintain local security during withdrawal.

(3) Leaders report updated accountability and status (ACE report) to the PL and PSG.

(l) Squads withdraw from the objective in the order designated in the FRAGO to the ORP.
   (1) Account for personnel and equipment.
   (2) Disseminate information.
   (3) Redistribute ammunition and equipment as required.
(m) The PL reports mission accomplishment to higher and continues the mission.
   (1) Reports raid assessment to higher.
   (2) Informs higher of any IR/PIR gathered.

This space intentionally left blank for notes.

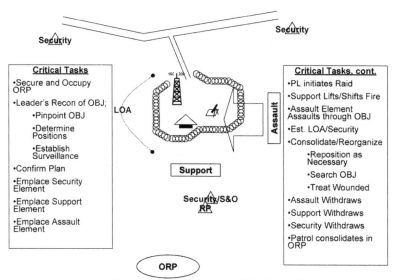

Figure 5-8. Actions on the Objective -- Raid

5-4. SUPPORTING TASKS. This section covers Passage of Friendly Lines, Link-up, Patrol Debriefing, and Occupation of an ORP.

(a) **Passage of Lines**. Movement in and around forward units must be controlled, coordinated, and kept to a minimum to preclude the possibility of being engaged by friendly forces and /or activating their reconnaissance, surveillance, and target acquisition devices. Additionally, the forward unit positions are considered danger areas and it must be assumed that they are under enemy surveillance at all times.

(1) Task Standards. The unit moves all personnel and equipment through the stationary unit NLT the time specified in the order. The enemy surprises neither unit main body during passage of lines.

(2) Planning Considerations.

(a) Fundamentals of Passage of Lines.

- Conduct the passage as quickly as possible.
- Avoid masking the fires of the forward unit.
- Coordinate early during the planning process and maintain coordination and liaison during execution.
- Plan for likely contingencies.
- When possible, bypass the stationary unit.
- When possible, avoid passing through a unit in contact.

(b) Coordination measures (to be used ICW the Coordination Checklists in Chapter 2-7).

- Identify both units.
- Provide the size of both units.
- Provide the times of departure and return.
- Provide the departing unit's AO (but not specific objectives or missions).
- Plan for exchange of intelligence.
- Plan for recon of the stationary unit's position.
- Plan for exchange of tactical plans.
- Plan for exchange of communication information.
- Plan for near and far recognition signals.
- Plan for guides and traffic control measures.
- Plan for security measures during the passage.
- Plan specific control measures for the passage (contact points, passage lanes and points, release points, assembly areas, and rally points).
- Coordinate fire support responsibilities and fire plans.
- Determine transfer of responsibility or action on enemy contact during passage.
- Coordinate any CSS.
- Coordinate contingency plans for both units.

(c) The PL should recon and locate the following if time permits:
- Passage lanes and passage points.
- Obstacles and safety lanes.
- Release Points.
- Assembly Areas.
- Contact points, start points, and routes.
- Positions of the stationary force.
- CS and CSS elements.
- Enemy positions in the AO.

(3) Execution (Forward Passage).

(a) The patrol moves at the specified time to a covered/concealed positionnear the contact point.

(b) Link up with stationary unit guides that lead the patrol from the contact point through the passage lanes and passage points to the release point (RP).

(c) Confirm or update the plan with the unit guide, and effect final coordination with the stationary unit commander.

(d) The guide leads the patrol to the Passage Point (PP). Enroute to the PP, the guide designates the Initial Rally Point (IRP) using the appropriate hand and arm signal, and all personnel ensure they know its location. This can easily be accomplished by passing by, moving through, or actually occupying.

(e) Patrol clears forward of the RP to the first covered and concealed position using security elements.

(f) Patrol moves forward to the RP once the area is cleared.

(g) PSG counts the patrol through the RP with the unit guide, and makes the following final coordination:
- Confirms the number of personnel in the patrol.
- Confirms the time the guide will wait at the RP.

- Confirms the running password.

(h) The patrol ensures continuous movement through the RP, and conducts a security halt to orient to the sights, sounds, and smells of the battlefield only once it has moved beyond the stationary unit FPF.

(4) Execution (Rearward Passage).

(a) The patrol occupies the reentry rally point.

(b) PL contacts the forward unit by radio and tells them that the platoon is ready to reenter.

(c) During good visibility the moving element has 2 chances at finding the break in the wire, during limited visibility they only have one chance.

(d) Upon confirmation of reentry with the stationary unit, the PL and a security team move to the contact point.

    (1) The security team establishes contact with the guide using far and near recognition signals.

    (2) Upon link-up with the guide, the security team leads the platoon forward to the passage point.

(e) The PSG and guide count each man through the passage point, and the PSG identifies each man.

(f) The patrol follows the guide without stopping to an assembly area to the rear of the stationary unit.

(g) The PL reports to the CP of the stationary unit and provides tactical information concerning the commander's area of responsibility.

(h) The PL rejoins the patrol and moves to the location designated in the order. Actions on Enemy Contact during Forward Passage.

    (1) If contact is made while the squad/platoon is at the security halt location and the squad/platoon leader is at the FFU's command post, the PSG will take command of the patrol and take guidance from the guide.

    (2) If contact is made while the patrol is moving toward the PP, the patrol will occupy the IRP as a security perimeter, call higher for orders, and stay in the IRP unless a representative from the friendly unit moves the squad/platoon.

    (3) If contact is made while the squad/platoon is the passage lane, they will turn around and move back through the PP and occupy the IRP. They will inform higher of the situation and await orders.

    (4) If the squad/platoon gets outside the PP but not yet gone beyond the friendly forward unit's FPF and contact is made, the squad leader will issue verbal instructions as to whether to go forward or back to the guide. If the squad/platoon goes back, they will use the running password to enter the PP and occupy the IRP and inform higher. Otherwise, the squad/platoon leader will simply attempt to break contact using the appropriate battle drill and then continue on the mission.

    (5) If the squad/platoon is already outside the FPF and makes contact, they will use the appropriate battle drill to react to or break contact.

b. **Link-Up.** A link-up is a meeting of friendly ground forces. Link-ups depend on control, detailed planning, communications, and stealth.

(1) Task Standard. The units link up at the time and place specified in the order. The enemy does not surprise the main bodies. The link-up units establish a consolidated chain of command.

(2) Link-up Site Selection. The leader identifies a tentative link-up site by map reconnaissance or higher headquarters designates a link-up site. The link-up site should have the following characteristics:
(a) Easy to recognize.
(b) Provides cover and concealment.
(c) Has no tactical value to the enemy.
(d) Away from natural lines of drift.
(e) Defendable.
(f) Provides multiple access and escape routes.

(3) Execution. Link-up procedure begins as the unit moves to the link-up point. The steps of this procedure are:
(a) The stationary unit performs link-up actions.
  (1) Occupies the link-up rally point NLT the time specified in the order.
  (2) Establishes all-around security, establishes commo, and prepares to accept the moving unit.
  (3) The security team clears the immediate area around the link-up point. It then marks the link-up point with the coordinated recognition signal. The unit moves to a covered and concealed position and observes the link-up point and immediate area around it.
(b) The moving unit performs link-up actions.
  (1) If using radio communications, the unit reports its location using phase lines, checkpoints, or other control measures.
  (2) Halts at a safe distance from the link-up point in a covered and concealed position (the link-up rally point).
(c) The PL and a contact team prepare to make physical contact with the stationary unit.
  (1) Issue a contingency plan to the PSG.
  (2) Maintain commo with the platoon; verify near and far recognition signals for link-up (Good Visibility and Limited Visibility).
  (3) Exchange far and near recognition signals with the link-up unit; conduct final coordination with the link-up unit.
(d) The stationary unit guides the patrol from its link-up rally point to the stationary unit link-up rally point.
  (1) Link-up is complete by the time specified in the order.
  (2) The main body of the stationary unit is alerted before the moving unit is brought forward.
(e) The patrol continues its mission IAW the order.

(4) Coordination Checklist. The PL coordinates or obtains the following information from the unit that his patrol will link-up with:
(a) Exchange frequencies, call signs, codes, and other communication information.
(b) Verify near and far recognition signals.
(c) Exchange fire coordination measures.

(d) Determine command relationship with the link-up unit; plan for consolidation of chain of command.

(e) Plan actions following link-up.

(f) Exchange control measures (contact points, phase lines, contact points, and others as appropriate).

c. **Debriefing.** Immediately after the platoon or squad returns, personnel from higher headquarters conduct a thorough debrief. This may include all members of the platoon or the leaders, RTO's, and any attached personnel. Normally the debriefing is oral. Sometimes a written report is required. Information on the written report should include:

- Size and composition of the unit conducting the patrol.
- Mission of the platoon (type of patrol, location, and purpose).
- Departure and return times.
- Routes. Use checkpoints, grid coordinates for each leg or include an overlay.
- Detailed description of terrain and enemy positions that were identified.
- Results of any contact with the enemy.
- Unit status at the conclusion of the patrol mission, including the disposition of dead or wounded soldiers.
- Conclusions or recommendations.

d. **Objective Rally Point (ORP).** The ORP is a point out of sight, sound, and small arms range of the objective area. It is normally located in the direction that the platoon plans to move after completion of actions on the objective. The ORP is tentative until the objective is pinpointed.

(1) Occupation of the ORP (Figure 5-9).

(a) The patrol halts beyond sight and sound of the tentative ORP (200-400m in good visibility, 100-200m in limited visibility).

(b) The patrol establishes a security halt IAW the unit SOP.

(c) After issuing a contingency plan to the PSG, the PL moves forward with a recon element to conduct a leader's recon of the ORP.

(d) For a squad-sized patrol, the PL moves forward with a compass man and one member of each fire team to confirm the ORP.

(1) After physically clearing the ORP location, the PL leaves two men at the 6 o'clock position facing in opposite directions.

(2) The PL issues a contingency plan and returns with the compass man to guide the patrol forward.

(3) The PL guides the patrol forward into the ORP, with one team occupying from 3 o'clock through 12 o'clock to 9 o'clock, and the other occupying from 9 o'clock through 6 o'clock to 3 o'clock.

(a) For a platoon-sized patrol, the PL follows the same sequence, taking one ammo bearer or assistant gunner from each gun team forward and positioning them at 10, 2, and 6 o'clock.

(1) The first squad in the order of march is the base squad, occupying from 10 to 2 o'clock.

(2) The trail squads occupy from 2 to 6 o'clock and 6 to 10 o'clock respectively.

(3) The patrol headquarters element occupies the center of the triangle.

(b) Actions in the ORP. The unit prepares for the mission in the ORP. During the leader's recon of the objective, once the objective is pinpointed, the PSG will generally line up rucks IAW unit SOP in the center of the ORP.

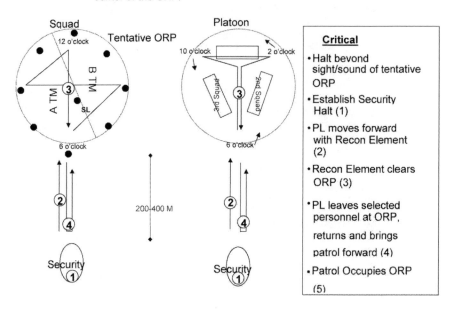

Figure 5-9. Occupation of the ORP

5-5. PATROL BASE. A patrol base is a security perimeter that is set up when a squad or platoon conducting a patrol halts for an extended period. Patrol bases should not be occupied for more than a 24 hour period (except in emergency). A patrol never uses the same patrol base twice. Patrol bases are typically used:

- To avoid detection by eliminating movement.
- To hide a unit during a long detailed reconnaissance.
- To perform maintenance on weapons, equipment, eat and rest.
- To plan and issue orders.
- To reorganize after infiltrating on an enemy area.

- To establish a base from which to execute several consecutive or concurrent operations.

a. Fundamentals. Keep the following fundamentals in mind during patrol base operations.
   (1) Site selection. The leader selects the tentative site from a map or by aerial reconnaissance. The site's suitability must be confirmed and secured before the unit moves into it. Plans to establish a patrol base must include selecting an alternate patrol base site. The alternate site is used if the first site is unsuitable or if the patrol must unexpectedly evacuate the first patrol base.
   (2) Planning Considerations. Leaders planning for a patrol base must consider the mission and passive and active security measures. A patrol base must be located so it allows the unit to accomplish its mission.
      (a) Security Measures. Security measures involve the following selection criteria and planning considerations:
         (1) Selection Criteria.
            - Select Terrain the enemy would probably consider of little tactical value.
            - Select Terrain that is off main lines of drift.
            - Select difficult terrain that would impede foot movement such as an area of dense vegetation, preferably bushes and trees that spread close to the ground.
            - Select Terrain near a source of water.
            - Select Terrain that can be defended for a short period of time and that offers good cover and concealment.
            - Avoid known or suspected enemy positions.
            - Avoid Built-up areas.
            - Avoid Ridges and hilltops, except as needed for maintaining communications.
            - Avoid Small valleys.
            - Avoid Roads and trails.
         (2) The leader plans for:
            - Observation posts and communication with observation posts.
            - Patrol or platoon fire plan.
            - Alert Plan.
            - Withdrawal plan from the patrol base to include withdrawal routes and a rally point, rendezvous point, or alternate patrol base.
            - A security system to make sure that specific soldiers are awake at all times.
            - Enforcement of camouflage, noise, and light discipline.
            - The conduct of required activities with minimum movement and noise.
            - Priorities of Work.

b. Occupation (Figure 5-10).

(1) A PB is reconned and occupied in the same manner as an ORP, with the exception that the platoon will typically plan to enter at a 90 degree turn (this is METT-TC dependent; if there is nothing to be gained by this step, the patrol does not do it). The PL leaves a two-man OP at the turn, and the patrol covers any tracks from the turn to the PB.

(2) The platoon moves into the PB. Squad-sized patrols will generally occupy a cigar-shaped perimeter; platoon-sized patrols will generally occupy a triangle-shaped perimeter.

(3) The PL and another designated leader start at 6 o'clock and move in a clockwise manner, inspecting and adjusting the perimeter as necessary.

(4) After the PL has checked each squad sector, each SL sends a two-man R&S team to the PL at the CP. The PL issues the three R&S teams a contingency plan, recon instructions, and detailed guidance on what to look for (enemy, water, built-up areas or human habitat, roads, trails, or possible rally points).

(5) Each R&S team departs at the left flank of its squad, moves a prescribed distance and direction, and reenters at the right flank of its own squad.

    (a) Squad-sized patrols do not normally send out an R&S team at night.

    (b) R&S teams will prepare a sketch of the area to the squad front if possible.

    (c) The patrol remains at 100 % alert during this recon.

    (d) If the PL feels the patrol was tracked or followed, he may elect to wait in silence at 100 % alert before sending out R&S teams.

    (e) The R&S teams may use methods such as the "I", the "Box", or the T". Regardless of the method chosen the R&S team must be able to provide the PL with the same information.

(6) Upon completion of R&S, the PL confirms or denies the patrol base location, and either moves the patrol or begins priorities of work.

c. Passive (Clandestine) Patrol Base (Squad)

    (1) The purpose of a passive patrol base is for the rest of a squad or smaller size element.

    (2) Unit moves as a whole and occupies in force.

    (3) Squad leader ensures that the unit moves in at a 90-degree angle to the order of movement.

    (4) A claymore mine is emplaced on route entering patrol base.

    (5) Alpha and Bravo teams sit back to back facing outward, ensuring that atleast one individual per team is alert and providing security.

d. Priorities of Work (Platoon and Squad) Once the PL is briefed by the R&S teams and determines area is suitable for a patrol base, the leader establishes or modifies defensive work priorities in order to establish the defense for the patrol base. Priorities of work is not a laundry list of tasks to be completed; to be effective, priorities of work must consist of a task, a given time, and a measurable performance standard. For each priority of work, a clear standard must be issued to guide element in the successful accomplishment of each task. It must also be designated whether the work will be controlled in a centralized or decentralized manner. Priorities of work are determined IAW METT-TC. Priorities of Work may include, but are not limited to the following tasks:

(1) Security (continuous).
- Prepare to utilize all passive and active measures to cover 100% of the perimeter 100% of the time, regardless of the percentage of weapons used to cover that 100% of the terrain.
- Readjust after R&S teams return, or based on current priority of work (such as weapons maintenance).
- Employ all elements, weapons, elements and personnel to meet conditions of the terrain, enemy or situation.
- Assign sectors of fire to all personnel and weapons. Develop squad sector sketches and platoon fire plan.
- Confirm location of fighting positions for cover, concealment, and observation and fields of fire. SLs supervise placement of aiming stakes and claymores.
- Only use one point of entry and exit, and count personnel in and out. Everyone is challenged IAW the unit SOP.
- Hasty fighting positions are prepared at least 18 inches deep (at the front), and sloping gently from front to rear, with a grenade sump if possible.

(2) Withdrawal Plan. The PL designates the signal for withdrawal, order of withdrawal, and the platoon rendezvous point and/or alternate patrol base.

(3) Communication (continuous). Commo must be maintained with higher headquarters, OP's, and within the unit. May be rotated between the patrol's RTOs to allow accomplishment of continuous radio monitoring, radio maintenance, act as runners for PL, or conduct other priorities of work.

(4) Mission preparation and planning. The PL uses the patrol base to plan, issue orders, rehearse, inspect, and prepare for future missions.

(5) Weapons and equipment maintenance. The PL ensures that machine guns, weapon systems, commo equipment, and night vision devices (as well as other equipment) is maintained. These items are not broken down at the same time for maintenance (NMT 25 % at one time), and weapons are not disassembled at night. If one machine gun is down, then security for all remaining systems is raised.

(6) Water Re-Supply. The PSG organizes watering parties as necessary. The watering party carries canteens in an empty rucksack or duffel bag, and must have commo and a contingency plan prior to departure.

(7) Mess plan. At a minimum, security and weapons maintenance areperformed prior to mess. No more than half of the platoon typically eats at one time, and men will typically eat 1-3 M behind their fighting positions.
    (a) Rest/sleep plan management. The patrol conducts rest as necessary to prepare for future operations.
    (b) Alert Plan and Stand-to. The PL states the alert posture and the stand-to time. He sets up the plan to ensure all positions are checked periodically, OP's are relieved periodically and that at least one leader is always alert.

The patrol typically conducts stand-to at a time specified by unit SOP (i.e., 30 minutes prior to and after BMNT or EENT).

(c) Re-supply. Distribute or cross-load ammunition, meals, equipment, etc.

(d) Sanitation and Personal Hygiene. The PSG and medic ensure a slit trench is prepared and marked, and that squads designate urine areas. All soldiers will shave, brush teeth, wash face, hands, armpits, groin, and feet, and darken (brush shine) boots daily. The patrol will not leave trash behind.

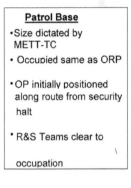

Patrol Base
- Size dictated by METT-TC
- Occupied same as ORP
- OP initially positioned along route from security halt
- R&S Teams clear to occupation

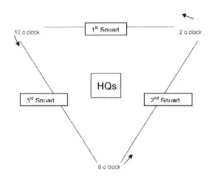

Patrol Base
- Machine Guns positioned at 2, 6, and 10 o'clock to cover the front of the squad to their left
- Slit Trench and urine holes designated
- Hasty fighting Positions (18" Deep)
- PL establishes priorities of work IAW METT-TC

Figure 5-10. Patrol Base

5-6. MOVEMENT TO CONTACT

a. Purpose/General: The movement to contact (MTC) is one of the five types of offensive operations. A MTC gains or regains contact with the enemy. Once contact is made, the unit develops the situation. Normally a platoon conducts a MTC as part of a larger force. There are two techniques of conducting a movement to contact: Approach march and search & attack.

(1) Search and Attack (S&A). This technique is utilized when the enemy is dispersed, is expected to avoid contact, disengage or withdraw, or you have to deny his movement in an area. The search and attack technique involves the use of multiple platoons, squads, and fire teams coordinating their actions to make contact with the enemy. Platoons typically attempt to find the enemy and then fix and finish him. They combine patrolling techniques with the requirement to conduct hasty or deliberate attacks once the enemy has been found. Planning considerations include:
- The factors of METT-TC.
- The requirement for decentralized execution.

- The requirement for mutual support.
- The length of operations.
- Minimize soldier's load to facilitate stealth and speed.
- Resupply and MEDEVAC.
- Positioning key leaders and equipment.
- Employment of key weapons.
- Requirement for patrol bases.
- Concept for entering the zone of action.
- The concept for link-ups while in contact.

    (2) Approach March. The concept of the approach march is to makecontact with the smallest element, allowing the commander the flexibility of destroying or bypassing the enemy. A platoon uses the approach march method as part of a larger unit. It can be tasked as the advance guard, move as part of the main body, or provide flank or rear security for the company or battalion. They may also receive on-order missions as part of the main body.

b. Fundamentals common to all movements to contact.
   (1) Make enemy contact with smallest element possible.
   (2) Rapidly develop combat power upon enemy contact.
   (3) Provide all-round security for the unit.
   (4) Support higher unit's concept.
   (5) Reports all information rapidly and accurately and strives to gain and maintain contact with the enemy.
   (6) Requires decentralized execution.
   (7) The following issues should be considered heavily for MTC operations:
      (a) Factors of METT-TC.
      (b) Reduced soldier's load.

c. Task Standards. The platoon moves NLT the time specified in the order. The platoon makes contact with the smallest element possible, and the main body is not surprised by the enemy. Once the platoon makes contact, it maintains contact. The platoon destroys squad and smaller-sized elements, and fixes elements larger than a squad. The platoon maintains sufficient fighting force capable of conducting further combat operations. Reports of enemy locations and contact are forwarded. If not detected by the enemy, the PL initiates a hasty attack. The platoon sustains no casualties from friendly fire. The platoon is prepared to initiate further movement within 25 minutes of contact, and all personnel and equipment are accounted for.

d. Critical Performance Measures (Search and Attack).
   (1) The platoon locates the enemy without being detected.
   (2) Once engaged, fixes the enemy in position and maneuvers against the enemy.
   (3) Maintains security throughout actions to avoid being flanked.

e. Critical Performance Measures (Approach March).
   (1) PL selects the appropriate movement formation based on likelihood of enemy contact.

(2) Maintains contact, once contact is made, until ordered to do otherwise.

This space intentionally left blank for notes.

CHAPTER SIX
BATTLE DRILLS

Infantry battle drills describe how platoons and squads apply fire and maneuver to commonly encountered situations. They require leaders to make decisions rapidly and to issue brief oral orders quickly.

6-1. DEFINITION. FM 25-101 defines a battle drill as "a collective action rapidly executed without applying a deliberate decision-making process."

a. Characteristics of a battle drill are—
   - They require minimal leader orders to accomplish and are standard throughout the Army.
   - Sequential actions are vital to success in combat or critical to preserving life.
   - They apply to platoon or smaller units.
   - They are trained responses to enemy actions or leader's orders.
   - They represent mental steps followed for offensive and defensive actions in training and combat.

b. A unit's ability to accomplish its mission often depends on soldiers and leaders to execute key actions quickly. All soldiers and their leaders must know their immediate reaction to enemy contact as well as follow-up actions. Drills are limited to situations requiring instantaneous response; therefore, soldiers must execute drills instinctively. This results from continual practice. Drills provide small units with standard procedures essential for building strength and aggressiveness.
   - They identify key actions that leaders and soldiers must perform quickly.
   - They provide for a smooth transition from one activity to another; for example, from movement to offensive action to defensive action.
   - They provide standardized actions that link soldier and collective tasks at platoon level and below. (Soldiers perform individual tasks to CTT or SDT standard.)
   - They require the full understanding of each individual and leader, and continual practice.

6-2. FORMAT. The format for drills discussed in this chapter include the TITLE, the SITUATION that would cue the unit or the leader into initiating the drill, the REQUIRED ACTIONS in sequence, and supporting illustrations. Where applicable, drills are cross-referenced with material in other chapters, or other drills, or both. Training standards for battle drills are in the mission training plan (MTP).

BATTLE DRILL I. PLATOON ATTACK

SITUATION: The platoon is moving as part of a larger force conducting a movement to contact or a hasty or deliberate attack.
REQUIRED ACTIONS: Refer to Steps 1-5

STEP 1. **Action on Enemy Contact.**
a. The platoon initiates contact. The platoon leader plans when and how his base-of-fire element initiates contact with the enemy to establish a base of fire. This element must be in position and briefed before it initiates contact. If the platoon has not been detected, STEPS 1 and 2 consist of positioning the support element and identifying the enemy's positions.
b. The enemy initiates contact. If the enemy initiates contact, the platoon takes the following actions:
  (1) The squad in contact reacts to contact (Battle Drill 2). It attempts to achieve suppressive fires with one fire team and maneuvers the other team to attack the enemy in the flank. The squad leader notifies the platoon leader of his action.
  (2) The platoon leader, his RTO, the platoon FO, the squad leader of the next squad, and one machine gun team move forward to link up with the squad leader of the squad in contact.
  (3) The squad leader of the trail squad moves to the front of his lead fire team.
  (4) The platoon sergeant moves forward with the second machine gun team and links up with the platoon leader. If directed, he assumes control of the base-of-fire element and positions the machine guns to add suppressive fires against the enemy.
  (5) The platoon leader assesses the situation. He follows the success of the squad's flank attack by leading the trail squads along the covered and concealed route taken by the assaulting fire team of the squad in contact.
  (6) If the squad in contact cannot achieve suppressive fire, the squad leader reports to the platoon leader.
    (a) The squad in contact establishes a base of fire. The squad leader deploys his squad to provide effective, sustained fires on the enemy position. The squad leader reports his final position to the platoon leader.
    (b) The remaining squads (not in contact) take up covered and concealed positions in place and observe to the flanks and rear of the platoon.
    (c) The platoon leader moves forward with his RATELO, the platoon FO, the squad leader of the nearest squad, and one machine gun team.

STEP 2. **Locate the Enemy.**
a. The squad leader of the squad in contact reports the enemy size and location, and any other information to the platoon leader. The platoon leader completes the squad leader's assessment of the situation.
b. The squad continues to engage the enemy's position.
c. The platoon sergeant moves forward with the second machine gun team and links up with the platoon leader.

STEP 3. **Suppress the Enemy.**
a. The platoon leader determines if the squad in contact can gain suppressive fire against the enemy based on the volume and accuracy of the enemy's return fire.
  (1) If the answer is **YES,** he directs the squad (with one or both machine guns) to continue suppressing the enemy:

      (a) The squad in contact destroys or suppresses enemy weapons that are firing most effectively against it (normally crew-served weapons).

      (b) The squad in contact places screening smoke (M203) to prevent the enemy from seeing the maneuver element.

    (2) If the answer is **NO,** the platoon leader deploys another squad and the second machine gun team to suppress the enemy position. (The platoon leader may direct the platoon sergeant to position this squad and one or both machine gun teams in a better support-by-fire position)

b. The platoon leader again determines if the platoon can gain suppressive fires against the enemy.

    (1) If the answer is **YES,** he continues to suppress the enemy with the two squads and two machine guns.

      (a) The platoon sergeant assumes control of the base-of-fire element (squad in contact, the machine gun teams, and any other squads designated by the platoon leader).

      (b) The machine gun team takes up a covered and concealed position and suppresses the enemy position.

      (c) The platoon FO calls for and adjusts fires based on the platoon leader's directions. (The platoon leader does not wait for indirect fires before continuing with his actions)

    (2) If the answer is still **NO,** the platoon leader deploys the last squad to provide flank and rear security and to guide the rest of the company forward as necessary, and reports the situation to the company commander. Normally the platoon will become the base-of-fire element for the company and may deploy the last squad to add suppressive fires. The platoon continues to suppress or fix the enemy with direct and indirect fire, and responds to orders from the company commander.

STEP 4. **Attack.**
If the squad(s) in contact together with the machine gun(s) can suppress the enemy, the platoon leader determines if the remaining squad(s) not in contact can maneuver. He makes the following assessment:

- Location of enemy positions and obstacles.
- Size of the enemy force engaging the squad. (The number of enemy automatic weapons, the presence of any vehicles, and the employment of indirect fires are indicators of enemy strength.)
- Vulnerable flank.
- Covered and concealed flanking route to the enemy position.

a. If the answer is **YES,** the platoon leader maneuvers the squad(s) into the assault:

    (1) Once the platoon leader has ensured that the base-of-fire element is in position and providing suppressive fires, he leads the assaulting squad(s) to the assault position.

    (2) Once in position, the platoon leader gives the prearranged signal for the base-of-fire element to lift or shift direct fires to the opposite flank of the enemy position (The assault element MUST pickup and maintain effective fires throughout the

assault. Handover of responsibility for direct fires from the base-of-fire element to the assault element is critical.)

(3) The platoon FO shifts indirect fires to isolate the enemy position.

(4) The assaulting squad(s) fight through enemy positions using fire and maneuver. The platoon leader controls the movement of his squads. He assigns specific objectives for each squad and designates the main effort or base maneuver element. (The base-of-fire element must be able to identify the near flank of the assaulting squad(s).)

(5) In the assault, the squad leader determines the way in which he will move the elements of his squad based on the volume and accuracy of enemy fire against his squad and the amount of cover afforded by the terrain. In all cases, each soldier uses individual movement techniques as appropriate.

   (a) The squad leader designates one fire team to support the movement of the other team by fires.

   (b) The squad leader designates a distance or direction for the team to move. He accompanies one of the fire teams.

   (c) Soldiers must maintain contact with team members and leaders.

   (d) Soldiers time their firing and reloading in order to sustain their rate of fire.

   (e) The moving fire team proceeds to the next covered position. Teams use the wedge formation when assaulting. Soldiers move in rushes or by crawling.

   (f) The squad leader directs the next team to move.

   (g) If necessary, the team leader directs soldiers to bound forward as individuals within buddy teams. Soldiers coordinate their movement and fires with within the buddy team. They maintain contact with their team leader.

   (h) Soldiers fire from covered positions. They select the next covered position before moving. They either rush forward (no more than 5 seconds), or use high or low crawl techniques based on terrain and enemy fires.

b. If the answer is **NO,** or the assaulting squad(s) cannot continue to move, the platoon leader deploys the squad(s) to suppress the enemy and reports to the company commander. The platoon continues suppressing enemy positions and responds to the orders of the company commander.

STEP 5. **Consolidate and Reorganize.**

a. Consolidate. Once the assaulting squad(s) has seized the enemy position, the platoon leader establishes local security. (The platoon must prepare to defeat an enemy counterattack. The platoon is most vulnerable at the conclusion of the assault)

   (1) The platoon leader signals for the base-of-fire element to move up into designated positions.

   (2) The platoon leader assigns sectors of fire for each squad.

   (3) The platoon leader positions key weapons to cover the most dangerous avenue(s) of approach.

   (4) The platoon sergeant begins coordination for ammunition resupply.

   (5) Soldiers take up hasty defensive positions.

   (6) The platoon leader and his FO develop a quick fire plan.

   (7) The squads place out OPs to warn of enemy counterattacks.

b. Reorganize.
    (1) The platoon performs the following tasks (only after it completes the consolidation of the objective):
        (a) Reestablish the chain of command.
        (b) Redistribute and resupply ammunition.
        (c) Man crew-served weapons first.
        (d) Redistribute critical equipment (radios, NBC, NVDs).
        (e) Treat casualties and evacuate wounded.
        (f) Fill vacancies in key positions.
        (g) Search, silence, segregate, safeguard, and speed EPWs to collection points.
        (h) Collect and report enemy information and materiel.
    (2) Squad leaders provide ammunition, casualty, and equipment (ACE) reports to the platoon leader.
    (3) The platoon leader consolidates ACE reports and passes them to the company commander (or XO).
    (4) The platoon continues the mission after receiving guidance from the company commander. The company follows the success of the platoon's flanking attack.

BATTLE DRILL 1A. SQUAD ATTACK

SITUATION: The squad is moving as part of the platoon conducting a movement to contact or a hasty or deliberate attack.
REQUIRED ACTIONS: Refer to Steps 1-5

STEP 1. **Action on Enemy Contact**.
a. Soldiers receiving fire take up nearest positions that afford protection from enemy fire (cover) and observation (concealment).
b. The fire team in contact immediately returns heavy volume of suppressive fire in the direction of the enemy.
    (1) Soldiers in the fire team in contact move to positions (bound or crawl) from which they can fire their weapons, position themselves to ensure that they have observation, fields of fire, cover, and concealment. They continue to fire and report known or suspected enemy positions to the fire team leader.
    (2) The team leader directs fires using tracers or standard fire commands.
    (3) The fire team not in contact takes covered and concealed positions and provides security to the flanks and rear of the squad.
    (4) The squad leader reports contact to the platoon leader and moves toward the fire team in contact.

STEP 2. **Locate the Enemy.**
a. Using sight and sound, the fire team in contact acquires known or suspected enemy positions.
b. The fire team in contact begins to place well-aimed fires on suspected enemy positions.
c. The squad leader moves to a position where he can observe the enemy and assess the situation.

d. The squad leader requests, through the platoon leader, immediate suppression indirect fires (normally 60-mm mortars).

e. The squad leader reports the enemy size, location, and any other information to the platoon leader. (As the platoon leader comes forward, he completes the squad leader's assessment of the situation.)

STEP 3. **Suppress the Enemy**.

The squad leader determines if the fire team in contact can gain suppressive fire based on the volume and accuracy of the enemy fire.

a. If the answer is **YES**, the fire team leader continues to suppress the enemy:

(1) The fire team destroys or suppresses enemy crew-served weapons first.

(2) The fire team places smoke (M203) on the enemy position to obscure it.

(3) The fire team leader continues to control fires using tracers or standard fire commands. Fires must be well aimed and continue at a sustained rate with no lulls.

(4) Buddy teams fire their weapons so that they are not reloading their weapons at the same time.

b. If the answer is **NO**, the squad leader deploys the fire team not in contact to establish a support-by-fire position. He reports the situation to the platoon leader. Normally, the squad will become the base-of-fire element for the platoon. The squad continues to suppress the enemy and respond to orders from the platoon leader. (The platoon leader, his RATELO, the platoon FO, one machine gun team, and the squad leader of the next squad, as well as the platoon sergeant and the other machine gun team, are already moving forward IAW Battle Drill 1, Platoon Attack.)

STEP 4. **Attack.**

- If the fire team in contact can suppress the enemy, the squad leader determines if the fire team not in contact can maneuver. He makes the following assessment:
- Location of enemy position(s) and obstacles.
- Size of enemy force engaging the squad. (The number of enemy automatic weapons, the presence of any vehicles, and the employment of indirect fires are indicators of enemy strength.)
- Vulnerable flank.
- Covered and concealed flanking route to the enemy position.

a. If the answer is **YES**, the squad leader maneuvers the fire team in the assault:

(1) The squad leader directs the fire team in contact to support the movement of the other fire team. He then leads or directs the assaulting fire team leader to maneuver his fire team along a route that places the fire team in a position to assault the enemy. (The assaulting fire team must pick up and maintain fire superiority throughout the assault. Handover of responsibility for direct fires from the supporting fire team to the assaulting fire team is critical.)

(2) Once in position, the squad leader gives the prearranged signal for the supporting fire team to lift fires or shift fires to the opposite flank of the enemy position.

(3) The assaulting fire team fights through enemy positions using fire and movement. (The supporting fire team must be able to identify the near flank of the assaulting fire team.)

   (a) The team leader selects the route that allows him to reach his objective, while providing the best available cover and concealment for his team. The team leader then leads his team, from up front, in a shallow wedge throughout the attack.

   (b) Fire team members conduct individual movement techniques as individuals or buddy-teams, while maintaining their relative position in the assault formation. At the end of each move, soldiers take up covered and concealed positions and resume firing.

b. If the answer is **NO** or the assaulting fire team cannot continue to move, the squad leader deploys the assaulting fire team to add its fires against the enemy, reports to the platoon leader and requests instructions. The squad continues suppressing enemy positions and responds to the orders of the platoon leader.

STEP 5. **Consolidate and Reorganize.**

a. Once the assaulting fire team has seized the enemy position, the squad leader establishes local security. (The squad leader must quickly prepare to defeat any enemy counterattack. At the conclusion of the assault, the squad is most vulnerable.)

   (1) The squad leader signals for the supporting fire team to move up into a designated position.
   (2) The squad leader assigns sectors of fire for both fire teams.
   (3) The squad leader positions key weapons.
   (4) All soldiers take up hasty defensive positions.
   (5) The squad leader develops an initial fire support plan against an enemy counterattack. (As the platoon moves up, he hands the plan to the platoon leader for further development.)
   (6) The squad leader posts an OP to warn of enemy activity.

b. The squad performs the following tasks:

   (1) Reestablish the chain of command.
   (2) Redistribute and resupply ammunition.
   (3) Man crew-served weapons first.
   (4) Redistribute critical equipment (for example, radios, NBC, NVDs).
   (5) Treat casualties and evacuate wounded.
   (6) Fill vacancies in key positions.
   (7) Search, silence, segregate, safeguard, and speed EPWs to collection points.
   (8) Collect and report enemy information and materiel.

c. Team leaders provide ammunition, casualty, and equipment (ACE) reports to the squad leader.

d. The squad leader consolidates the ACE report and passes it to the platoon leader (or platoon sergeant).

e. The squad continues the mission after receiving instructions from the platoon leader. (The platoon follows the success of the squad's flanking attack with the remaining squads as part of the platoon attack.)

f. The squad leader reports the situation to the platoon leader.

BATTLE DRILL 2. REACT TO CONTACT

SITUATION: A squad or platoon receives fires from enemy individual or crew-served weapons.
REQUIRED ACTIONS: (Figure 6-1.)
1. Soldiers immediately take up the nearest covered positions and return fire in the direction of contact.
2. Team/squad leaders locate and engage known or suspected enemy positions with well-aimed fire, and pass information to the squad/platoon leader.
3. Fire team leaders control fire using standard fire commands (initial and supplemental) containing the following elements:
    - Alert.
    - Direction.
    - Description of target.
    - Range.
    - Method of fire (manipulation and rate of fire).
    - Command to commence firing.
4. Soldiers maintain contact with the soldiers on their left and right.
5. Soldiers maintain contact with their team leaders and report the location of enemy positions.
6. Leaders check the status of their personnel.
7. The team/squad leaders maintain contact with the squad/platoon leader.
8. The squad/platoon leader—
    a. Moves up to the fire team/squad in contact and links up with its leader. (The platoon leader brings his RATELO, platoon FO, the squad leader of the nearest squad, and one machine gun team. The squad leader of the trail squad moves to the front of his lead fire team. The platoon sergeant also moves forward with the second machine gun team and links up with the platoon leader, ready to assume control of the base-of-fire element.)
    b. Determines whether or not his squad/platoon must move out of an engagement area.
    c. Determines whether or not he can gain and maintain suppressive fires with his element already in contact (based on the volume and accuracy of enemy fires against the element in contact).
    d. Makes an assessment of the situation. He identifies:
        - The location of the enemy position and obstacles.
        - The size of the enemy force. (The number of enemy automatic weapons, the presence of any vehicles, and the employment of indirect fires are indicators of the enemy strength.)
        - Vulnerable flanks.
        - Covered and concealed flanking routes to the enemy position.
    e. Determines the next course of action (for example, fire and movement, assault, breach, knock out bunker, enter and clear a building or trench).

f. Reports the situation to the platoon leader/company commander and begins to maneuver.

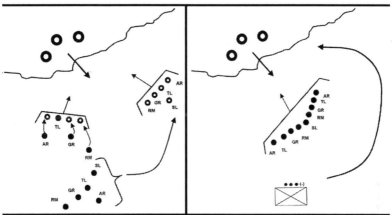

Figure 6-1. React to Contact

g. Calls for and adjusts indirect fire (mortars or artillery). (Squad leaders relay requests through the platoon leader.)

Team leaders lead their teams by example; for example, "Follow me, do as I do." Leaders relay all commands and signals from the platoon chain of command.

BATTLE DRILL 3. BREAK CONTACT

'UATION: The squad/platoon is under enemy fire and must break contact.
QUIRED ACTIONS: (Figure 6-2.)

The squad/platoon leader directs one fire-team/squad in contact to support the disengagement of the remainder of the unit.

The squad/platoon leader orders a distance and direction, or a terrain feature, or last objective rally point for the movement of the first fire team/squad.

The base of fire (fire team/squad) continues to suppress the enemy.

The moving element uses fragmentation, concussion, and smoke grenades to mas its movement.

The moving element takes up the designated position and engages the enemy position.

The platoon leader directs the base-of-fire element to move to its next location. (Based on the terrain and the volume and accuracy of the enemy's fire, the moving fire team/squad may need to use fire and movement techniques.

The squad/platoon continues to bound away from the enemy until (the squad/platoon must continue to suppress the enemy as it breaks contact):

•   It breaks contact.

- It passes through a higher level support-by-fire position.
- Its fire teams/squads are in the assigned position to conduct the next mission.
8. The leader should consider changing the direction of movement once contact is broken. This will reduce the ability of the enemy to place effective indirect fires on the unit.
9. If the squad or platoon becomes disrupted, soldiers stay together and move to the last designated rally point.
10. Squad/platoon leaders account for soldiers, report, reorganize as necessary and continue the mission.

This space intentionally left blank for notes.

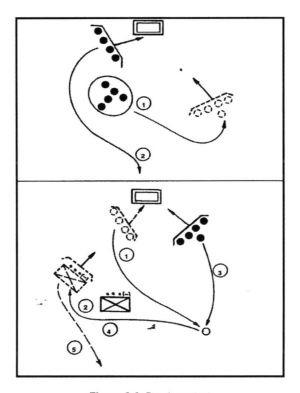

Figure 6-2. Break contact

BATTLE DRILL 4. REACT TO AMBUSH

SITUATION: If the squad/platoon enters a kill zone and the enemy initiates an ambush with a casualty-producing device and a high volume of fire, the unit takes the following actions.

REQUIRED ACTIONS: (Figure 6-3.)

1. In a near ambush (within hand-grenade range), soldiers receiving fire immediately return fire, take up covered positions, and throw fragmentation, concussion, and smoke grenades.

   a. Immediately after the grenades detonate, soldiers in the kill zone assault through the ambush using fire and movement.

   b. Soldiers not in the kill zone immediately:

     • Identify enemy positions.

     • Initiate immediate suppressive fires against the enemy.

- Take up covered positions.
- Shift fires as the soldiers in the kill zone assault through the ambush.

2. In a far ambush (beyond hand-grenade range), soldiers receiving fire immediately return fire, take up covered positions, and suppress the enemy by:
   - Destroying or suppressing enemy crew-served weapons first.
   - Obscuring the enemy position with smoke (M203).
   - Sustaining suppressive fires.
      a. Soldiers (teams/squads) not receiving fires move by a covered and concealed route to a vulnerable flank of the enemy position and assault using fire and movement techniques.
      b. Soldiers in the kill zone continue suppressive fires and shift fires as the assaulting team/squad fights through the enemy position.

3. The platoon FO calls for and adjusts indirect fires as directed by the platoon leader. On order, he lifts fires or shifts them to isolate the enemy position, or to attack them with indirect fires as they retreat.

4. The squad/platoon leader reports, reorganizes as necessary, and continues the mission.

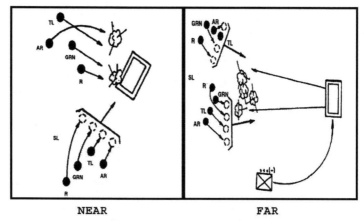

NEAR   FAR

Figure 6-3. React to ambush

BATTLE DRILL 5. KNOCK OUT BUNKERS

SITUATION: The platoon identifies enemy in bunkers while moving as a part of a larger force.

REQUIRED ACTIONS: (Figures 6-4)

1. The platoon initiates contact:
   a. The squad in contact establishes a base of fire.

    b. The platoon leader, his RATELO, platoon FO, and one machine gun team move forward to link up with the squad leader of the squad in contact.

    c. The platoon sergeant moves forward with the second machine gun team and assumes control of the base-of-fire element.

    d. The base-of-fire element–

        (1) Destroys or suppresses enemy crew-served weapons first.

        (2) Obscures the enemy position with smoke (M203).

        (3) Sustains suppressive fires at the lowest possible level.

    e. The platoon FO calls for and adjusts indirect fires as directed by the platoon sergeant.

2. The platoon leader determines that he can maneuver by identifying–

    a. The enemy bunkers, other supporting positions, and any obstacles.

    b. The size of the enemy force engaging the platoon. (The number of enemy, automatic weapons, the presence of any vehicles, and the employment of indirect fires are indicators of enemy strength.)

    c. A vulnerable flank of at least one bunker.

    d. A covered and concealed flanking route to the flank of the bunker.

3. The platoon leader determines which bunker is to be assaulted first and directs one squad (not in contact) to knock it out.

4. If necessary, the platoon sergeant repositions a squad, fire team, or machine gun team to isolate the bunker as well as to continue suppressive fires.

5. The assaulting squad, with the platoon leader and his RATELO, move along the covered and concealed route and take action to knock out the bunker.

    a. The squad leader moves with the assaulting fire team along the covered and concealed route to the flank of the bunker.

        (1) The assaulting fire team approaches the bunker from its blind side and does not mask the fires of the base-of-fire element.

        (2) Soldiers constantly watch for other bunkers or enemy positions in support of it.

    b. Upon reaching the last covered and concealed position–

        (1) The fire team leader and the automatic rifleman remain in place and add their fires to suppressing the bunker (includes the use of LAW/AT4s).

        (2) The squad leader positions himself where he can best control his teams. On the squad leader's signal, the base-of-fire element lifts fires or shifts fires to the opposite side of the bunker from the assaulting fire team's approach.

        (3) The grenadier and rifleman continue forward to the blind side of the bunker. One soldier takes up a covered position near the exit, while one soldier cooks off (two seconds maximum) a grenade, shouts "FRAG OUT!" and throws it through an aperture.

        (4) After the grenade detonates, the soldier covering the exit enters the bunker, firing short bursts, to destroy the enemy. The soldier who throws the grenade should not be the first one to clear the bunker.

    c. The squad leader inspects the bunker to ensure that it has been destroyed. He reports, reorganizes as needed, and continues the mission. The platoon follows the success of the attack against the bunker and continues the attack of other bunkers.

6. The platoon leader repositions base-of-fire squads as necessary to continue to isolate and suppress the remaining bunkers, and maintain suppressive fires.
7. The platoon leader either redesignates one of the base-of-fire squads to move up and knock out the next bunker; or, directs the assaulting squad to continue and knock out the next bunker.
   NOTE: The platoon leader must consider the condition of his assaulting squad(s) (ammunition and exhaustion) and rotate squads as necessary.
   a. On the platoon leader's signal, the base-of-fire element lifts fires or shifts fires to the opposite side of the bunker from which the squad is assaulting.
   b. At the same time, the platoon FO shifts indirect fires to isolate enemy positions.
8. The assaulting squad takes action to knock out the next bunker (see paragraph 5, above).
9. The platoon leader reports, reorganizes as necessary, and continues the mission. The company follows up the success of the platoon attack and continues to assault enemy positions.

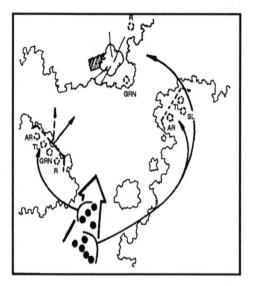

Figure 6-4. Knock out bunker (squad)

BATTLE DRILL 6. ENTER/CLEAR A TRENCH

SITUATION: The platoon is attacking as part of a larger force and identifies enemy in a trench line. The platoon deploys and establishes a base of fire. The platoon leader determines that he has sufficient combat power to maneuver and assault the trench line.

REQUIRED ACTIONS: (Figures 6-5,6-6, and 6-7)

1. The platoon leader directs one squad to enter the trench and secure a foothold.
2. The platoon leader designates the entry point of the trench line and the direction of movement once the platoon begins clearing.
3. The platoon sergeant positions soldiers and machine guns to suppress the trench and isolate the entry point.
4. The assaulting squad executes actions to enter the trench and establish a foothold. The squad leader directs one fire team to assault and one fire team to support by fire initially, then follow and support the assaulting fire team. He designates the entry point of the trench line.
   a. The squad leader and the assault fire team move to the last covered and concealed position short of the entry point.
      (1) The squad leader marks the entry point.
      (2) The base-of-fire element shifts direct fires away from the entry point and continues to suppress adjacent enemy positions or isolate the trench as required.
      (3) The assault fire team leader and the automatic rifleman remain in a position short of the trench to add suppressive fires for the initial entry.
      (4) The two remaining soldiers of the assault fire team (rifleman and grenadier) continue toward the entry point. They move in rushes or by crawling.
      (5) The squad leader positions himself where he can best control his teams.
   b. The first two soldiers (rifleman and grenadier) of the assault fire team move to the edge of the trench; parallel to the trench and on their backs; on the squad leader's command, cook-off grenades (two seconds maximum), shout FRAG OUT, and throw the grenades into the trench.
      (1) After ensuring that both grenades detonate, the soldiers roll into the trench, landing on their feet, and back-to-back. They fire their weapons down the trench in opposite directions. Immediately, both soldiers move in opposite directions down the trench, continuing to fire three-round bursts. Each soldier continues until he reaches the first corner or intersection. Both soldiers halt and take up positions to block any enemy movement toward the entry point.
      (2) Upon detonation of the grenades, the assault fire team leader and the automatic rifleman immediately move to the entry point and enter the trench. The squad leader directs them to one of the secured corners or intersections to relieve the rifleman or grenadier who then rejoins his buddy team at the opposite end of the foothold.
   c. The squad leader remains at the entry point and marks it.
   d. The squad leader reports to the platoon leader that he has entered the trench and secured a foothold. The platoon follows the success of the seizure of the foothold with the remainder of the platoon as part of the platoon actions to clear a trench line.
   e. The squad reorganizes as necessary. Leaders redistribute ammunition.
5. The platoon leader directs one of the base-of-fire element squads to move into the trench and begin clearing it in the direction of movement from the foothold.

6. The base-of-fire element repositions as necessary to continue suppressive fires.
7. The platoon leader moves into the trench with the assaulting squad.
8. The assaulting squad passes the squad that has secured the foothold and executes actions to take the lead and clear the trench.
   a. The squad leader designates a lead fire team and a trail fire team.
   b. The lead fire team and the squad leader move to the forward most secure corner or intersection. The squad leader tells the team securing that corner or intersection that his squad is ready to continue clearing the trench. The trail fire team follows maintaining visual contact with the last soldier of the lead team.

NOTE: Throughout this technique, the team leader positions himself at the rear of the fire team to have direct control (physically, if necessary) of his soldiers. Other soldiers in the fire team rotate the lead. Soldiers rotate the lead to change magazines and prepare grenades. Rotating the lead provides constant suppressive fires down the trench and maintains the momentum of the attack as the squad clears the trench.

   c. The lead fire team passes the element securing the foothold.
      (1) The lead soldier of the fire team moves abreast of the soldier securing the corner or intersection, taps him, and announces TAKING THE LEAD.
      (2) The soldier securing the corner or intersection acknowledges that he is handing over the lead by shouting OKAY. He allows the fire team to pass him.
   d. The lead fire team starts clearing in the direction of movement. They arrive at a corner or intersection.
      (1) Allowing for cook-off (two seconds maximum) and shouting FRAG OUT, the second soldier prepares and throws a grenade around the corner.
      (2) Upon detonation of the grenade, the lead soldier moves around the corner firing three round bursts and advancing as he fires. The entire fire team follows him to the next corner or intersection.
   e. The squad leader:
      (1) Follows immediately behind the lead team.
      (2) Ensures that the trailing fire team moves up and is ready to pass the lead at his direction.
      (3) Rotates fire teams as necessary to keep his soldiers fresh and to maintain the momentum of the attack.
      (4) Requests indirect fires, if necessary, through the platoon leader.

DANGER
The fire teams must maintain sufficient interval to prevent them from being engaged by the same enemy fires.

   f. At each corner or intersection, the lead fire team performs the same actions described above (paragraph d).
   g. If the lead soldier finds that he is nearly out of ammunition before reaching a corner or intersection, he announces AMMO.
      (1) Immediately, the lead soldier stops and moves against one side of the trench, ready to let the rest of the team pass. He continues to aim his weapon down the trench in the direction of movement.
      (2) The next soldier ensures that he has a full magazine, moves up abreast of the lead soldier, taps him and announces TAKING THE LEAD.

(3) The lead soldier acknowledges that he is handing over the lead by shouting OKAY, positions rotate, and the squad continues forward.

h. The trailing fire team secures intersections and marks the route within the trench as the squad moves forward. The trailing fire team leader ensures that follow-on squads relieve his buddy teams to maintain security.

i. The squad leader reports the progress of the clearing operation. (The base-of-fire element must be able to identify the location of the lead fire team in the trench at all times)

9. The platoon leader rotates squads to keep soldiers fresh and to maintain the momentum of the assault.

10. The platoon sergeant calls forward ammunition resupply and organizes teams to move it forward into the trench.

11. The base-of-fire element ensures that all friendly forces move into the trench ONLY through the designated entry point. (All movement must be made in the trench to avoid casualties by friendly fires)

12. The platoon leader reports to the company commander that the trench line is secured, or that he is no longer able to continue clearing.

This space intentionally left blank for notes.

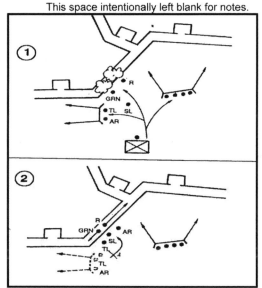

Figure 6-5. Enter a trench (squad)

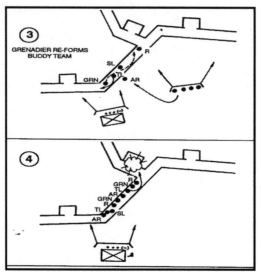

Figure 6-6. Clear a trench line (squad) (continued)

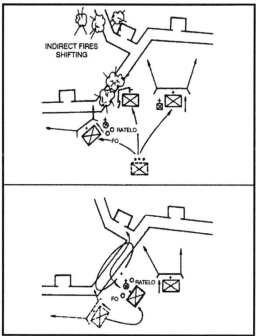

Figure 6-7. Clear a trench line (platoon)

BATTLE DRILL 7. CONDUCT INITIAL BREACH OF A MINED WIRE OBSTACLE

SITUATION: The platoon is operating as part of a larger force. The lead squad identifies a wire obstacle, reinforced with mines that cannot be bypassed and enemy positions on the far side of the obstacle.

REQUIRED ACTIONS: (Figures 6-8.)

1. The platoon leader, his RATELO, platoon FO, and one machine gun team move forward to link up with the squad leader of the lead squad.
2. The platoon leader determines that he can maneuver by identifying–
   a. The obstacle and enemy positions covering it by fire.
   b. The size of the enemy force engaging the squad. (The number of enemy automatic weapons, the presence of any vehicles, and the employment of indirect fires are indicators of enemy strength.)
   c. A breach point.
   d. A covered and concealed route to the breach point.
   e. A support-by-fire position large enough for a squad reinforced with machine guns.

3. The platoon leader directs one squad to support the movement of another squad(s) to the breach point. He indicates the support-by-fire position, the route to it, the enemy position to be suppressed, the breach point, and the route that the rest of the platoon will take to it. He also gives instructions for lifting and shifting fires.
4. The platoon leader designates one squad as the breach squad, and the remaining squad, as the assault squad once the breach has been made. (The assault squad may add its fires to the base-of-fire element. Normally, it follows the covered and conceled route of the breach squad and assaults through immediately after the breach is made)
5. The designated squad moves to and establishes a base of fire.
6. The platoon sergeant moves forward to the base-of-fire element with the second machine gun team and assumes control of the element.
7. On the platoon leader's signal, the base-of-fire element:
   a. Destroys or suppresses enemy crew-served weapons, first.
   b. Obscures the enemy position with smoke (M203).
   c. Sustains suppressive fires at the lowest possible level.
8. The platoon leader designates the breach point and leads the breach and assault squads along the covered and concealed route to it.
9. The platoon FO calls for and adjusts indirect fires as directed by the platoon leader.
10. The breach squad executes actions to breach the obstacle.
   a. The squad leader directs one fire team to support the movement of the other fire team to the breach point.
   b. The squad leader identifies the breach point.
   c. The base-of-fire element continues to provide suppressive fires and isolates the breach point.
   d. The breaching fire team, with the squad leader, move to the breach point using the covered and concealed route.
      (1) The squad leader and breaching fire team leader employ smoke grenades to obscure the breach point. The platoon base-of-fire element shifts direct fires away from the breach point and continue to suppress key enemy positions. The platoon FO lifts indirect fires or shifts them beyond the obstacle.
      (2) The breaching fire team leader positions himself and the automatic rifleman on one flank of the breach point to provide close security.
      (3) The grenadier and rifleman of the breaching fire team probe for mines, and cut the wire obstacle, marking their path as they proceed. (Bangalore is preferred, if available)
      (4) Once the obstacle has been breached, the breaching fire team leader and the automatic rifleman move to the far side of the obstacle and take up covered and concealed positions with the rifleman and grenadier. The team leader signals to the squad leader when they are in position and ready to support.
   e. The squad leader signals the supporting fire team leader to move his fire team up and through the breach. He then moves through the obstacle and joins the breaching fire team, leaving the grenadier and rifleman of the supporting fire team on the near side of the breach to guide the rest of the platoon through.

f. Using the same covered and concealed route as the breaching fire team, the supporting fire team moves through the breach and takes up covered and concealed positions on the far side.

g. The squad leader reports to the platoon leader and consolidates as needed.

11. The platoon leader leads the assault squad through the breach in the obstacle and positions them beyond the breach to support the movement of the remainder of the platoon or assaults the enemy position covering the obstacle.

12. The platoon leader reports the situation to the company commander and directs his base-of-fire element to move up and through the obstacle. The platoon leader leaves guides to guide the company through the breach point.

13. The company follows up the success of the platoon as it conducts the breach and continues the assault against the enemy positions.

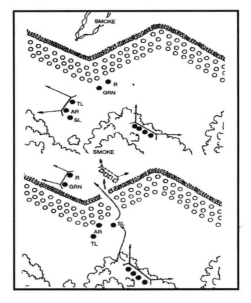

Figure 6-8. Conduct initial breach of a mined wire obstacle (squad)

This page intentionally left blank for notes.

CHAPTER SEVEN
COMMUNICATIONS

GENERAL. The AN/PRC-119 is composed of a receiver and a transmitter. Together, the receiver-transmitter has many capabilities and features that enable you to perform your mission more effectively. The radio can operate in Single Channel mode or Frequency Hopping mode. The radio has approximately 2,320 SC Channels and includes voice and digital communication. The operating voltage for the manpack radio is 13.5 volts from the primary battery. The range of the manpack radio is 5-10 KM on Hi power. This range is based upon line of sight and is derived from averages achieved under normal atmospheric and weather conditions. Ranges depend upon location, sighting, weather, and surrounding noise level, among other factors. The AN/PRC-126 set covers the 30 to 88 MHZ band in 25 KHZ increments. It is a lightweight radio that is best utilized for squad operations. If properly maintained the AN/PRC-126 is an excellent complement for the larger more powerful AN/PRC-119. The following chapter outlines assembly, operation, and trouble-shooting for both radios.

7-1.THE AN/PRC-119

a. Manpack Radio Assembly. To assemble a manpack radio you must first check and install a battery.
    (1) Inspect the battery box for dirt or damage
    (2) Stand RT on front panel guards
    (3) Check battery life condition (you will be using the rechargeable BB-390 batteries)
    (4) Place battery in box
    (5) Close battery cover, and secure using latches
    (6) Return radio to upright position
    (7) If used battery was installed, enter the battery life condition into radio by performing the following
    (8) Set FCTN to LD
    (9) Press BAT; then CLR
    (10) Enter number recorded on side of battery
    (11) Press STO
    (12) Set FCTN to SQ ON

b. Antenna
    (1) Inspect whip antenna connector on antenna and on radio for damage
    (2) Screw whip antenna into base
    (3) Hand tighten
    (4) Carefully mate antenna base with RT ANT connector
    (5) Hand tighten
    (6) Position antenna as needed by bending goose neck

NOTE: Keep antenna straight, if possible. If the antenna is bent to a horizontal position, it may be necessary to turn the radio in order to receive and transmit messages.

c. Handset
   (1) Inspect the handset for damage
   (2) Push handset on AUD/DATA and twist clockwise to lock in place

d. Field Pack
   (1) Place RT in field pack with antenna on the left shoulder
   (2) Fold top flap of field over RT and secure flap to field pack using straps and buckles

e. Setting Presets
   (1) Set CHAN to 1
   (2) Set MODE to SC
   (3) Set RF PWR to HI
   (4) Set VOL to mid range
   (5) Set DIM full clockwise
   (6) Set FCTN to LD
   (7) Set DATA RATE to off

f. Single Channel Loading Frequencies
   (1) Obtain Ranger SOI
   (2) Set FCTN to LD
   (3) Set mode to SC
   (4) Set CHAN to MAN, Cue, or desired channel(1-6) where frequency is to be stored
   (5) Press FREQ(display will show "00000", or frequency RT is currently turned on)
   (6) Press CLR(display will show five lines)
   (7) Enter the number of the new frequency
   (8) If you make a mistake with a number press CLR
   (9) Press STO(display will blink)
   (10) Set FCTN to SQ ON

g. Clearing Frequencies
   (1) Set mode to SC
   (2) Set CHAN to MAN, Cue or desired channel where frequency is to be cleared
   (3) Press FREQ
   (4) Press CLR
   (5) Press Load; then press STO
   (6) Set FCTN to SQ ON

h. Scanning more than one frequency

(1) Load all desired frequencies using "Single Channel Loading Frequencies" instructions (reference 7-2.f)
(2) Set CHAN to CUE
(3) Set SC to FH
(4) Set FCTN to SQ ON
(5) Press STO (display will say SCAN)
(6) Press 8. You will now be able to scan more than one frequency

i. Troubleshooting

PROBLEM	CORRECTIVE ACTION
1. No power	1.a. Check DIM switch
	1.b. Check battery
2. High pitch in handset	2.a. Clean handset contacts with an eraser
3. No side tone in Lo, Med, or Hi power	3.a. Change Handset
4. Continuous keying	4.a. Press push to talk button on hand mike
	4.b. Check for side tone by blowing into handset
	4.c. If no tone replace handset
5. Will not key	5.a. Change handset
6. Will not transmit	6.a. Check antenna
	6.b. Check handset
	6.c. Check frequency
7. Will not receive	7.a. Check frequency
	7.b. Check antenna
	7.c. Check handset

7-3.THE AN/PRC-126

e. Radio assembly
    (1) Check and install the battery
    (2) Inspect the battery box for dirt and damage
    (3) Check battery life condition (you will be using the rechargeable BB-388 battery)
    (4) Place battery in box
    (5) Close battery cover and secure latches

b. Antenna
    (1) Inspect antenna for damage
    (2) Screw antenna into radio (screw into base first if using the whip antenna)

c. Handset
    (1) Inspect the handset for damage
    (2) Push handset onto audio connector and twist to lock into place

d. Operation and frequency setting
   (1) Press set button and turn radio on
   (2) Press INCR button to cycle through to first number of desired frequency
   (3) Press the SET button
   (4) Repeat the process of pressing INCR and SET button until desired
       frequency is displayed
   (5) Press SET button once more to LOAD frequency
   (6) If a beeping noise is heard turn the black antenna knob until beeping noise
       is no longer heard

e. Troubleshooting

PROBLEM	CORRECTIVE ACTION
1. No power	1.a. Check battery
2. High pitch in handset	2.a. Clean handset and audio connector with eraser
3. Continuous keying	3.a. Press push to talk button on handset
4. Will not key	4.a. Press push to talk button on radio
	4.b. Change handset
5. Will not transmit	5.a. Check frequency
	5.b. Check antenna
	5.c. Check handset
6. Will not receive	5.a. Check frequency
	5.b. Check antenna
	5.c. Check handset

CHAPTER EIGHT
ARMY AVIATION

8-1. GENERAL
Army aviation and infantry units can be fully integrated with other members of the combined arms team to form powerful and flexible air assault task forces that can project combat power throughout the entire depth, width, and breadth of the modern battlefield with little regard for terrain barriers. These combat operations are deliberate, precisely planned, and vigorously executed. They are assigned to strike the enemy when and where he is most vulnerable (See Chapter 2, pages 2-6 & 2-22, AIR Movement Annex, 2-32 Army Aviation coordination).

8-2. AIR ASSAULT.
a. Successful air assault execution is based on a careful analysis of METT-TC and detailed, precise reverse planning. Five basic plans that comprise the reverse planning sequence are developed for each air assault operation. They are:
   (1) Ground Tactical Plan. The foundation of a successful air assault operation is the commander's ground tactical plan. All additional plans must support this plan. The plan specifies actions in the objective area to ultimately accomplish the mission and address subsequent operations.
   (2) The Landing Plan. The landing plan must support the ground tactical plan. This plan outlines a sequence of events that allows elements to move into the area of operations, and ensures that units arrive at designated locations at prescribed times prepared to execute the ground tactical plan.
   (3) The Air Movement Plan. The air movement plan is based on the ground tactical and landing plans. It specifies the schedule and provides instructions for air movement of troops, equipment, and supplies from PZs to LZs.
   (4) The Loading Plan. The loading plan is based on the air movement plan. It ensures that troops, equipment, and supplies are loaded on the correct aircraft. Unit integrity is maintained when aircraft loads are planned. Cross-loading may be necessary in order to ensure survivability of command and control assets, and the mix of weapons arriving at the LZ are ready to fight.
   (5) The Staging Plan. The staging plan is based on the loading plan and prescribes the arrival time of ground units (troops, equipment and supplies) at the PZ in the order of movement

b. The battalion is the lowest level that has sufficient personnel to plan, coordinate, and control air assault operations. When company size or lower operations are conducted, the bulk of the planning takes place at battalion or higher headquarters.

c. Selection and Marking of PZs/LZs.
  (1) Small unit leaders should consider the following when selecting a PZ/LZ:
    (a) Size. Minimal circular landing point separation from other aircraft and obstacles is needed:
- Observation helicopters – 25 meters
- UH-1, AH-1 – 35 meters
- UH-60, AH-64 – 50 meters
- Cargo helicopters – 80 meters

    (b) Surface conditions. Avoid potential hazards e.g. sand, blowing dust, snow, tree stumps, large rocks.
    (c) Ground slope.
- 0% - 6 % -- land upslope
- 7% - 15% -- land sideslope
- over 15% -- no touchdown (aircraft may hover)

    (d) Obstacles. An obstacle clearance ratio of 10 to 1 is used in planning approach and departure of the PZ and LZ (Eg: a ten foot tall tree requires 100 feet of horizontal distance for approach or departure). Obstacles will be marked with a red chem light at night or red panels during the daytime. Markings will not be used if they cause the position to be seen by the enemy.
    (e) Approach/Departure. Approach and departure are made into the wind and along the long axis of the PZ/LZ.
    (f) Loads. The greater the load, the larger the PZ/LZ must be to accommodate the insertion or extraction.
  (2) Marking PZs and LZs.
    (a) Day. A ground guide will mark the PZ or LZ for the lead aircraft by holding an M16/M4 rifle over his head, by displaying a folded VS-17 panel chest high, or by other coordinated and identifiable means.
    (b) Night. The code letter Y (Inverted Y) is used to mark the landing point of the lead aircraft at night (figure 8-1). Chemical lights or "beanbag" lights are used to maintain light discipline. A swinging chem light may also be used to mark the landing point.

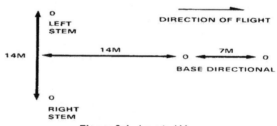

Figure 8-1. Inverted Y.

d. Air Assault Formations. Aircraft supporting an operation may use any of the following PZ/LZ configurations which are prescribed by the Air Assault Task Force (AATF) Commander working in conjunction with the Air Mission Commander (AMC):

    (1) Heavy Left or Right. Requires a relatively long, wide landing area; presents difficulty in pre-positioning loads; restricts suppressive fire by inboard gunners; provides firepower to front and flank.

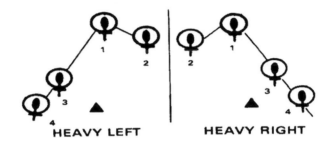

Figure 8-2. Heavy Left/Heavy Right

    (2) Diamond. Allows rapid deployment for all-round security; requires small landing area; presents some difficulty in pre-positioning loads; restricts suppressive fire of inboard gunners.

Figure 8-3. Diamond

(3) Vee. Requires a relatively small landing area; allows rapid deployment of forces to the front; restricts suppressive fire of inboard gunners; presents some difficulty in pre-positioning loads.

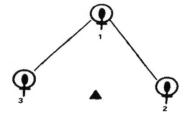

Figure 8-4. Vee

(4) Echelon Left or Right. Requires a relatively long, wide landing area; presents some difficulty in pre-positioning loads; allows rapid deployment of forces to the flank; allows unrestricted suppressive fire by gunners.

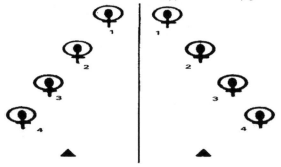

Figure 8-5. Echelon Left/Echelon Right

(5) Trail. Requires a relatively small landing area; allows rapid deployment of forces to the flank; simplifies pre-positioning loads; allows unrestricted suppressive fire by gunners.

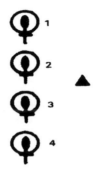

Figure 8-6. Trail

(6) Staggered Trail Left or Right. Requires a relatively long, wide landing area; simplifies pre-positioning loads; allows rapid deployment for all round security; gunners' suppressive fire restricted somewhat.

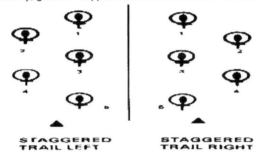

Figure 8-7. Staggered Trail Left/Staggered Trail Right

e. PZ Operations. Prior to arrival of aircraft, the PZ is secured, PZ control party is positioned, and the troops and equipment are positioned in platoon/squad assembly areas.

 (1) Occupation of patrol/squad assembly area. Patrol leader/squad leader should accomplish the following:

  (a) Maintain all-around security of the assembly area.

  (b) Maintain communications.

  (c) Organize personnel and equipment into chalks and loads.

8-5

(d) Conduct safety briefing and equipment check of troops.

An example of a large, one sided PZ is depicted in Figure 8-8.

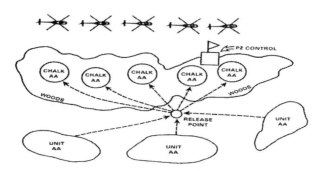

Figure 8-8. Large, one sided PZ

(2) UH-60 Loading Sequence.

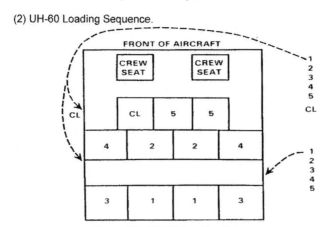

Figure 8-9. UH-60 Loading Sequence.

(3) Unloading.

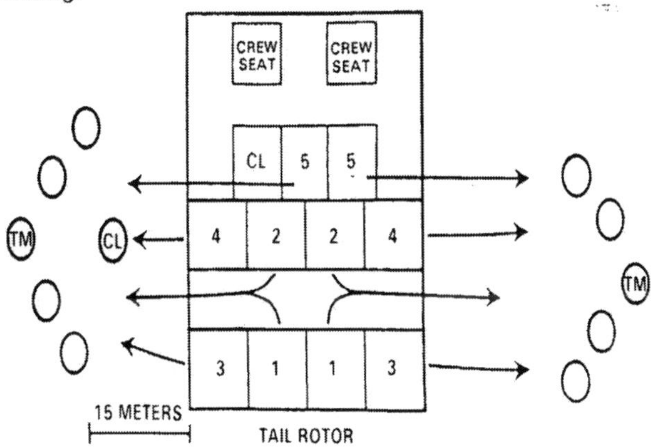

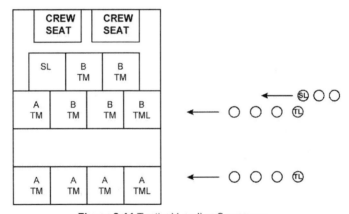

Figure 8-10. Unloading Sequence.

(4) Tactical loading sequence

Figure 8-11.Tactical Loading Sequence

(5) Tactical unloading
NOTE: Is best using 1xdoor, nearest the cover and concealment

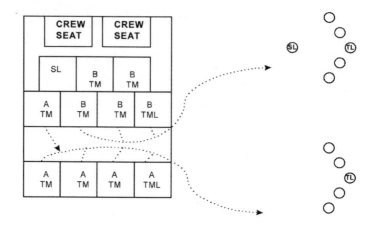

Figure 8-12. Tactical Unloading Using 1 Door

f.   Safety. Safety is the primary concern of all leaders when operating in/around
     aircraft. The inclusion of aircraft into Ranger operations carries an inherent
     "high" risk factor. The following guidelines are to be considered.
     (1)   Approach the aircraft from 90 degrees to 45 degrees off the
     (2)   nose.
     (3)   Weapons with blank firing adapters are pointed muzzles up.
     (4)   Weapons loaded with live ammunition are muzzles down.
     (5)   The ballistic helmet is worn.
     (6)   When possible, an air crew safety brief is conducted with all
     (7)   personnel. At a minimum it will include loading and offloading,
           emergencies, and egress procedures.
     (8)   Leaders need to carry a manifest and turn a copy into higher.

CHAPTER NINE
WATERBORNE OPERATIONS

9-1. GENERAL. The availability of ready-made bridges to a Ranger Patrol is not only uncertain, but is highly unlikely. Therefore, it may become necessary for the patrol to employ expedient stream crossing techniques. The leader will need to know various techniques in order to make a successful stream crossing. The stream crossing team is designated and instructed to prepare ropes and equipment, and to conduct team rehearsals. This team is highly proficient in the mechanics of a stream crossing. This proficiency is gained by realistic rehearsals, close inspections, organization and good control.

9-2. ORGANIZATION OF RIVER CROSSING TEAM.

(a) Number 1 man: Lead safety swimmer and far side lifeguard.

(b) Number 2 man: Rope puller, swims water obstacle pulling 150-foot rope, ties off rope on far side anchor point.

(c) Number 3 man: Near side lifeguard is the last man to cross water obstacle.

(d) Number 4 man: Bridge Team Commander (BTC).

(e) Number 5 and 6 men: Rope Tighteners.

9-3. ONE ROPE BRIDGE (WET CROSSING).
(a) Special Equipment:
    (1) Two snaplinks per piece of heavy equipment.
    (2) Two snaplinks for every 120 feet of rope.
    (3) One 14-foot utility rope per person.
    (4) Two snaplinks per person.
    (5) One waterproof bag per RATELO.
    (6) Three B-7 life preservers.
    (7) Three floatation work vests.
    (8) Two 150-foot nylon ropes.

(b) Planning. A stream crossing annex is prepared in conjunction with the unit's operation order. Special organization is accomplished at this time. For a platoon size patrol, a squad is normally given the task of providing the bridge team, with the squad leader as the Bridge Team Commander (see Chapter 2, page 2-6 e).

(c) Rehearsals and inspections:
    (1) **The stream crossing team always rehearses.**
    (2) Rehearse the entire stream crossing emphasizing:
        (a) Security and actions on enemy contact.
        (b) Actual construction of the rope bridge within EIGHT minutes on dry land.
        (c) Individual preparation.

(d) Order of crossing.
(e) All signals and control measures.
(f) Reorganization.
(3) Conduct rehearsals as realistically as possible.
(4) Ensure personnel are proficient in the mechanics of a stream crossing operation.
(5) Inspect for equipment completeness, correct rigging and preparation, personnel knowledge and understanding of the operation.
(6) Actions of the #4 man (Bridge Team Commander(BTC) during the preparation phase.
(a) Rehearse the bridge team.
(b) Accounts for all equipment in the bridge kit.
(c) Ensures 120-foot rope is coiled.

(d) Execution Phase:
(1) Steps for the establishment and conduct of bridge stream crossing.
(a) Unit leader halts short of the river, local security is established, and a recon is conducted of the area for the presence of the enemy and for crossing site suitability/ necessity. He directs the BTC to construct the bridge.
(b) Security is established up and downstream while unit leader briefs BTC on anchor points. The unit leader counts individuals across.
(c) The bridge team begins to establish the rope bridge while unit members begin individual preparation.
(d) The BTC is responsible for construction of one-rope bridge and selection of the near side anchor point as well as the far side anchor point if visibility permits. He will tie a swimmer's safety line to anchor himself into the bridge. Tying a bowline around the waist secured with an overhand knot, and on the free running end, an end of line bowline with an overhand knot. A snap link will be placed on the loop portion of the end of line bowline, which will extend no further than arms length away from the soldier (standard waterborne uniform). This will ensure that the soldier is never more than arms length away from the rope bridge should he lose his grip.
(e) Noise and light discipline is enforced and security is maintained.
(f) Individual soldiers put a snaplink in their end-of-the rope bowline and the sight blade of every M-4/M16 or M203. M240 gunners put a snaplink through the front sight blade and rear swivel of their M240 MG. RATELOS (and others with heavy rucksacks) place an additional snaplink on their rucksack frame, top center.
(2) The responsibilities of the bridge team while erecting the rope bridge are as follows:
(a) Number 1 man (Lead safety swimmer and far side lifeguard).
(1) Grounds rucksack (with snaplink through top of frame) to the rear of the near side anchor point. Wears equipment in the following order (body out): Waterborne Uniform (top button buttoned, pants unbloused), B7 life preserver-or engineer work vest, LCE, weapon (across the back), carrying a safety line to assume duties of far side lifeguard.
(2) The Number 1 man enters the water upstream from the Number 2 man and stays an arms length away from the Number 2 man on the upstream side. He identifies the far side anchor point upon exiting the water and once the Number 2 man has exited the water moves to his far side lifeguard position downstream

of the rope bridge with knotted safety line on wrist, LCE/weapon grounded, and work vest held in throwing hand. He continues to wear the B7.

(b) Number 2 man (rope puller) in waterborne uniform (same as Number 1 man) wears his equipment in the following order, Work vest, LCE, weapon (across the back), Australian rappel seat with snaplink to the rear. He grounds his rucksack (with snaplink through top of frame) to the rear of the near side anchor point. His duties are to swim across the water obstacle pulling the rope. He ties off the rope on the anchor point identified by the Number 1 man with a round turn and two half hitches with a quick release. The direction of the round turn is the same direction as the flow of water (current) to facilitate exit off the rope bridge.

(c) Number 3 man (near side lifeguard) in the same waterborne uniform as the far side lifeguard. The Number 3 man positions himself on the downstream side of the bridge before the number 1 and 2 men enter the water, grounding his rucksack (with snaplink through top of frame) on rear of near-side anchor point. His duties include untying the quick release at the near side anchor point after the PSG crosses and verifies the headcount. The Number 3 man reties his safety line into an Australian rappel seat, hooks the end of line bowline into his snaplink, connects his snaplink to the snaplink on the end-of-line bowline of the rope, and is the last man pulled across the water obstacle. He puts on the work vest prior to crossing the water obstacle with his equipment in order of B7, work vest, LCE and weapon.

(d) Number 4 man (Bridge Team Commander - BTC)

    (1) He is in the standard waterborne uniform with LCE and sling rope tied in safety line (round the waist bowline with end of line bowline at arms length). He is responsible for construction of rope bridge and organization of bridge team. He is also responsible for back feeding the rope and tying end of line bowlines.

    (2) He designates the near side anchor point, ties the wireman's knot of the transport tightening system, and hooking all personnel to the rope bridge. He ensures that the transport tightening knot is on the upstream side of the rope bridge. He ensures that all individuals are in the waterborne uniform, hooked into the rope facing the current with the safety line routed through the trailing shoulder of the individual's LCE and rucksack. He ensures that the weapon is hooked onto the rope. He controls the flow of traffic on the bridge. He is responsible for crossing with the Number 1 man's rucksack. He is generally the next to the last man to cross (follows PSG who is keeping headcount).

(e) Number 5 and 6 men (rope tighteners) in waterborne uniform with LCE and safety line. They are responsible for tightening the transport tightening knot. They are also responsible for taking the rucksacks of the Number 2 and 3 men across. Once on the far side, they are responsible for pulling the last man (Number 3 man) across.

(f) The rucksacks of 1/2/3 men are transported across by 4/5/6 men. The rucksacks of 1/2/3 are hooked into the rope by the snaplink through the top of the frames and the 4/5/6 men pull them across. The weapons of 4/5/6 men are attached between the 4/5/6 men and the rucksack that they are pulling across the bridge.

(g) Bridge Team Commander rehearses the bridge team during the planning sessions and directs construction and emplacement. The unit leader selects the crossing site which complements the tactical plan.

(1) Number 3 man positions himself downstream of crossing site.

(2) Number 1 man enters water upstream of number 2. He stays one arm's length from the number 2 man and is prepared to render any assistance to the number 2 man. Both swim in conjunction upstream to compensate for the current. BTC feeds rope out of rucksack positioned on the downstream side of near side anchor point.

(h) The number 1 man exits and identifies (hugs) the far side anchor point (if BTC cannot identify it for the Number 2 man). Number 2 man exits on the upstream side of the far side anchor point. The rope is now routed to facilitate movement onto and off the bridge.

(i) Radios and heavy equipment are waterproofed and rigged. All individuals don waterborne uniform and tie safety lines. PSG moves to anchor point and maintains accountability through headcount.

(j) Number 2 man signals the BTC that the rope is at the far side anchor point, and the BTC pulls out excess slack and ties a round turn with two (2) half hitches and emplaces snaplink. The BTC signals the number 2 man who pulls the rope 1/5 of the way across. The number 2 man selects a point on the far side anchor point that is 18 - 24 inches off the water. After this is done, the number 2 man ties a round turn and two half hitches, the first half hitch is tied in a quick release. Number 2 man signals the BTC and the pulling team (4,5,6) tightens the bridge, pulling the wireman's knot as close as possible to the near side anchor point.

(k) The number 1 man moves downstream and assumes his duties as the far side lifeguard.

(1) The bridge team commander will tie off the rope with a round turn and two half hitches around the near side anchor point. The BTC will place himself on the upstream side of the bridge (facing downstream). He begins to hook individuals into the rope inspecting them for safety. **NOTE: Any Ranger identified as a weak swimmer will cross with no other personnel on the rope bridge**. The weak swimmer crosses individually to allow the near and far side lifeguards to focus their attention exclusively on the weak swimmer and not be distracted by other personnel crossing the bridge.

(l) Number 2 man moves upstream to provide far side security. Number 5 and Number 6 cross (taking the rucks of 2/3). The number 5 man maintains far side headcount and unhooks all individuals on the far side (he positions himself on the upstream side of the bridge facing downstream). Number 6 precedes the remainder of the patrol.

(m)The BTC maintains the flow of traffic ensuring that no more than three individuals are on the bridge at any one time (one hooking up, one near the center, and one being unhooked). Once the PSG has accounted for all individuals on the near side, he withdraws L/R security sending them across. PSG follows security across. Number 3 man hooks the BTC (with number I's rucksack) onto the rope. Once the BTC has crossed, number 3 unhooks near side anchor point and the BTC unties far side anchor Point. Number 3 man ties an Australian rappel seat with snaplink to the front, hooks onto the snaplink that is in the end of the line bowline on the 120-foot rope-and signals 4/5/6 men to take in slack. Number 3 man extends arms in front of his head, slightly upstream to fend off debris and is pulled across by

4/5/6. All individuals (except 1/2/3 and RATELOs) wear rucksacks across. The 4/5/6 men hook the rucksacks of 1/2/3 men onto bridge by the snaplink. All individuals cross facing upstream.

(n) Once the far side headcount, weapons and equipment are verified (between PSG and Number 5 man), personnel reorganize and continue mission.

(o) Personnel with heavy equipment:

(1) M240 - all major groups are tied together with 1/4-inch cord. An anchor line bowline runs through the rear swivel, down the left side of gun. Tie a round turn through the trigger guard. Route the cord down the right side and tie off two half hitches around the forearm assembly with a round turn and two half hitches through the front sight posts. The remainder of the working end is tied off with an end of the rope bowline approximately one foot from the front sight post large enough to place leading hand through. The M240 is secured to the bridge by snaplinks on the front sight post and rear swivel. The M240 is pulled across by the trailing arm of the M240 gunner.

(2) PRC II9's are waterproofed prior to conducting a one rope bridge crossing. A snaplink is placed in the top center of the rucksack frame (same as for 1/2/3 men). The BTC will hook the rucksack to the rope.

NOTE: The use of 2 snaplinks invariably leads to the load binding on the rope. The arm straps are adjusted all the way out and the radio is pulled across the rope bridge by the RTO.

9-4. PONCHO RAFT. Normally a poncho raft is constructed to cross rivers and streams when the current is not swift. A poncho raft is especially useful when the unit is still dry and the platoon leader desires to keep the individuals equipment dry.

a. Equipment Requirements:
   (1) Two serviceable ponchos.
   (2) Two weapons (poles can be used in lieu of weapons).
   (3) Two rucksacks per team.
   (4) 10 feet of utility cord per team.
   (5) One sling rope per team.

b. Conditions: Poncho rafts are used to cross water obstacles when any or all of the following conditions are found:
   (1) The water obstacle is too wide for 120-foot rope.
   (2) No sufficient near or far shore anchor points are available to allow rope bridge construction.
   (3) Under no circumstances will poncho rafts be used as a means to cross a water obstacle if an unusually swift current is present.

c. Choosing a crossing site: Before a crossing site is used, a thorough reconnaissance of the immediate area is made. Analyzing the situation using METT-TC, the patrol leader chooses a crossing site that offers as much cover and concealment as possible and has entrance and exit points that are as shallow as possible. For speed of movement it is best to choose a crossing site that has near and far shore banks that are easily traversed by an individual Ranger.

d. Execution Phase: Steps for the construction of a poncho raft:
   (1) Pair off the unit/patrol in order to have the necessary equipment.
   (2) Tie off the hood of one poncho and lay out on the ground with the hood up.
   (3) Weapons are then placed in the center of the poncho, approximately 18 inches apart, muzzle to butt.
   (4) Next, rucksacks and LCE are placed between the weapons with the two individuals placing their rucksacks as far apart as possible.
   (5) The two will then start to undress (bottom to top), first with their boots, taking the laces completely out for subsequent use as tie downs if necessary).
   (6) The boots are then placed over muzzle/butt of weapon toe in.
   (7) Members continue to undress, folding each item neatly and placing on top of their boots.
   (8) Once all of the equipment is placed between the two weapons or poles, the poncho is snapped together. The snapped portion of the poncho is then lifted into the air and tightly rolled down to the equipment. Start at the center and work out to the end of the raft creating pigtails at the end. This is accomplished much easier if done by both soldiers together. The pigtailed ends are then folded in toward the center top of the raft and tied off with a single boot lace.
   (9) The other poncho is then laid out on the ground with the hood up and the first poncho with equipment is placed in its center. The second poncho is then snapped, rolled and tied in the same manner as the first poncho. The third and fourth boot laces (or utility cord) are then tied around the raft approximately one foot from each end for added security. The poncho raft is now complete.

NOTE: The patrol leader must analyze the situation using METT-TC and make a decision on the uniform for crossing the water obstacle, i.e., weapons inside the poncho raft or slung across the back, remaining dressed or stripped down with clothes inside raft.

9-5. GENERAL. Use of inland and coastal waterways may add flexibility, surprise, and speed to tactical operations. Use of these waterways will also increase the load carrying capacity of normal dismounted units.

9-6. EQUIPMENT F470 COMMANDO ZODIAC ASSAULT BOAT

a. Description of uses, reconnaissance and assault operations.

b. Inflatable with foot pumps using four separate valves located on the inside of the buoyancy tubes. Each of the four valves are used to section off the assault boat into eight separate airtight compartments. To pump air into the boat, turn all valves into the "orange" or "inflate" section of the valve. Once the assault boat is filled with air, turn all valves onto the "green" or "navigation" section. This will section the assault boat into eight separate compartments.

c. Overall length - 15 feet, 5 inches.

d. Overall width - 6 feet, 3 inches.

e. Weight - 265 pounds.

f. Maximum payload - 2,710.

g. Crew - 1 coxswain, 10 paddlers or can be powered by 65 HP short shaft outboard motor.

This space intentionally left blank for notes.

9-7. ORGANIZATION.

(a) Assign each individual a specific boat position (see figure 9-1).

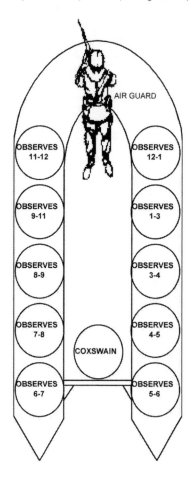

FIGURE 9-1. Boat positions

(b) Designate a commander for each boat, (normally coxswain)

(c) Designate a navigator (normally a leader within the platoon) - observer team as necessary.

(d) Crew is positioned as shown in figure 9-2.

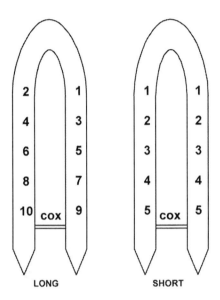

FIGURE 9-2. Crew positions, long count and short count

(e) Duties of the Coxswain.

    (1) Responsible for control of the boat and actions of the crew.

    (2) Supervises the loading, lashing and distribution of equipment.

    (3) Maintains the course and speed of the boat.

    (4) Gives all commands.

(f) Number two paddler (long count) is responsible for setting the pace.

(g) Number one paddler is the observer and responsible for the storage and use of the bowline if no observer has been assigned.

9-8. PREPARATION OF PERSONNEL AND EQUIPMENT.

a. All personnel will wear work vest or kapoks (or another suitable Positive flotation device)

b. LCE is worn over the work vest, unbuckled at the waist.

c. Individual weapon is slung across the back, muzzle pointed down and facing toward the inside of the boat.

d. Crew served weapons, radios, ammunition and other bulky equipment is lashed securely to the boat to prevent loss if the boat should overturn. Machine guns with hot barrels are cooled prior to being lashed inside the boats.

e. Radios and batteries are waterproofed.

f. Pointed objects are padded to prevent puncturing the boat.

9-9. COMMANDS. Commands are issued by the coxswain to ensure the boat is transported over land and controlled in the water. All crew members learn and react immediately to all commands issued by the coxswain. The various commands are as follows:

(a) "Short Count......count off," Crew counts off their position by pairs, i.e., 1,2,3,4,5 (passenger #1, #2, if applicable) coxswain.

(b) "Long Count----count off," Crew counts off the position by individual, i.e., 1,2,3,4,5,6,7,8,9,10, (Passenger #1, #2, if applicable), coxswain.

(c) "Boat Stations", Crew takes positions along side the boat.

(d) "High Carry----Move", (used for long distance move overland).
    (1) On the preparatory command of "High Carry", the crew faces the rear of the boat and squats down grasping carrying handles with the inboard hand.
    (2) On the command "Move", the crew swivels around, lifting the boat to the shoulders so that the crew is standing and facing to the front with the boat on their inboard shoulders.
    (3) Coxswain guides the crew during movement.

(e) "Low Carry----Move", (Used for short distance moves overland).
    (1) On preparatory command of "Low Carry", the crew faces the front of the boat, bent at the waist, and grasps the carrying handles with their inboard hands.
    (2) On the command of "Move", the crew stands up straight raising the boat approximately six to eight inches off the ground.

(3) Coxswain guides the crew during movement.

(f) "Lower the Boat----Move", Crew lowers the boat gently to the ground using the carrying handles.

(g) "Give Way Together", Crew paddles to front with number 2 setting the pace.

(h) "Hold", Entire crew keeps paddles straight downward motionless in the water stopping the boat.

(i) "Left side hold (Right)", Left crew holds, right continues with previous command.

(j) "Back paddle", Entire crew paddles backward propelling the boat to the rear.

(k) "Back Paddle Left" (Right), Left crew back paddles causing the boat to turn left, right crew continues with previous command.
  (1) "Rest Paddles", Crew members place paddles on their laps with blades outboard. This command may be given in pairs (e.g., "Number 1's, rest paddles").

9-10. EMBARKING AND DEBARKING PROCEDURES.

(a) When launching, the crew will maintain a firm grip on the boat until they are inside it: similarly, when beaching or debarking, they hold on to the boat until it is completely out of the water. Loading and unloading is done using the bow as the entrance and exit point.

(b) Keep a low center of mass when entering and existing the boat to avoid capsizing. Maintain 3 points of contact at all times.

(c) The long count is a method of loading and unloading by which the boat crew embarks or debarks individually over the bow of the boat. It is used at river banks, on loading ramps, and when deep water prohibits the use of the short count method.

(d) The short count is a method of loading or unloading by which the boat crew embarks or debarks in pairs over the sides of boat while the boat is in the water. It is used in shallow water allowing the boat to be quickly carried out of the water.

(e) Beaching the boat is a method of debarking the entire crew at once into shallow water and quickly carrying the boat out of the water.

9-11. SECURING THE LANDING SITE.

(a) If the landing site cannot be secured prior to the waterborne force landing, some form of early warning (e.g. scout swimmers) is considered. These personnel swim to shore from the assault boats and signal the boats to land. All signals and actions are rehearsed prior to the actual operation.

(b) If the patrol is going into an unsecured landing site it can provide security by having a security boat land, reconnoiter the landing site and then signal to the remaining boats to land. This is the preferred technique.

(c) The landing site can be secured by force with all the assault boats landing simultaneously in a line formation. While this is the least desirable method of securing a landing site, it is rehearsed in the event the tactical situation requires its use.

(d) Arrival at the debarkation point.
    (1) Unit members disembark according to leaders order.
    (2) Local security is established.
    (3) Leaders account for personnel and equipment.
    (4) Unit continues movement.

Direction of Movement

Establish local security 15-25 meters in from shore based on terrain

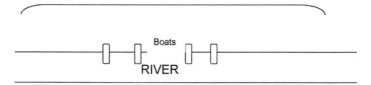

Boats

RIVER

- Soldiers pull security initially with work vest on
- Coxswains and two men unlash and de-rig rucksacks
- Soldiers return in buddy teams to secure rucksack and drop off work vest
- Boats are camouflaged/cached if necessary prior to movement

Figure 9-3. Debarkation

9-12. CAPSIZE. The following commands and procedures are used for capsize drills or to right an over-turned boat,

(a) "Prepare to capsize", This command alerts the crew and they raise paddles above their heads, with the blade pointed outward. Before capsizing, the coxswain will conduct a long count.

(b) "Pass paddles", All paddles are passed back and collected by the number nine and ten men.

(c) "Capsize the boat", All personnel slide into the water except the number three, five, and seven men. The number one man secures the bowline. They grasp the capsize lines (ensuring the lines are routed under the safety lines) and stand on the buoyancy tubes opposite the capsize lines anchor points. The boat is then turned over by the three, five and seven men by leaning back and straightening their legs as they pull back on the capsize lines. As the boat lifts off the water, the number four man grasps the center carrying handle and rides the boat over. Once the boat is over, the number four man helps the number three and seven men back onto the boat at which time the number five man holds onto the center carrying handle and again, the boat is turned over the same way. The number five man rides the boat back over and helps the rest of the crew into the boat.

(d) Coxswain's duties. As soon as the boat is capsized, the coxswain commands a long count to ensure that no one is trapped under the boat or sank. Every time the boat is turned over, a long count must be conducted.

9-13. RIVER MOVEMENT.

(a) Characteristics of River:
  (1) Know local conditions prior to embarking on river movement.
  (2) A bend is a turn in the river course.
  (3) A reach is a straight portion of river between two curves.
  (4) A slough is a dead end branch from a river. They are normally quite deep and can be distinguished from the true river by their lack of current
  (5) Dead water is a part of the river, due to erosion and changes in the river course that has no current. Dead water is characterized by excessive snags and debris.
  (6) An island is usually a pear-shaped mass of land in the main current of the river. Upstream portions of islands usually catch debris and are avoided.
  (7) The current in a narrow part of a reach is normally greater than in the wide portion.
  (8) The current is greatest on the outside of a curve; sandbars and shallow water are found on the inside of the curve.
  (9) Sandbars are located at those points where a tributary feeds into the main body of a river or stream.
  (10) The coxswain and the #1 man must (and the observer, if designated) watch the water for obstacles and overhanging vegetation and projections from the bank.

(b) Navigation. The Patrol Leader is responsible for navigation. There are three acceptable methods of river navigation which are used:
  (1) Checkpoint and general route. These methods are used when the drop site is marked by a well-defined checkpoint and the waterway is not confused by a lot of branches and tributaries. They are best used during daylight hours and for short distances.
  (2) Navigator-observer method. This method is the most accurate means of river navigation and is used effectively in all light conditions.

(a) Equipment needed:
- Compass
- Photo map(1st choice)
- Topographical map (2nd choice)
- Poncho (for night use)
- Pencil/Grease pencil
- Flashlight (for night use)

(b) Navigator is positioned in center of boat and does not paddle. During hours of darkness, he uses his flashlight under the poncho to check his map. The observer (or #1 man) is at the front of the boat.

(c) The navigator keeps his map and compass oriented at all time.

(d) (d)The navigator keeps the observer informed of the configuration of the river by announcing bends, sloughs, reaches and stream junctions as shown on his map.

(e) The observer compares this information with the bends, sloughs, reaches and stream junctions he actually sees. When these are confirmed the navigator confirms the boat's location on his map.

(f) The navigator also keeps the observer informed of the general azimuths of reaches as shown on his map and the observer confirms these with actual compass readings of the river.

(g) The navigator announces only one configuration at a time to the observer and does not announce another until it is confirmed and completed.

(h) A strip-map drawn on clear acetate backed by luminous tape may be used. The drawing is to scale or a schematic. It should show all curves and the azimuth and distance of all reaches. It may also show terrain features, stream junctions and sloughs.

9-14. FORMATIONS. Various boat formations are used (day and night) for control, speed and security. The choice of which is used depends on the tactical situation and the discretion of the patrol leader. He should use hand and arm signals to control his assault boats. The formations are:

(a) Wedge
(b) Line
(c) File
(d) Echelon
(e) VEE

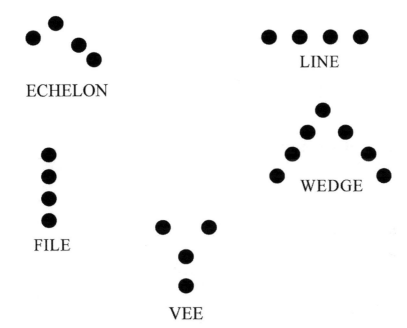

ECHELON

LINE

FILE

WEDGE

VEE

Figure 9-4. Formations

CHAPTER TEN
MILITARY MOUNTAINEERING

10-1. GENERAL. The success of a unit operating in mountainous terrain depends on its ability to use a number of skills in over coming a great variety of obstacles. These skills include knot tying, construction of rope installations, mountain evacuation, rappelling and mountain climbing techniques on rock, snow and ice. Rangers performing mountaineering are familiar with TC 90-6-1 (Military Mountaineering) and have received adequate training.

10-2. SPECIAL EQUIPMENT.

(a) Ropes
(1) Ropes are intended to provide security for climbers and equipment in operations involving steep ascents and descents. They are also used for establishing rope installations and hauling equipment.
(2) Selection. Nylon laid ropes or Kernmantle ropes can be used in military mountaineering. Nylon laid ropes are used by most units to perform most mountaineering tasks. Nylon laid ropes are easy to inspect and have many uses but are not as durable or flexible as kernmantle. Kernmantle ropes come in two types: dynamic and static. Dynamic ropes are used in climbing and in mountaineering operations where rope stretch is needed. A dynamic rope stretches 8-12% of its length. Static kernmantle ropes stretch approximately 2% of their length. Static ropes are used in mountaineering operations where rope stretch is not needed, as in installations (Rope Bridge or fixed rope). Criteria for rope selection are:
(a)   Selection is based on intended use and mission.
(b)   Impact force (the jerk on a climber caused by a fall) should be minimal.
(c)   Elasticity (stretch)is considered (dynamic vs. static ropes for ascending and descending).
(d)   Weight is considered (rope length and tensile strength).
(e)   Versatile, select multi-use ropes.
(f)   Know the tensile strength, characteristics and capabilities of the rope you select.

(b)   Care of ropes:
(1) Inspect ropes thoroughly before, during and after use for cuts, frays, abrasions, mildew, soft or worn spots.
(2) When wet, hang rope to drip dry on a rounded wooden peg, at room temperature (do not apply heat).
(3) Do not step on the rope or drag it on the ground unnecessarily.
(4) Avoid running rope over sharp or rough edges (pad if necessary).
(5) Keep ropes away from oil, acids and other corrosive substances.
(6) Avoid running ropes across one another under tension (nylon to nylon contact will damage ropes).
(7) Do not leave ropes knotted or under tension longer than necessary.

(8) Clean in cool water, loosely coil and hang to dry out of direct sunlight. Ultraviolet light rays harm synthetic fibers. Store in a cool dry shaded area on a peg.

10-3. KNOTS.

a. BASIC KNOTS.
(1) Square knot (Figure 10-1). Two interlocking bites, running ends exit on same side of standing portion of rope, 180 degrees away from each other. Each running end is secured with an overhand knot on the standing end flush with the bight.

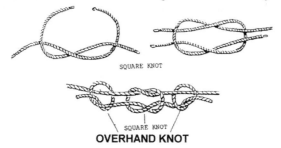

SQUARE KNOT

SQUARE KNOT

OVERHAND KNOT

Figure 10-1. Square knot with overhand safeties

(a) Used to tie two ropes of equal diameter together.
(b) Always secure with an overhand knot.

(2) Round turn two half hitches (Figure 10-2). Used to tie the end of a rope to an anchor. It must have constant tension. Rope forms a complete round turn around the anchor point with both ropes parallel to each other touching, but not crossing. Both half hitches are tightly dressed against the round turn with the locking bar on top and have a minimum of 4 inches in length.

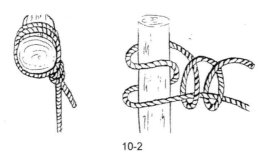

10-2

Figure 10-2. Round turn with two half hitches

(3) <u>End of the rope clove hitch</u> (Figure 10-3). The end of the rope clove hitch is an intermediate anchor knot, which requires constant tension. Two turns around the anchor with a locking bar that runs diagonally from one side to the other. No more than one rope width between turns of rope. Locking bar is opposite direction of pull. Minimum of 4 inch tail remaining after the knot is dressed.

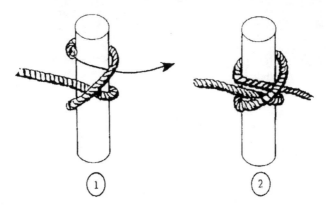

Figure 10-3. End of rope clove hitch

(4) <u>Middle of the rope clove hitch</u> (Figure 10-4). The middle of the rope clove hitch is a middle of the rope anchor knot used to secure the middle of the rope to an anchor. Knot forms two turns around the anchor with a locking bar that runs diagonally from one side to the other. No more than one rope width between turns. Locking bar is opposite direction of pull. Tails are within 6 inches of being equal in length.

Figure 10-4. Middle of rope clove hitch

(5) <u>Rappel seat left hand brake</u> (Figure 10-5). The rappel seat is utilized to form a rope harness for rappelling and can be tied for use with the left or right hand.

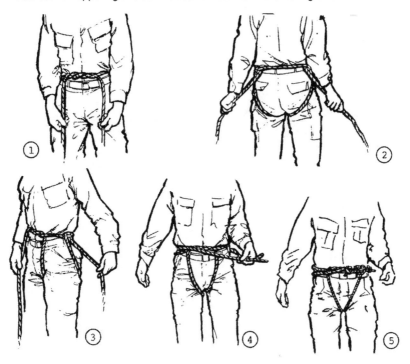

Figure 10-5. Rappel seat left hand brake

Leg straps do not cross, and are centered on buttocks and tight. Leg straps form locking half-hitches on rope around waist. Square knot properly tied on right hip and finished with two overhand knots. Tails even within 6 inches. Carabiner properly inserted around all ropes with opening gate opening up and away. Carabiner will not come in contact with square knot or overhand knot. Rappel seat is tight enough not to allow a fist to be inserted between the rappeller's body and the harness.

b. FIGURE 8 KNOTS.

(1) <u>Figure 8 loop</u> (Figure 10-6). Figure 8 loop knot is utilized to form a fixed loop in the end of the rope. It can be tied at the end of the rope or anywhere along the length of the rope. Figure 8 loop knots are formed by two ropes parallel to each other in the shape of a figure 8, no twists are in the figure eight. Fixed loops are

large enough to insert a carabiner. Minimum of a four inch tail remains after dressing the double figure eight.

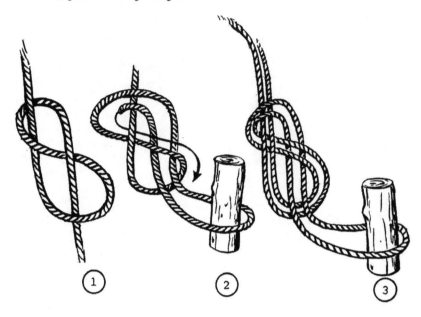

Figure 10-6. Rerouted figure 8 loop knot

(2) <u>Rerouted figure 8 knot</u> (10-7). The rerouted figure 8 knot is utilized to attach a climber to the climbing rope with two ropes running parallel. Figure 8 is approximately the diameter of the anchor point away from the anchor point. A minimum of a four inch tail remains after dressing the knot.

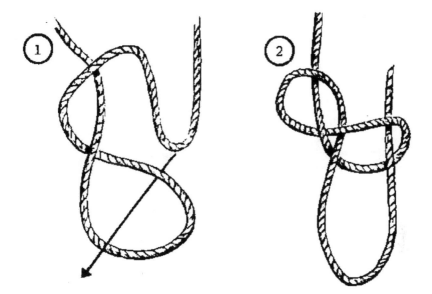

Figure 10-7. Figure 8 slip knot

(3) <u>Figure 8 slip</u> - The figure 8 slip is utilized to form an adjustable loop in the middle of a rope. Knot is in the shape of a figure 8. Both ropes of the bight pass through the same loop of the figure 8. The bight is adjustable by means of a sliding section.

c. SPECIALTY KNOTS.
   (1) <u>End of the rope prusik</u> (Figure 10-8). The end of the rope prusik is utilized to attach a movable rope to a fixed rope. The knot consists of two round turns with a locking bar perpendicular to the standing end of the rope. A bowline is tied no more than 6 inches from the locking bar. Minimum of 4 inch tail after dressing the bowline. Knot does not move freely on fixed rope.

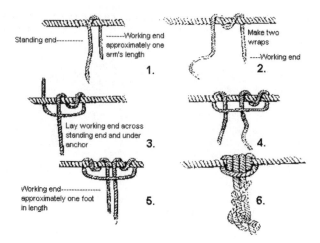

Figure 10-8. End of rope prusik

(2) <u>Middle of the rope prusik</u> (Figure 10-9). The middle of the rope prusik is utilized to attach a movable rope to a fixed rope anywhere along the length of the fixed rope.

Figure 10-9. Middle of rope prusik

10-7

Two round turns with a locking bar perpendicular to the standing end. Wraps do not cross, overhand knot is no more than 6 inches from horizontal locking bar. Knot does not move freely on fixed rope.

    (3) Bowline on a coil (Figure 10-10). The bowline on a coil is utilized to secure a climber to the end of the climbing rope. Utilize a minimum of three wraps parallel to each other and laying between the hip bone and lower set of ribs. All coils touch and are tight enough to ensure that a fist cannot be inserted between the wraps and the body. Wraps are free of clothing. Three distinct coils show through the bight of the bowline. The rope coming off the bottom of the coils is on the right side, forward of the hip and forms the bight and the overhand knot. The rope coming off the top of the coils is on the left side, forward of the hips and forms the third and final coil showing through the bight

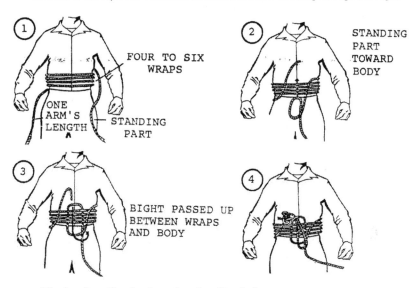

of the bowline. Bowline is centered on the gig line.

Figure 10-10. Bowline on a coil

10-4. BELAYS. Belaying is a method of applying friction to the rope to control the amount of rope that is paid out or taken in. It is also used to arrest a climber that has fallen or to control the rate of descent of a load from a higher elevation to a lower elevation. The belay man must be anchored to a suitable anchor to prevent him from being pulled out of his belay position.

a. Body belay (Figure 10-11). Is used where the rope runs around the belayer's body creating friction. To control the rope there are two basic types of body belays: Standing and Sitting. Sitting is preferred because it offers the most stable position.

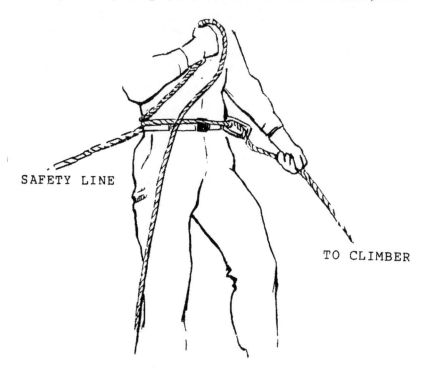

SAFETY LINE

TO CLIMBER

Figure 10-11. Body belay

b. Mechanical belays (Figure 10-12). Equipment is used to provide the friction to control the rate of descent. There are a variety of devices in mountaineering that are used to construct a mechanical belay. One of the most often used that requires little equipment is the munter hitch belay. Ensure when conducting a munter hitch belay that you use a locking carabiner.

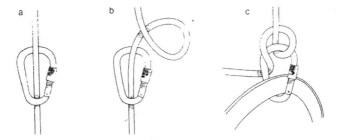

Figure 10-12. Mechanical belay (munter hitch)

c. Actions taken when performing duties as a belay man.
   (1) "Brake" Command given to the belay man to secure the rope and to not pay any more rope out.
   (2) "Slack" This is a command given to the belay man to move to the slack position so rope can be paid out. The belay man does not push rope to the climber or load, the climber pulls what he needs.
   (3) "Up rope" This command is given to the belay man to tell him to take in all the slack between him and the climber or load. Once all slack is taken in, the belay man will go to the brake position.
   (4) "Tension" This command is given to the belay man to tell him to take up all the slack between him and the climber or load, pull the rope tight, and go to the brake position.

10-5. TIGHTENING SYSTEMS. Tightening systems are used to tighten ropes in installations such as rope bridges, suspension traverses and fixed ropes.

a. Knots used for tightening systems are: figure eight slip, directional figure 8 slip and prusiks.

b. Most systems should be constructed with static ropes since their working elongation is only 2 percent. Dynamic ropes stretch 8-12 percent and will require more adjustment and maintenance.

10-6. ROCK CLIMBING TECHNIQUES.

a. Balance climbing: Adequate hand and foot holds are available

b. Tension climbing or direct aid climbing
   (1) Limited hand and foot holds
   (2) Relying on artificial hand and foot holds (ateriers)

10-7. SPECIALIZED CLIMBING EQUIPMENT.

a. Mountaineering / Safety Harness: Consists of CAMP body harness, one locking steel carabiner, one steel figure eight descender, one aluminum locking carabiner and a double headed safety line (sling rope, two steel ovals). The harness is worn as shown (figure 10-13).

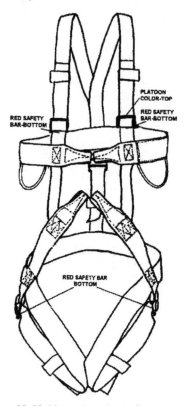

Figure 10-13. Mountaineering/safety harness

10-8. INSTALLATIONS. Assault climbers move forward of the main element and install installations for the main body. Assault climbers install fixed ropes, vertical hauling lines and suspension traverses for troops to overcome mountain obstacles. It is the responsibility of the climbing team that installed the installation to manage and maintain the installation.

(a) <u>A-frame</u> (Figure 10-14). Is used to gain artificial height when needed. Two systems requiring artificial height are the vertical hauling line and the suspension traverse.

(b) <u>Fixed rope</u>. Is in place to assist personnel moving on difficult terrain. Allows personnel with heavy loads to negotiate dangerous mountain routes quickly and safely.
  (1) Most suitable location, ease of negotiation, avoids obstacles.
  (2) Availability of anchors (natural and artificial)
  (3) Area is safe from fallen rock and ice.
  (4) Tactical considerations are met.
  (5) Rope routed between knee and chest high.
  (6) Fairly tight except at obstacles which a climber must avoid. At these
  (7) points, the rope should be loose enough to permit passage.
  (8) No rope crossovers. The climber should not have to cross over the top of the rope at any point.
  (9) An adequate number of intermediate anchor points.

(c) <u>Vertical hauling line</u> (Figure 10-14). Is an installation used to move men and equipment up vertical or near vertical slopes. It is often used in conjunction with the fixed rope.

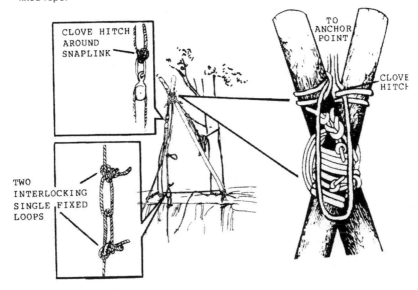

CLOVE HITCH AROUND SNAPLINK

TWO INTERLOCKING SINGLE FIXED LOOPS

TO ANCHOR POINT

CLOVE HITCH

Figure 10-14. A-frame / vertical hauling line

10-12

(1) Most suitable location.
(2) Availability of anchors (natural and artificial).
(3) Good loading and off loading platforms.
(4) Sufficient clearance for load.
(5) A-Frame used for artificial height.
(6) Hauling line used to move personnel and equipment up and down slope.
(7) Pulley or locking carabiner on A-Frame to ease friction on hauling line.
(8) Knotted hand line used to assist personnel up installation.
(9) Personnel placed at top and bottom of installation to monitor safe operation.

(d) <u>Suspension traverse</u> (Figure 10-15). Is an installation used to move men and equipment over rivers, ravines, chasms, and up and down a vertical rock face. The system may be established from horizontal to near vertical slopes.
(1) A-Frame to add height if needed.
(2) Upper and lower anchors.
(3) Loading and unloading anchors.
(4) Sufficient clearance for loads.
(5) Location.
(6) Personnel placed at top and bottom of installation to monitor safe operation.

Figure 10-15. Suspension traverse

(e) <u>Rope bridges</u> (Figure 10-16). A rope bridge is employed in mountainous terrain when streams are more than thigh deep. Such crossings are dangerous since the force of flowing water may be great. Sudden rain or thaws can change a placid stream into a roaring torrent. The maximum span that can be bridged with a standard 120 ft climbing rope is 20 meters.
(1) Personnel are trained in water survival techniques to include unexpected entry into the water.
(2) Good site selection.
(3) Suitable near and far anchors.
(4) Good on and off loading platforms.
(5) Preparation of men and equipment.

10-13

(6) Rescue swimmers posted.
(7) Bridge is as tight as possible with no more than 6 man tightening team.
(8) Bridge is knee to waist high.
(9) Methods of crossings: Commando crawl, Monkey crawl, Tyrolean traverse
(10) One man at a time on one rope bridge.
(11) Up to three on a two rope bridge (one mounting, one in center, one dismounting).

Figure 10-16. 1-Rope bridge

10-9. RAPPELLING (Figure 10-17): Rappelling is the most dangerous task performed in mountaineering. The ranger relies totally on his equipment. When establishing a rappel point the following must be considered:

(a) Types
    (1) Body rappel
    (2) Hasty rappel
    (3) Seat hip shoulder.
    (4) Seat hip

Figure 10-17. Rappelling

(b) Establishment
 (1) Select a suitable primary and secondary anchor and test them.
 (2) Rappel point has primary and secondary anchors.
 (3) Rappel point has equal tension between all anchor points.
 (4) Double rope is used when possible.
 (5) Ropes must reach the off loading platform.
 (6) Site has suitable on and off loading platforms.
 (7) Personnel working near the edge are tied in.
 (8) Select a smooth route free of loose rock and debris.

(c) Operation
 (1) Personnel at the top of the rappel point must have communication with the bottom of the rappel point.
 (2) Belay men are used at the bottom of each lane.
 (3) Rappellers move down the cliff in a controlled descent.
 (4) Rappeller wears gloves and helmet.
 (5) Rappeller clears the ropes once off rappel.

> **Note**- Bounding is discouraged since this stresses the anchor and causes undue wear and friction on the rope.

CHAPTER ELEVEN
EVASION/SURVIVAL

11-1. EVASION. When you become isolated or separated in a hostile area, either as an individual or as a group, your evasion and survival skills will determine whether or not you return to friendly lines.

a. When unable to continue the mission or unable to rejoin your unit, leave the immediate area and move to your last rally point.

b. Observe activity in the area and form a plan.

c. Traveling alone offers the least possibility of detection, but traveling in groups of two to three is more desirable.

d. Plan a primary and alternate route. Consider distance, cover, food and water. The easiest and shortest route may not be the best.

e. Food and water are daily requirements. You can do without food for several days; water, however, is essential.

f. Move at night. Use the daylight to observe, plan, and rest in a hide position.

g. Linkup only during daylight hours. Place friendly lines under observation.

h. Attempt to identify the unit you approach, note their movements and routine.

i. After carefully considering your approach route, make voice contact with the unit as soon as possible.

11-2. SURVIVAL.

a. With training, equipment, and the WILL TO SURVIVE, you will find you can overcome any obstacle you may face. You will survive. You must understand the emotional states associated with survival, "knowing thyself" is extremely important in a survival situation. It bears directly on how well you cope with serious stresses, anxiety, pain, injury, illness; cold, heat, thirst, hunger, fatigue, sleep deprivation, boredom, loneliness and isolation.

b. You can overcome and reduce the shock of being isolated behind enemy lines if you keep the key word S-U-R-V-I-V-A-L foremost in your mind. Its letters can help guide you in your actions.
(1) **S** - Size up the situation; size up your surroundings; size up your physical condition; size up your equipment.
(2) **U** - Undue haste makes waste; don't be too eager to move. Plan your moves.

(3) **R** - Remember where you are in relation to, the location of enemy units and controlled areas. The location of friendly units and controlled areas. The location of local water sources (this is especially important in the desert). Areas that will provide good cover and concealment. The above information will allow you to make intelligent decisions when you are in a survival/evasion situation.

(4) **V** - Vanquish fear and panic.

(5) **I** – Improvise; the situation can be improved. Learn to use natural things around you for different needs. Use your imagination.

(6) **V** - Value living. Remember your goal - getting out alive. Stubbornness, a refusal to give into problems and obstacles that face you, will give you the mental and physical strength to endure.

(7) **A** - Act like the natives; watch their daily routines. When, where, and how they get their food. Where they get their water.

(8) **L** - Live by your wits. Learn basic skills.

11-3. NAVIGATION. In a survival situation, an individual may well find himself without a compass. The ability to determine directions may enable an individual to navigate back to his unit or to a friendly sanctuary. Two methods that are easy to use when there is sunlight are the shadow-tip and the watch.

a. Use the sun to find approximate true north. This method can be used any time the sun is bright enough for a stick to cast a shadow. Find a fairly straight stick about three feet long and follow the diagram below (figure 11-I).

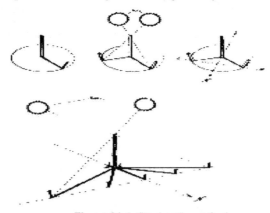

Figure 11-1. Shadow-tip method.

b. Watch method. You can also determine direction using a watch (figure 11-2). The steps you take will depend on whether you are in the northern Temperate Zone or in the southern Temperate Zone. The northern temperate zone is located between

23.4 north and 26.6 north. The southern Temperate Zone is located between 23.4 south and 66.6 south.

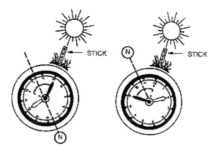

NORTH TEMPERATE ZONE   SOUTH TEMPERATE ZONE

Figure 11-2. Watch method

c. Procedures in the northern temperate zone using a conventional watch are as follows:
   (1) Place a small stick in the ground so that it casts a definite shadow.
   (2) Place your watch on the ground so that the hour hand points toward and along the shadow of the stick.
   (3) Find the point on the watch midway between the hour hand and 12 o'clock and draw an imaginary line from that point through and beyond the center of the watch. This imaginary line is a north-south line. You can then tell the other directions,

   NOTE: If your watch is set on daylight savings time, then use the midway point between the hour hand and 1 o'clock to draw your imaginary line.

d. Procedures in the southern temperate zone using a conventional watch are as follows:
   (1) Place a small stick in the ground so that it casts a definite shadow.
   (2) Place your watch on the ground so that 2 o'clock points to and along the shadow.
   (3) Find the midway point between the hour and 12 o'clock and draw an imaginary line from the point through and beyond the center of the watch. This is a north-south line.

e. A hasty shortcut using a conventional watch is simply to point the hour hand at the sun in the northern temperate zone (or point the 12 at the sun in the southern temperate zone) and then follow the last step of the watch method above to find your directions. This shortcut, of course, is not as accurate as the regular method but quicker. Your situation will dictate which method to use.

11-3

11-4. WATER. Water is one of your most urgent needs in a survival situation. You can't live long without it, especially in hot areas where you lose so much through sweating. Even in cold areas, you need a minimum of 2 quarts of water a day to maintain efficiency. More than three-fourths of your body is composed of fluids. Your body loses fluid as a result of heat, cold, stress, and exertion. The fluid your body loses must be replaced for you to function effectively. So, one of your first objectives is to obtain an adequate supply of water.

a. Purification. Purify all water before drinking, either (1) by boiling for at least one minute (plus 1 minute for each additional 1,000 feet above sea level) or boil for 10 minutes no matter where you are; (2) by using water purification tablets or (3) by adding 8 drops of 2-1/2% solution of iodine to a quart (canteen full) of water and letting it stand for 10 minutes before drinking. Rain water collected directly in clean containers or on plants is generally safe to drink without purifying. Don't drink urine or sea water -- the salt content is too high -- Old bluish sea ice can be used, but new, gray ice may be salty. Glacier ice is safe to melt and drink.

b. Desert Environment. In a desert environment water has a tremendous physiological effect on soldiers. If a unit does not plan properly and cannot be re-supplied, their water supply could run out. There are four indicators or signs of water that you should look for in the desert. They are, animal trails, vegetation, birds, and civilization. Adequate water supply is critical in a hot desert environment if a unit is to survive and maintain the soldier's physical condition necessary to accomplish the mission. Unit leaders must enforce water discipline and plan for water re-supply. The leader can use the following planning considerations for water re-supply.
(1) Units average water consumption.
(2) Drop sites.
(3) Aviation support.
(4) DZ and LZ parties.
(5) Caches.
(6) Targets of opportunity (enemy).

c. Survival water still. For the below ground still (Figure 11-3) you will need a digging tool.
(1) You should select a site where you believe the soil will contain moisture (such as a dry stream bed or a spot where rain water has collected), where the soil is easy to dig, and where sunlight hits most of the day. Proceed as follows:
(a) Dig a bowl-shaped hole approximately 3 feet across and 2 feet deep.
(b) Dig a sump in center of the hole. The depth and the perimeter of the sump will depend on the size of the container that you have to set in it. The bottom of the sump should allow the container to stand upright.
(c) Anchor the tubing to the bottom of the container by forming a loose overhand knot in the tubing.
(d) Place the container upright in the sump.

11-4

(e) Extend the unanchored end of the tubing up, over, and beyond the lip of the hole.

(f) Place plastic sheeting over the hole covering the edge with soil to hold it in place.

(g) Place a rock in the center of the plastic.

(h) Allow the plastic to lower into the hole until it is about 15 inches below ground level. The plastic now forms an inverted cone with the rock at its apex. Make sure that the apex of the cone is directly over your container. Also make sure the plastic cone does not touch the sides of the hole because the earth will absorb the condensed water.

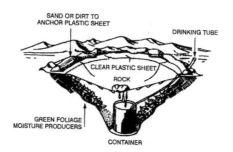

Figure 11-3. Survival water still

(i) Put more soil on the edges of the plastic to hold it securely in place and to prevent loss of moisture.

(j) Plug the tube when not being used so that moisture will not evaporate.

d. You can drink water without disturbing the still by using the tube as a straw. You may want to use plants in the hole as a moisture source. If so, when you dig the hole you should dig out additional soil from the sides of the hole to form a slope on which to place the plants. Then proceed as above.

11-5. PLANT FOOD. There are many plants throughout the world. Tasting or swallowing even a small portion of some can cause severe discomfort, extreme internal disorders, or death. Therefore, if you have the slightest doubt as to the edibility of a plant, apply the universal edibility test described below before eating any part of it.

a. Universal Edibility Test. Before testing a plant for edibility, make sure there are a sufficient number of plants to make testing worth your time and effort. You need more than 24 hours to apply the edibility test outlined below:

(1) Test only one part of a potential food plant at a time.

(2) Break the plant into its basic components, leaves, stems, roots, buds, and flowers.

11-5

(3) Smell the food for strong or acid odors. Keep in mind that smell alone does not indicate a plant is edible.

(4) Do not eat for 8 hours before starting the test.

(5) During the 8 hours you are abstaining from eating, test for contact poisoning by placing a piece of the plant you are testing on the inside of your elbow or wrist. Usually 15 minutes is enough time to allow for reaction.

(6) During the test period, take nothing by mouth except purified water and the plant part being tested.

(7) Select a small portion and prepare it the way you plan to eat it.

(8) Before putting the prepared plant part in your mouth, touch a small portion (a pinch) to the outer surface of the lip to test for burning or itching.

(9) If after 3 minutes there is no reaction on your lip, place the plant part on your tongue, holding there for 15 minutes.

(10) If there is no reaction, thoroughly chew a pinch and hold it in your mouth for 15 minutes. DO NOT SWALLOW.

(11) If no burning, itching, numbing, stinging, or other irritation occurs during the 15 minutes, swallow the food.

(12) Wait 8 hours. If any ill effects occur during this period, induce vomiting and drink a lot of water.

(13) If no ill effects occur eat 1/2 cup of the same plant part prepared the same way. Wait another 8 hours. If no ill effects occur, the plant part as prepared is safe for eating.

b. DO NOT eat unknown plants that have the below characteristics:

(1) Have a milky sap or a sap that turns black when exposed to air.

(2) Are mushroom like.

(a) Resemble onion or garlic.

(b) Resemble parsley, parsnip, or dill.

(c) Have carrot-like leaves, roots, or tubers.

11-6. ANIMAL FOOD.

a. Animal Food. Animal food contains the most food value per pound. Anything that creeps, crawls, swims, or flies is a possible source of food, however you must first catch, kill and butcher it before this is possible. There are numerous methods for catching fish and animals in a survival situation. You can catch fish by using a net across a small stream, (figure 11-4) or by making fish traps and baskets.

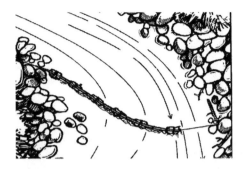

Figure 11-4. Setting a gill net in the stream

b. Improvise fish hooks and spears as indicated in figure 11-5, and use them for conventional fishing, spearing and digging.

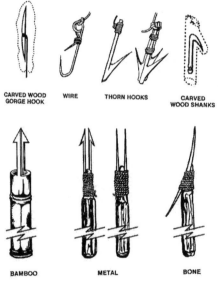

CARVED WOOD GORGE HOOK   WIRE   THORN HOOKS   CARVED WOOD SHANKS

BAMBOO   METAL   BONE

Figure 11-5. Spears and fish hooks

11-7. TRAPS AND SNARES

a. For an unarmed survivor or evader, or when the sound of a rifle shot could be a problem, trapping or snaring wild game is a good alternative. Several well-placed traps have the potential to catch much more game than a man with a rifle is likely to shoot. To be effective with any type of trap or snare, you must--
(1) Be familiar with the species of animal you intend to catch.
(2) Be capable of constructing a proper trap.
(3) Not alarm the prey by leaving signs of your presence.

b. There are no catchall traps you can set for all animals. You must determine what species are in a given area and set your traps specifically with those animals in mind. Look for the following:
(1) Runs and trails.
(2) Tracks.
(3) Droppings.
(4) Chewed or rubbed vegetation.
(5) Nesting or roosting sites.
(6) Feeding and watering areas.

c. Position your traps and snares where there is proof that animals pass through. You must determine if it is a "run" or a "trail." A trail will show signs of use by several species and will be rather distinct. A run is usually smaller and less distinct and will only contain signs of one species. You may construct a perfect snare, but it will not catch anything if haphazardly placed in the woods. Animals have bedding areas, waterholes, and feeding areas with trails leading from one to another. You must place snares and traps around these areas to be effective.

d. For an evader in a hostile environment, trap and snare concealment is important. It is equally important, however, not to create a disturbance that will alarm the animal and cause it to avoid the trap. Therefore, if you must dig, remove all fresh dirt from the area. Most animals will instinctively avoid a pitfall-type trap. Prepare the various parts of a trap or snare away from the site, carry them in, and set them up. Such actions make it easier to avoid disturbing the local vegetation, thereby alerting the prey. Do not use freshly cut, live vegetation to construct a trap or snare. Freshly cut vegetation will "bleed" sap that has an odor the prey will be able to smell. It is an alarm signal to the animal.

e. You must remove or mask the human scent on and around the trap you set. Although birds do not have a developed sense of smell, nearly all mammals depend on smell even more than on sight. Even the slightest human scent on a trap will alarm the prey and cause it to avoid the area. Actually removing the scent from a trap is difficult but masking it is relatively easy. Use the fluid from the gall and urine bladders of previous kills. Do not use human urine. Mud, particularly from an area with plenty of rotting vegetation, is also good. Use it to coat your hands when handling the trap and to coat the trap when setting it. In nearly all

11-8

parts of the world, animals know the smell of burned vegetation and smoke. It is only when a fire is actually burning that they become alarmed. Therefore, smoking the trap parts is an effective means to mask your scent. If one of the above techniques is not practical, and if time permits, allow a trap to weather for a few days and then set it. Do not handle a trap while it is weathering. When you position the trap, camouflage it as naturally as possible to prevent detection by the enemy and to avoid alarming the prey.

   f. Traps or snares placed on a trail or run should use canalization. To build a channel, construct a funnel-shaped barrier extending from the sides of the trail toward the trap, with the narrowest part nearest the trap. Canalization should be inconspicuous to avoid alerting the prey. As the animal gets to the trap, it cannot turn left or right and continues into the trap. Few wild animals will back up, preferring to face the direction of travel. Canalization does not have to be an impassable barrier. You only have to make it inconvenient for the animal to go over or through the barrier. For best effect, the canalization should reduce the trail's width to just slightly wider than the targeted animal's body. Maintain this constriction at least as far back from the trap as the animal's body length, then begin the widening toward the mouth of the funnel.

     (1) Treadle Spring Snare. Use a treadle snare against small game on a trail (Figure 11-6). Dig a shallow hole in the trail. Then drive a forked stick (fork down) into the ground on each side of the hole on the same side of the trail. Select two fairly straight sticks that span the two forks. Position these two sticks so that their ends engage the forks. Place several sticks over the hole in the trail by positioning one end over the lower horizontal stick and the other on the ground on the other side of the hole. Cover the hole with enough sticks so that the prey must step on at least one of them to set off the snare. Tie one end of a piece of cordage to a twitch-up or to a weight suspended over a tree limb. Bend the twitch-up or raise the suspended weight to determine where you will tie a 5 centimeter or so long trigger. Form a noose with the other end of the cordage.

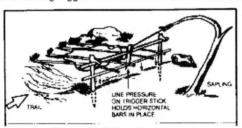

Figure 11-6. Treadle snare

Route and spread the noose over the top of the sticks over the hole. Place the trigger stick against the horizontal sticks and route the cordage behind the sticks so that the tension of the power source will hold it in place. Adjust the bottom horizontal stick so that it will barely hold against the trigger. As the animal places its foot on a stick across the hole, the bottom horizontal stick moves down, releasing the trigger and allowing the noose to catch the animal by the foot. Because of the disturbance on the trail, an animal will be wary. You must therefore use canalization.

g. Trapping game can be accomplished through the use of snares, traps, or deadfalls. A snare is a noose that will slip and strangle or hold any animal caught in it. You can use inner core strands of parachute suspension lines, wire, bark of small hardwood saplings as well as hide strips from previously caught animals to make snares.

(1) The drag noose snare, figure 11-7, is usually the most desirable in that it allows you to move away from the site, plus it is one of the easiest to make and fastest to set.

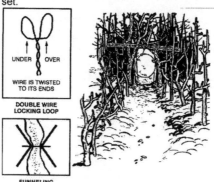

Figure 11-7. Drag noose snare

It is especially suitable for catching rabbits. To make the drag noose snare, make a loop in the string using a bowline or wireman's knot. (When using wire, secure the loop by intertwining the end of the wire with the wire at the top of the loop). Pull the other end of the string (or wire) through the loop to form a noose that is large enough for the animal's head but too small for its body; tie the string (or attach the wire) to a sturdy branch. The branch should be large enough to span the trail and rest on the bush or support (two short forked sticks) you have selected. A snared animal will dislodge the drag stick, pulling it until it becomes entangled in the brush. Any attempt to escape tightens the noose, strangling or holding the animal.

(2) Another type snare is the locking type snare loop (figure 11-8) that will lock when pulled tight, ensuring the snared animal cannot escape.

11-10

Figure 11-8. Forming a locking-type snare loop

Use lightweight wire to make this snare, i.e., trip wire, from vehicle or aircraft electrical system. To construct this snare, cut a piece of wire twice the length of the desired snare wire. Double the wire and attach the running ends to a securely placed object, such as the branch of a tree. Place a stick about 1/2 inch in diameter through the loop end of the wire; holding the wire taut, turn the stick in a winding motion so that the wire is twisted together. You should have four to five twists per inch. Detach the wire from the branch and then remove the loop from the stick; make a figure 8 in the I/2-inch loop by twisting the loop over itself then fold the figure 8 so the small loops are almost overlapping; run the loose wire ends through these loops. This forms a stiff noose that is strong. Tie the loose end to the stick (for a drag noose square) or branch you are using to complete the snare. This is an excellent snare for catching large animals.

(3) Another means of obtaining game is the use of the deadfall trap as indicated at figure 11-8A and figure 11-8B.

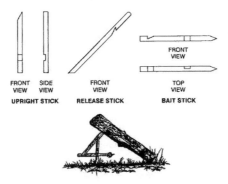

Figure 11-8A. Trigger with deadfall

Figure 11-8B. Trip-string deadfall trap

h. Once you have obtained your fish or game you must clean/butcher and cook/store it. Improper cleaning storing can result in inedible fish and game.

(1) Fish. You must know how to tell if fish are free of bacterial decomposition that makes the fish dangerous to eat. Although cooking may destroy the toxin from bacterial decomposition, do not eat fish that appear spoiled. Signs of spoilage are:

- A peculiar odor.
- A suspicious color. (Gills should be red or pink. Scales should be a pronounced-not faded shade of gray).
- A dent remaining after pressing the thumb against the flesh.
- A slimy rather than moist or wet body.
- A sharp or peppery taste.

(a) Eating spoiled or poisoned fish may cause diarrhea, nausea, cramps, vomiting, itching; paralysis, or a metallic taste in the mouth. These symptoms appear suddenly 1 to 6 hours after eating. If you are near the sea, drink sea water immediately upon on set of such symptoms and force yourself to vomit.

(b) Fish spoil quickly after death, especially on a hot day, so prepare fish for eating as soon as possible after you catch them.

(c) Cut out the gills and large blood vessels that lie next to the backbone. (You can leave the head if you plan to cook the fish on a spit).

(d) Gut fish that are more than 4 inches long cut along the abdomen and scrape out the intestines.

(e) Scale or skin the fish.

(f) You can impale a whole fish on a stick and cook it over an "open fire". However, boiling the fish with the skin on is the best way to get the most food value. The fats and oil are under the skin, and by boiling the fish, you can save the juices for broth. Any of the methods used for cooking plant food can be used for cooking fish. Fish is done when the meat flakes off.

(g) To dry fish in the sun, hang them from branches or spread them on hot rocks. When the meat has dried splash it with sea water, if available, to salt the outside. Do not keep any seafood unless it is well dried or salted.

11-12

(2) Snakes. All poisonous and nonpoisonous fresh water and land snakes are edible.

CAUTION: Take extreme care in securing snakes as the bite of some poisonous snakes can be fatal. Even after a snake's head is cut off, its reflex action can cause it to bite, injecting poison. The best time to capture snakes is in the early morning or late evening when temperatures are low and they move slow. Kill or use a long stick to pin down its head and capture it. To pick up a snake, place the index finger on the top rear of its head with your thumb and middle finger on either side of the head behind the jaws. Keep your index finger on top of snake's head to prevent it from turning inside its skin and biting you. To prepare snakes for eating use the following steps (figure 11-9):

    (a) Grip the snake firmly behind the head and cut off the head with a knife.

    (b) Slit the belly and remove the innards. (You can use the innards for baiting traps and snares).

    (c) Skin the snake. (You can use the skin for improvising, belts, straps, or similar items).

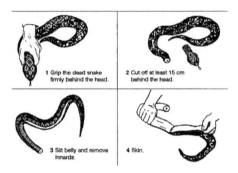

1 Grip the dead snake firmly behind the head.

2 Cut off at least 15 cm behind the head.

3 Slit belly and remove innards.

4 Skin.

Figure 11-9. Cleaning a snake

(3) Fowl. Your first step after killing a fowl for eating or preserving is to pluck its feathers. If plucking is impractical, you can skin the fowl. Keep in mind, however, that a fowl cooked with the skin on retains more food value. Waterfowl are easier to pluck while dry, but other fowl are easier to pluck after scalding. After you pluck the fowl:

    (a) Cut off its neck close to the body.

    (b) Cut an incision in the abdominal cavity and clean out the insides. Save the neck, liver, and heart for stew. Thoroughly clean and dry the entrails to use for cordage.

(c) Wash out the abdominal cavity with fresh clean water. You can boil fowl or cook it on a spit over a fire. You should boil scavenger birds such as vultures and buzzards for at least 20 minutes to kill any parasites. Use the feathers from fowl for insulating your shoes clothing, or bedding. You can also use feathers for fish lures.

(4) Medium-sized Mammals. The game you trap or snare will generally be alive when you find it and therefore dangerous. Be careful when you approach a trapped animal. Use a spear or club to kill it so you can keep a safe distance from it. After you kill an animal, immediately bleed it by cutting its throat. If you must drag the carcass any distance, do so before you cut off the hide so that the carcass is protected from dirt and debris that might contaminate it. Clean the animal near a stream if possible so that you can wash and *cool* the carcass and edible parts. Fleas and parasites will leave a cooled body so if the situation allows, wait until the animal cools before cleaning and dressing the carcass. To skin and dress the animal (figure 11-10 and 11-11).

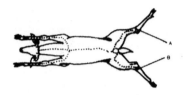

Figure 11-10. Skinning and butchering large game

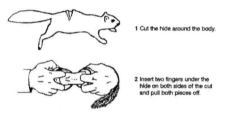

Figure 11-11. Skinning small game

(a) Place carcass, belly up, on a slope if available. You can use rocks or brush to support it.

(b) Remove genitals or udder.

(c) Remove musk glands to avoid tainting meat.

(d) Split hide from tail to throat. Make the cut shallow so that you do not pierce the stomach.

(e) Insert your knife under the skin, taking care not to cut into the body cavity. Peel the hide back several inches on each side to keep hair out of the meat.

(f) Open the chest cavity by splitting the sternum. You can do this by cutting to one side of the sternum where the ribs join.

(g) Reach inside and cut the windpipe and gullet as close to the base of the skull as possible.

(h) With the forward end of the intestinal tract free, work your way to the rear lifting out internal organs and intestines. Cut only where necessary to free them.

(i) Carefully cut the bladder away from the carcass so that you do not puncture the bladder (urine can contaminate meat). Pinch the urethra tightly and cut it beyond the point you are pinching.

(j) Remove the bladder.

(k) From the outside of the carcass, cut a circle around the anus.

(l) Pull the anus into the body cavity and out of the carcass.

(m) Lift or roll the carcass to drain all blood. **NOTE: Try to save as much blood as you can as it is a vital source of food and salt. Boil the blood.**

(n) Remove the hide, make cuts along the inside of the legs to just above the hoof or paw. Then peel the skin back, using your knife in a slicing motion to cut the membrane between the skin and meat. Continue this until the entire skin is removed.

(o) Most of the entrails are usable. The heart, liver, and kidneys are edible. Cut open the heart and remove the blood from its chambers. Slice the kidneys and if enough water is available, soak or rinse them. In all animals except those of the deer family, the gall bladder (a small, dark-colored, clear-textured sac) is attached to the liver.

(p) Sometimes the sac looks like a blister on the liver. To remove the sac, hold the top portion of it and cut the liver around and behind the sac. If the gall bladder breaks and gall gets on the meat, wash it off immediately so the meat will not become tainted. Dispose of the gall.

(q) Clean blood splattered on the meat will glaze over and help preserve the meat for a short time. However, if an animal is not bled properly, the blood will settle in the lowest part of its body and will spoil in a short time. Cut out any meat that becomes contaminated.

(r) When temperatures are below 40 degrees, you can leave meat hanging for several days without danger of spoilage. If maggots get on the meat, remove the maggots and cut out the discolored meat. The remaining meat is edible. Maggots, which are the larvae of insects, are also edible.

(s) Blood, which contains salts and nutrients is a good base for soups.

(t) Thoroughly clean the intestines and use them for storing or smoking food or lashings for general use. Make sure they are completely dry to preclude rotting.

(u) The head of most animals contains a lot of meat, which is relatively easy to get. Skin the head, saving the skin for leather. Clean the mouth thoroughly and cut out the tongue. Remove the outer skin from the tongue after cooking. Cut or scrape the meat from the head. If you prefer, you can roast the head over an open fire before cutting off the meat. Eyes are edible. Cook them but discard the retina (this is a plastic like disc). The brain is also edible; in fact, some people consider it a delicacy. The brain is also used to tan leather, the theory being that the brain of an animal is adequate to tan its hide.

(v) Use the tendons and ligaments of the body of large animals for lashings.

(w) The marrow in bones is a rich-food source. Crack the bones and scrap out the marrow, and use bones to make weapons.

(x) If the situation and time allow, you should preserve the extra meat for later use. If the air is cold enough, you can freeze the meat. In warmer climates however, you will need to use a drying or smoking process to preserve it. One night of heavy smoking will make meat edible for about 1 week. Two nights will make it remain edible for 2 to 4 weeks. To prepare meat for drying or smoking, cut it with the grain in quarter inch strips. To air dry the meat, hang it in the wind and hot sun out the reach of animals; cover it so that blow flies cannot land on it.

(y) To smoke meat, you will need an enclosed area – for instance, a teepee (figure 11-12) or a pit. You will also need wood from deciduous trees, preferably green. Do not use conifer trees such as pines, firs, spruces, or cedars as the smoke from these trees give the meat a disagreeable taste.

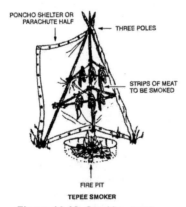

PONCHO SHELTER OR PARACHUTE HALF

THREE POLES

STRIPS OF MEAT TO BE SMOKED

FIRE PIT

TEPEE SMOKER

Figure 11-12. Smoking meat

(z) When using the para-teepee or other enclosed area with a vent at the top, set the fire in the center and let it burn down to coals, then stoke it with green wood. Place the strips of meat on a grate or hang them from the top

11-16

of the enclosure so that they are about 2 feet above the smoking coals. To use the pit method of smoking meat dig, a hole about 3 feet (1 meter) deep and 1 1/2 feet (1/2 meter) in diameter. Make a fire at the bottom of the hole. After it starts burning well, add chipped green wood or small branches of green wood to make it smoke. Place a wooden grate about 1 1/2 feet (1/2 meter) above the fire and lay the strips of meat on the grate. Cover the pit with poles, boughs, leaves, or other material.

11-8. SHELTERS. A shelter can protect you from the sun, insects, wind, rain, snow, hot or cold temperatures, and enemy observation. In some areas your need for shelter may take precedence over your need for food, possibly even your need for water.

a. Types of shelters. After determining your shelter site, you should keep in mind the type of shelter (protection) you need. The below listed factors are considered:
(1) How much time and effort are needed to build the shelter?
(2) Will the shelter adequately protect you from the elements (rain, snow, wind, sun, etc.)?
(3) Do you have tools to build it? If not, can you improvise tools from materials in the area?
(4) Do you have the type and amount of manmade materials needed to build it? If not, are there sufficient natural materials in the area? You need to know how to make different types of shelters. Only two are described in this handbook. Additional information is available in FM 21-76.

b. Poncho Lean-to. It takes only a short time and minimal equipment to build this lean-to (figure 10-13). You need a poncho, 6 to 10 feet of rope, three stakes about 6 inches long, and two trees (or two poles) 7 to 9 feet apart. Before you select the trees you will use (or decide where to place the poles), check the wind direction. Make sure the back of your lean-to will be into the wind. To make the lean-to:

(1) Tie off the hood of the poncho. To do this, pull the draw cord tight; roll the hood long ways, fold it into thirds, and tie it with the draw cord
(2) Cut the rope in half, on one long side of the poncho, tie half of the rope to one corner grommet and the other half to the other corner grommet.
(3) Attach a drip stick (about a 4-inch stick) to each rope 1/4 to 3/4 inches away from the grommet. These drip sticks will keep rainwater from running down the ropes into the lean-to. Using drip lines is another way to prevent dripping inside the shelter. Tie lines or string about 4 inches long to each grommet along the top edge of the shelter. This allows water to run to and down the line without dripping into the shelter.
(4) Tie the ropes about waist high on the trees (uprights). Use a round turn and two half hitches with quick-release knot.
(5) Spread the poncho into the wind and anchor to the ground. To do this, put three sharpened sticks through the grommets and into the ground.

Figure 11-13. Poncho lean-to

(6) If you plan to use the lean-to for more than one night, or if you expect rain, make a center support to the lean-to. You can do this by stretching a rope between two upright poles or trees that are in line with the center of the poncho.
(7) Tie another rope to the poncho hood; pull it upward so that it lifts the center of the poncho, and tie it firmly to the rope stretched between the two uprights.
(8) Another method is to cut a stick to place upright under the center of the lean-to. This method, however, will restrict your space and movements in the shelter.
(9) To give additional protection from wind and rain, place boughs, brush, your rucksack, or other equipment at the sides of the lean-to.
(10) To reduce heat loss to the ground, place some type of insulating material, such as leaves or pine needles, inside your lean-to. **NOTE: When at rest, as much as 80 percent of your body heat can be lost to the ground**.
(11) To increase your security from enemy observation, lower the silhouette of the lean-to by making two modifications.
  (a) Secure the support lines to the trees knee-high rather than waist-high.
  (b) Use two knee-high sticks in the two center grommets (sides of lean-to), and angle the poncho to the ground, securing it with sharpened sticks as above.

c. Field Expedient Lean-to. If you are in a wooded area and have sufficient natural materials, you can make an expedient lean-to (figure 11-14) without the aid of tools or with only a knife. You need more time to make it than the shelter previously mentioned, but it will protect you from most environmental elements. You will need two trees, (or two upright poles), about 6 feet apart; one pole about 7 feet long and 1 inch in diameter. Five to eight poles about 10 feet long and 1 inch in diameter for beams, cord or vines for securing, the horizontal support to the trees and other poles, saplings, or vines to crisscross the beams. To make this lean-to:

Figure 11-14. Field Expedient Lean-to

(1) Tie the 7-foot pole to the two trees at point about waist to chest high. This is your horizontal support. If there is a fork in the tree, you can rest the pole in it instead of tying the pole in place. If a standing tree is not available, construct a bipod using an Y-shaped sticks or two tripods.

(2) Place one end of the beams (10-foot poles) one side of the horizontal support. As with all lean-to type shelters, make sure the backside of the lean-to is placed into the wind.

(3) Crisscross sapling or vines on the beams.

(4) Cover the framework with brush, leaves, pine needles, or grass, starting at the bottom and working your way up like shingling.

(5) Place straw, leaves, pine needles, or grass inside the shelter for bedding.

(6) In cold weather you can add to the comfort of your lean-to by building a fire-reflector wall (figure 11-14). Drive four stakes about 4 feet long into the ground to support the wall. Stack green logs on top of one another between the support stales. Bind the top of the support stakes so the green logs will stay in place. Fill in the spaces between the logs with twigs or small branches. With just a little more effort you can have a drying rack: Cut a few 3/4 inch diameter poles (length depends on distance between the lean-to support and the top of the fire-reflector wall). Lay one end of the poles on the lean-to horizontal support and the other ends on top of the reflector wall. Place and tie into place smaller sticks across these poles. You now have a place to dry clothes, meat, or fish.

11-9. FIRE BUILDING. A fire can full fill several needs. It can keep you warm, it can keep you dry: you can use it to cook food, to purify water, and to signal. It can also cause you problems when you are in enemy territory: it creates smoke, which can be smelled and seen from a long distance: It causes light which can be seen day or night and it leaves signs of your presence. Remember you should always weigh your need for a fire against your need to avoid enemy protection. When operating in remote areas you should always take a supply of matches in a waterproof case and keep them on your person.

a. When selecting a site to build a fire, you should consider the following:
   (1) The area (terrain and climate) in which you are operating.
   (2) The material and tools available.
   (3) How much time you have.
   (4) Why you need a fire.
   (5) The nearness of the enemy.

b. To prepare a site for a fire, look for a dry spot that has the following:
   (1) That is protected from the wind.
   (2) That is suitably placed in relation to your shelter (if any).
   (3) That will concentrate the heat in the direction you desire.
   (4) Where a supply of wood or other fire burning material is available.
   (5) If you are in a wooded or brush-covered area, clear brush away, and scrape
       the surface soil from the spot you selected. The cleared circle should be at
       least 3 feet (1 meter) in diameter so that there is little chance of the fire
       spreading.

c. Dakota fire hole. In some situations you may find that an underground fireplace will
   best meet your need. It conceals the fire to some extent and serves well for
   cooking food. To make an underground fireplace or Dakota fire hole (figure 11-15):

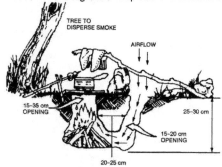

Figure 11-15. Dakota Fire Hole

   (1) Dig a hole in the ground.
   (2) On the upwind side of this hole, poke one large connecting hole for ventilation.

d. Above ground fire. If you are in a snow covered or wet area, you can use green
   logs to make a dry base for your fire (figure 11-16). Trees with wrist-size trunks
   are easily broken in extreme cold. Cut or break several green logs and lay them
   side by side on top of the snow. Add one or two more layers, laying the top layer
   logs in a direction opposite those of the layer below it.

Figure 11-16. Base for fire in snow covered area

e. There are several methods for laying a fire for quick fire making. Three easy methods are Tepee, lean-to, and cross-ditch. Tepee (figure 11-17). Arrange tinder and a few sticks of kindling in the shape of a cone. Fire the center. As the cone burns away, the outside logs will fall inward, feeding the heart of the fire. This type of fire burns well even with wet wood.

    (1) Lean-to (figure 11-17). Push a green stick into the ground at a 30 degree angle. Point the end of the stick in the direction of the wind. Place some tinder (at least a handful) deep inside this lean-to stick. Light the tinder. As the kindling catches fire from the tinder, add more kindling.

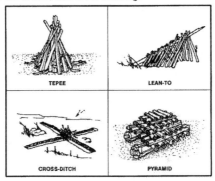

Figure 11-17. Methods for Laying a Fire

    (2) Cross-ditch (figure 11-17). Scratch a cross about 1 foot in size in the ground. Dig the cross 3 inches deep. Put a large wad of tinder in the middle of the cross. Build a kindling pyramid above the tinder. The shallow ditch allows air to sweep under the fire to provide a draft.

This space intentionally left blank for notes.

CHAPTER TWELVE
FIRST AID

12-1. GENERAL. The nature of patrolling operations causes casualties to become a greater consideration than on other missions. It is essential that all personnel know how to diagnose and treat injuries, wounds, and illnesses. The unit should also have a plan for handling KIA's.

12-2. LIFESAVING STEPS (Applies to all injuries).

a. Open the airway and restore breathing.
b. Stop the bleeding and protect the wound.
c. Check, treat and monitor for shock.

12-3. STINGS AND BITES.

BITES AND STINGS	
TYPE	FIRST AID
Snakebite	1. Get the casualty away from the snake. 2. Remove all rings and bracelets from the affected extremity. 3. Reassure the casualty and keep him quiet. 4. Apply constricting band(s) 1-2 finger widths proximal to the bite. One finger should be able to be slipped between the band and skin. ARM or LEG Bite - Place one band above and one band below the bite site. HAND or FOOT Bite - Place one band above the wrist or ankle. 5. Immobilize the affected limb in a position below the level of the heart. 6. Kill the snake, if possible, (without damaging its head or endangering yourself) and send it with the casualty. 7. Seek medical treatment immediately.
Brown recluse Black Widow Spider bites	1. Keep the casualty calm. 2. Wash the area. 3. Apply ice or a freeze pack, if available. 4. Seek medical treatment.
Tarantula bite, Scorpion sting, Ant bites	1. Wash the area. 2. Apply ice or a freeze pack, if available. 0. Apply baking soda, calamine lotion, or meat tenderizer to the bite site to relieve pain and itching. 4. If site of bite(s) or sting(s) is on the face, neck (possible airway blockage), or genital area, or if reaction is severe, or if the sting is by the dangerous Southwestern scorpion, keep the casualty as quiet as possible and seek immediate medical aid.

1. If the stinger is present, remove by scraping with a knife or finger nail. DO NOT squeeze venom sack on stinger, more venom may be injected.
2. Wash the area.
3. Apply ice or freeze pack, if available.
4. If allergic signs or symptoms appear, be prepared to perform CPR and seek medical assistance.

1. Cleanse the wound thoroughly with soap or detergent solution.
2. Flush bite well with water.
3. Cover bite with a sterile dressing.
4. Immobilize injured extremity.
5. Transport casualty to a medical treatment facility.
6. Kill the animal, if possible, without damaging its head or endangering yourself, and send it with the casualty.

1. Control the bleeding.
2. Prevent shock.
3. Provide basic life support.
4. Splint any orthopedic injuries.
5. Provide immediate medical attention.

1. Clean the wound(s) thoroughly.
2. Splint if necessary.

1. Gently remove clinging tentacles with a towel.
2. Apply diluted ammonia, alcohol, meat tenderizer, or talcum powder.
3. Seek medical attention.

1. Soak the wound in warm water for 30-60 minutes.
2. Seek further first aid as necessary.

VAC - Nine line call format:

	EXPLANATION
ɔf te.	Encrypt the grid coordinates of the pick-up site. When using the DRYAD Numeral Cipher, the same "SET" line is used to encrypt both the grid zone letters and the coordinates. To preclude misunderstanding, a statement should be made that grid zone letters are included in the message. (Unless unit SOP specifies its use at all times.)

, call fix.	Encrypt the frequency of the radio at the pick-up site and not a relay frequency. The call sign (and suffix if used) of person to be contacted at the pick-up site may be transmitted in the clear.
f y :e	Report only applicable information and encrypt the appropriate amount(s) and brevity number(s). (#)-1-Urgent - Save life/limb/eyesight EVAC w/in 2 hours (#)-2-Priority - Evac w/in 4 hours. (#)-3-Routine - Evac w/in 24 hours. (#)-4-Tactical Immediate - ASAP. If two or more categories must be reported in the same request, insert the word "BREAK" between each category.
t	Encrypt the appropriate brevity number(s). 5 – None 6 – Hoist 7 - Stokes Litter 8 - Forest/Jungle Penetrator
f y	Report only applicable information and encrypt the appropriate amount(s) and brevity number(s). If requesting MEDEVAC for both types, insert the proword "BREAK" between the litter entry and ambulatory entry. (#) – Litter (#) – Ambulatory (sitting)
)f	1 – No enemy troops in area. 2 – Possibly enemy troops in area (approach with caution). 3 - Enemy troops in area (approach with caution). 4 – Enemy troops in area (armed escort required). 5 – Peacetime
ick-up	Encrypt the appropriate brevity number(s): 5 - Panels. 6 - Pyrotechnic signal. 7 - Smoke signal. 8 - Signal person. 9 - Strips of fabric or parachute. 0 - Tree branches, pieces of wood, or stones placed together. 1 - Signal lamp or flashlight. 2 - Vehicle lights. 3 - Open flame.
and	The number of patients in each category need not be transmitted. Encrypt only the appropriate brevity number(s): 4 - US military. 5 - US civilian. 6 - Non-US military. 7 - Non-US civilian. 8 - EPW.

9	NBC Contamination	Include this line only when applicable. Encrypt the appropriate brevity number(s). 9 - Nuclear 0 - Biological 1 – Chemical - Peacetime

12-5. HEAD INJURY.

a. Symptoms:
   (1) Bleeding
   (2) Deformity
   (3) Unconsciousness
   (4) Memory loss
   (5) Clear fluid or blood leaking from nose and ears
   (6) Staggering/dizziness
   (7) Change in pulse
   (8) Breathing problems
   (9) Nausea or vomiting
   (10) Convulsions
   (11) Slurred speech
   (12) Confusion
   (13) Sleepiness
   (14) Black eyes
   (15) Eye problems
   (16) Paralysis
   (17) Headache

b. Treatment:
   (1) Maintain open airway.
   (2) Place a dressing over wounded area.
   (3) Do not attempt to clean the wound.
   (4) Keep casualty warm.
   (5) Do not attempt to remove an impaled object from the head.
   (6) Do not give the casualty anything to eat or drink.
   (7) Do not administer morphine or similar drugs.
   (8) Do not attempt to push any brain matter back into the head.
   (9) Keep the airway clean.
   (10) Position the casualty on his side opposite the site of injury.

12-6. ENVIRONMENTAL INJURIES.

NJURY	SIGNS/SYMPTOMS	FIRST AID
	COLD INJURIES	
_BLAIN	Red, swollen, hot, tender, itching skin. Continued exposure may lead to infected (ulcerated bleeding) skin lesions.	1. Area usually responds to locally applied warming (body heat). 2. Do Not rub or massage area. 3. Seek medical treatment.
RSION)T/ ICH FOOT	Affected parts are cold, numb, and painless. As parts warm they may be hot, with burning and shooting pains. Advanced stage: skin pale with bluish cast: pulse decreases, blistering, swelling, heat hemorrhages, and gangrene may follow.	1. Gradual warming by exposure to warm air. 2. DO NOT massage or moisten skin. 3. Protect affected parts from trauma. 4. Dry feet thoroughly: avoid walking. 5. Seek medical treatment.
;T BITE : 1	SUPERFICIAL: Redness, blisters in 24-36 hours and sloughing of the skin. DEEP: Preceded by superficial frostbite; skin is painless, pale-yellowish, waxy, "wooden" or solid to touch, blisters form in 12-36 hours	SUPERFICIAL: 1. Keep casualty warm; gently warm affected parts. 2. Decrease constricting clothing, increase exercise and insulation. DEEP: 1. Protect the part from additional injury. 2. Seek medical treatment as fast as possible.
V)NESS	Eyes may feel scratchy, watering, redness, headache, increased pain with exposure to light can occur.	1. Cover the eyes with a dark cloth. 2. Seek medical treatment.
'DRATION	Similar to heat exhaustion.	1. Keep warm, loosen clothes. 2. Replace lost fluids, rest, and additional medical treatment.
)THERMIA	Casualty is cold, uncontrolled shivering, until shivering stops, rectal (core)temp less 95 degrees F consciousness may be altered, uncoordinated movements may occur, shock and coma occur as body	MILD HYPOTHERMIA: 1. Warm body evenly and without delay. (Heat source must be provided.) 2. Keep dry, protect from elements. 3. Warm liquids may be given to conscious casualty only. 4. Be prepared to start CPR. 5. Seek medical treatment immediately.

		temperature drops.	SEVERE HYPOTHERMIA: 1. Quickly stabilize body temperature. 2. Attempt to prevent further heat loss. 3. Handle the casualty gently. 4. Evacuate to nearest medical treatment facility as soon as possible.

HEAT INJURIES			NOTE 2, 3
CRAMPS	Casualty experiences muscle cramps in arms, legs and/or stomach, may also have wet skin and extreme thirst.	1. Move the casualty to a shaded area and loosen clothing. 2. Allow casualty to drink 1 quart of cool water slowly per hour. 3. Monitor casualty and provide water as needed. 4. Seek medical attention if cramps persist.
AUSTION	Casualty experiences loss of appetite, headache, excessive sweating, weakness or faintness, dizziness, nausea, muscle cramps. The skin is moist, pale and clammy.	1. Move the casualty to a cool, shaded area and loosen clothing. 2. Pour water on casualty and fan to increase cooling effect of evaporation. 3. Provide at least one quart of water to replace lost fluids. 4. Elevate legs. 5. Seek medical aid if symptoms continue.
STROKE NSTROKE) 4	Casualty stops sweating (hot, dry skin), may experience headache, dizziness, nausea, vomiting, rapid pulse and respiration, seizures, mental confusion. Casualty may suddenly collapse and lose consciousness. THIS IS A MEDICAL EMERGENCY!	1. Move casualty to a cool, shaded area, loosen clothing, remove outer clothing if the situation permits. 2. Immerse in cool water. If cool bath is not available, massage arms and legs with cool water. Fan casualty to increase the cooling effect of evaporation. 3. If conscious, slowly consume one quart of water. 4. SEEK MEDICAL AID AND EVACUATE AS SOON AS POSSIBLE. Perform any lifesaving measures.

NOTE 1: DO NOT attempt to thaw deep frostbite. There is less danger of walking on feet while frozen than after they have thawed.
NOTE 2: The first aid procedure for heat related injuries caused by wearing individual protective equipment is to move the casualty to a clear area and give him water to drink.
NOTE 3: When in a chemical environment, DO NOT loosen or remove casualty's protective garments.
NOTE 4: Can be fatal if not treated promptly and quickly.

This space intentionally left blank for notes.

CHAPTER THIRTEEN
DEMOLITIONS

8-1. CHARACTERISTICS OF EXPLOSIVES. There are two categories of explosives, Low and High.

a. Low Explosives are characterized by having a detonating velocity up to 1300 feet per second, producing a pushing or shoving effect.

b. High Explosives are characterized by having a detonating velocity between 3,280 - 27,888 feet per second, producing a shattering effect.

8-2. INITIATION SYSTEMS. Demolition systems are primed utilizing Modernized Demolition Initiators (MDI). MDI consists of blasting caps attached to various lengths of time fuse or shock tube. These blasting caps, along with a fuse igniter and detonating cord, can be used to create numerous firing systems.

8-3. MDI COMPONENTS.

a. Shock tube.
  (1) Thin, plastic tube of extruded polymer with a layer of special explosive material on the interior surface.
  (2) Explosive material propagates a detonation wave which moves along the shock tube to a factory crimped and sealed blasting cap.
  (3) Detonation is normally contained within the plastic tubing. However, burns may occur if the shock tube is held.
  (4) Advantages of shock tube.
    (a) The shock tube offers the instantaneous action of electric initiation without the risk of accidental initiation caused by radio transmitters, static electricity, etc.
    (b) Extremely reliable.
    (c) May be extended using left over pieces from previous operations.

b. Blasting caps. Five MDI blasting caps are available which replace the M6 electric and M7 Non-electric blasting cap. Three of these are high-strength caps and two are low-strength.
  (1) High-strength blasting caps. Can be used to prime all standard military explosives (including detonating cord) or to initiate the shock tube of other MDI blasting caps.
    (a) M11.
      (1) Factory crimped to 30-foot length of shock tube.
      (2) A movable "J" hook is attached for quick and easy attachment to detonating cord.
      (3) A red flag is attached 1 meter from the blasting cap and a yellow flag 2 meters from the blasting cap.
    (b) M14.

(1) Factory crimped to 7 1/2 foot length of time fuse.
(2) May be initiated utilizing fuse igniter or match.
(3) Burn-time for total length is approximately five minutes.
(4) Yellow bands indicate calibrated one minute time intervals.

NOTE: Burn time will increase with altitude and colder temperatures.

(c) M15.
(1) Two blasting caps factory crimped to a 70 foot length of shock tube.
(2) Each blasting cap has delay elements to allow for staged detonations.

(2) Low-strength blasting caps. Used as a relay device to transmit a shock tube detonation impulse from an initiator to a high strength blasting cap. NOTE: Low strength blasting caps cannot reliably set off explosives. They should only be used to set off additional shock tubes.
(a) M12. Factory crimped to a 500 foot length of shock tube on a cardboard spool.
(b) M13. Factory crimped to a 1,000 foot length of shock tube.

c. M81 Fuse igniter. Used to ignite time blasting fuse or to initiate the shock tube of MDI blasting caps. NOTE: The M60 fuse igniter may still be used to ignite time blasting fuse. However, it will not reliably initiate the shock tube.

8-4. DETONATION SYSTEMS. There are two types of firing systems: MDI as a stand alone firing system and combination (MDI and detonating cord).

a. MDI Firing system (Stand Alone). An MDI firing system is one in which the initiation sets and transmission and branch lines are constructed using MDI components and the explosive charges are primed with MDI blasting caps. Construct the charge in the following manner.
(1) Emplace and secure explosive charge (C4, TNT, cratering charge, etc.) on target.
(2) Place a sandbag or other easily identifiable marker over the M11, M14, or M15 blasting cap to be used.
(3) Connect to an M12 or M13 transmission line if desired.
(4) Connect blasting cap with shock tube to an M14 cap with time fuse. Cut time blasting fuse to the desired delay time.
(5) Prime the explosive charge by inserting the blasting cap into the charge.
(6) Visually inspect firing system for possible misfire indicators.
(7) Return to the firing point and secure a fuse igniter to the cut end of the time fuse.
(8) Remove the safety cotter pin from the igniter's body.
(9) Actuate the charge by grasping the igniter body with one hand while sharply pulling the pull ring.

b. Combination (MDI and detonating cord) Firing system. Construct the charge utilizing the above steps for MDI stand alone system. Incorporate detonating cord branch lines into the system utilizing the "J" hooks of the M11 shock tube.

8-5. SAFETY CONSIDERATIONS.

a. MDI is not recommended for below ground use, except in quarry operations with water-gel or slurry explosives. Utilize detonating cord when it is necessary to bury primed charges.

b. Do not handle misfires downrange until the required 30 minute waiting period for both primary and secondary initiation systems has elapsed and other safety precautions have been accomplished.

c. Never yank or pull hard on the shock tube. This may actuate the blasting cap.

d. Do not dispose of used shock tubes by burning because of potentially toxic fumes given off from the burning plastic.

e. Do not use M1 dynamite with the M15 blasting cap. The M15 delay blasting cap should be used only with water-gel or slurry explosives.

8-6. DEMOLITION EFFECTS SIMULATOR (DES) Demolition Effects Simulators are a simple and cost effective way to conduct demolition training and rehearsals. DES charges can be constructed of materials immediately available through normal supply channels.

a. Materials.
  (1) Cardboard box (Not MRE box)
  (2) 1 roll 100mph Tape
  (3) Approx 2½ lbs 50/50 chalk/sand mix
  (4) Det Cord, approx 4ft
  (5) Cap, Blasting, M14
  (6) Fuse Igniter, M81

b. Construction.
  (1) Cut out the cardboard box utilizing the template below (figure 13-1).

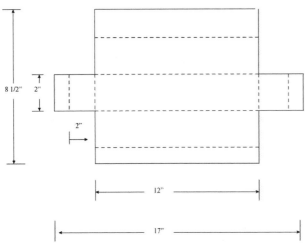

Figure 13-1. DES template

(2) Assemble the box by folding along creases. Tape the box to prevent it from unfolding.

(3) Fill half of the box with a 50/50 mix of chalk and sand. Ensure no rocks or other large objects are the sand mixture.

(4) Place a Uli knot in the box.

(5) Finish filling the box with the chalk and sand mixture.

(6) Make a small hole in the top flap. Thread the free end of the detonating cord through the hole at least 18 inches.

(7) Close the top flap and completely tape the outside with 100 mph tape.

(8) Prime charge utilizing desired amount of time fuse and M81 igniter.

CHAPTER FOURTEEN
RANGER URBAN OPERATIONS

14-1. GENERAL. Urban operations are defined as all military actions that are planned and conducted on terrain where man-made construction affects the tactical options available. Urban terrain is likely to be one of the most significant future areas of operations for American forces throughout the world. Expanding urban development affects military operations as the terrain is altered. The increasing focus on stability and support operations, urban terrorism, and civil disorder emphasizes that combat in urbanized areas is unavoidable. Urban areas are the power centers, the centers of gravity, and thus the future battlefield. References for further study are: FM 90-10-1, FM 90-10, FM 90-1, FM 7-8, 75th Ranger Regiment Advanced MOUT SOP, Ranger Training Circular 350-1-2.

14-2. TYPES OF URBAN OPERATIONS

(a) High-Intensity Conditions of Urban Combat. Infantry units must be trained to conduct urban combat under high-intensity conditions. High-intensity urban combat requires the employment of combat power of the joint combined arms team. An Infantry unit's mission is normally to recon, isolate, penetrate, systematically clear, defend the urban area, and engaging and defeating the enemy with decisive combat power. Although the changing world situation may have made urban combat under high-intensity conditions less likely for US forces, it represents the high end of the combat spectrum, and units must be trained for it. High-intensity urban operations can be casualty-intensive for both sides. With the integrated firepower of the joint, combined arms team, leaders must make every attempt to limit unnecessary destruction of critical infrastructure and casualties among noncombatants.

(b) Precision Conditions of Urban Combat. Infantry units train to defeat an enemy that is mixed with non-combatants in precision urban combat. Leaders plan to limit civilian casualties and collateral damage through the establishment of strict rules of engagement (ROE) and the employment of precision weapons and munitions. The ROE provides the focus for the use and restraint of combat power. The ROE may be significantly more restrictive than under high-intensity conditions.

(c) Surgical Conditions of Urban Combat. Operations conducted under surgical conditions include special-purpose raids, small precision strikes, or small-scale personnel seizure or recovery operations in an urban environment (for example, hostage rescue). Joint special operation forces usually conduct these operations. They may closely resemble US police operations performed by Special Weapons and Tactics (SWAT) teams. They may even involve cooperation between US forces and host nation police. Though regular units may not usually be involved in the actual surgical operation, they may support it by isolating the area, by providing security or crowd control, or providing search and rescue teams.

(d) Leaders must always be prepared to transition rapidly from one type of urban combat to another, and back. Lessons learned from combat demonstrate that urban operations can rapidly deteriorate with little or no forewarning to combatants. It is quite possible for a force involved in stability and support operations, to suddenly find themselves in a high-intensity combat situation.

14-3. PRINCIPLES OF MOUT.
(a) Surprise. Strike the enemy at a time or place or in a manner for which he is unprepared. **Key to success: gives the assaulting element the advantage.**
(b) Security. Never permit the enemy to acquire unexpected advantage.
    (1) Maintain during all phases of the operation.
    (2) Four-dimensional battlefield (height, depth, width, subterranean).
    (3) Always maintain 360 degree security (include elevated and subterranean areas).
    (4) Mission is never complete as long as you remain in the urban environment. The status of actors in the urban environment does not afford the sense of security offered by "open" terrain. The key to survivability is a constant state of situational awareness.
(c) Simplicity. Prepare clear, uncomplicated plans, and provide subordinates with concise orders to ensure thorough understanding.
    (1) Always keep plans simple.
    (2) Ensure everyone understands the mission and the commander's intent.
    (3) Plan and prepare for the worst.
(d) Speed. Rate of military action.
    (1) Acts as security.
    (2) Move in a careful hurry.
    (3) Smooth is fast and fast is smooth.
    (4) Never move faster than you can accurately engage targets.
    (5) Exercise tactical patience.
(e) Violence of Action. Eliminate the enemy with sudden, explosive force.
    (1) Combined with speed gives surprise.
    (2) Prevents enemy reaction.
    (3) Both physical and mental.

14-4. METT-TC CONSIDERATIONS. To effectively plan combat operations in urban environments, leaders must utilize Troop Leading Procedures and conduct a thorough analysis utilizing METT-TC factors. The following lists specific planning guidance that must be incorporated when planning for urban operations. For more specifics on mission planning, refer to Chapter 2, Ranger Handbook.

a. Mission: Know correct Task Organization to accomplish the mission (Offense, Defense, or Stability and Support Operations).

b. Enemy.
   (1) Disposition. Analyze the arrayal of enemy forces in and around your objective, known and suspected. Example: Known or suspected locations of minefields, obstacles, and strong points.
   (2) Composition and Strength. Analyze the enemy's task organization, troops available, suspected strength, and amount of support from local civilian populace based on intelligence estimates. Is the enemy a conventional or unconventional force?
   (3) Morale. Analyze the enemy's current operational status based on friendly intelligence estimates. Example: Is the enemy well supplied, have they had recent success against friendly forces, taken many casualties, current weather?
   (4) Capabilities. Determine what the enemy can employ against your forces. Example: Enemy's weapons, artillery assets, engineer assets, air defense assets, NBC threats, thermal/NVG capabilities, close air support, armor threat, etc.
   (5) Probable Course(s) of Action. Based on friendly intelligence estimates, determine how the enemy will fight within his area of operation (in and around your area of operation).

c. Terrain.
   (1) Leaders conduct a detailed terrain analysis of each urban setting, considering the types of built-up areas and composition of existing structures
   (2) Utilize OCOKA when analyzing terrain, in and around the area of operation.
      (a) Observation and Fields of Fire: Always be prepared to conduct urban operations under limited visibility conditions. This includes the effects of reduced illumination, as well as natural and manmade obscuration. Leaders should ensure that soldiers are equipped with adequate resources, which allow them to successfully operate in the urban environment under these types of conditions.
      (b) Cover and Concealment: Leaders must perform a thorough analysis of peripheral as well as intra-urban areas. Leaders should identify routes to objectives, which afford assault forces with the best possible cover and concealment. Additionally, leaders should take advantage of limited visibility conditions, which would allow for forces to move undetected to their final assault / breaching positions. When in the final assault position, forces should move as rapidly as tactically possible to access structures, which afford additional cover and concealment. Leaders must learn to properly employ obscurants and exercise "tactical patience" to fully take advantage of these effects. Finally, all members of the urban force must practice noise and light discipline. Soldiers must avoid unnecessary voice communications, learn the

proper use of white light, and limit contact with surfaces that may alert the enemy of their presence.

(c) Obstacles: There are many manmade and natural obstacles on the periphery, as well as within the urban environment. Leaders should conduct a detailed reconnaissance of routes and objectives (this must include subterranean complexes), taking into consideration route adjustments and special equipment needs.

(d) Key Terrain: Analyze which buildings, intersections, bridges, LZ/PZ, airports, and elevated areas that provide a tactical advantage to you or the enemy. Additionally, the leader must identify critical infrastructure within his area of operations, which would provide the enemy with a tactical advantage on the battlefield. These may include, but are not limited to, communication centers, medical facilities, governmental facilities, and facilities that are of psychological significance.

(e) Avenues of Approach: Consider roads, intersections, inland waterways, and subterranean constructions (subways, sewers, and basements). Leaders should classify areas as go, slow go, or no-go based on the navigability of the approach.

NOTE: Military maps may not provide enough detail for urban terrain analysis or reflect the underground sewer systems, subways, water systems, or mass transit routes.

(d) Troops: Analyze your forces utilizing their disposition, composition, strength, morale, capabilities, etc. Leaders must also consider the type and size of the objective to plan effective use of troops available.

(e) Time: Operations in an urban environment have a slower pace and tempo. Leaders must consider the amount of time required to secure, clear, or seize the urban objective and stress and fatigue soldiers will encounter. Additional time must also be allowed for area analysis efforts, these may include, but are not limited to:

- Maps and urban plans Recon and analysis
- Hydrological data analysis
- Line-of-sight surveys
- Long Range Surveillance and Scout reconnaissance

Similar to the conduct of other military operations, leaders need to designate time for rehearsals. Urban operations require a variety of individual, collective, and special tasks, which are not associated with operations on less complex terrain. These task require additional rehearsal time for clearing, breaching, obstacle reduction, casualty evacuation, and support teams. Additionally, rehearsal time must be identified for rehearsals with combined arms elements. These may include, but are not limited to:

- Artillery
- Armor
- Aviation
- Armor
- Engineers

(f) Civilians: Authorities such as the National Command will establish the Rules of Engagement. Commanders at all levels, may provide further guidance regarding civilians occupying the area of operations (AO). Leaders must daily reiterate the ROE to subordinates, and immediately inform them of any changes to the ROE. Rangers must have the discipline to identify the enemy from noncombatants and ensure civilians understand and follow all directed commands.

NOTE: Civilians may not speak English, may be hiding (especially small children), or dazed from a breach. Civilians must not be given the means to resist. Rehearse how clearing/search teams will react to these variables. Never compromise the safety of your Rangers.

14-5. CLOSE QUARTERS COMBAT (CQC).

a. Due to the very nature of a CQC encounter, engagements will be very close (within 10 meters) and very fast (targets exposed for only a few seconds). Most close quarter's engagements are won by who hits first and puts the enemy down. It is more important to knock a man down as soon as possible than it is to kill him. In order to win a close quarters engagement, Rangers must make quick, accurate shots by mere reflex. This is accomplished by reflexive fire training. Remember, no matter how proficient you are, always fire until the enemy goes down. All reflexive fire training is conducted with the eyes open.

Note: Research has determined, that on average, only three individuals out of ten actually fire their weapons when confronted by an enemy during room clearing operations. Close quarters combat success for the Ranger begins with the Ranger being psychologically prepared for the close quarter's battle. The foundation for this preparedness begins with the Ranger's proficiency in basic rifle marksmanship. Survival in the urban environment does not depend on advanced skills and technologies. Rangers must be proficient in the basics.

b. Stance. Feet are shoulder width apart, toes pointed straight to the front (direction of movement). The firing side foot is slightly staggered to the rear of the non-firing foot. Knees are slightly bent and the upper body leans slightly forward. Shoulders are not rolled or slouched. Weapon is held with the butt stock in the pocket of the shoulder. The firing side elbow is kept in against the body. The stance should be modified to ensure the Ranger maintains a comfortable boxer stance.

(1) Low Carry Technique. The butt stock of the weapon is placed in the pocket of the shoulder. The barrel is pointed down so the front sight post and day optic is just out of the field of vision. The head is always up identifying targets. This technique is safest and is recommended for use by the clearing team once inside the room.

(2) High Carry Technique. The butt stock of the weapon is held in the armpit. The barrel is pointed slighted up with the front sight post in the peripheral vision of the individual. Push out on the pistol grip and thrust the weapon forward and pull straight back into the pocket of the shoulder to assume the proper firing position. This technique is best suited for the line-up outside the door. Exercise caution with this technique always maintaining situational awareness, particularly in a multi-floored building.

NOTE: Muzzle awareness is critical to the successful execution of close quarter's operations. Rangers must never point their weapons or cross the bodies of their fellow Rangers at any time. Additionally Rangers should always avoid exposing the muzzle of their weapons around corners; this is referred to as "flagging".

c. Malfunction. If a Ranger has a malfunction with his weapon during any CQC training, he will take a knee to conduct immediate action. Once the malfunction is cleared there is no need to immediately stand up to engage targets. Rangers can save precious seconds by continuing to engage from one knee. Whenever other members of the team see a Ranger down, they must automatically clear his sector of fire. Before rising to his feet, the Ranger warns his team members of his movement and only rises after they acknowledge him. If a malfunction occurs once committed to a doorway, the Ranger must enter the room far enough to allow those following him to enter and move away from the door. This drill must be continually practiced until it is second nature.

d. Approaching the Building or Breach Point. One of the trademarks of ranger operations is the use of limited visibility conditions. Whenever possible, breaching and entry operations should be executed during hours and conditions of limited visibility. Rangers should always take advantage of all available cover and concealment when approaching breach and entry points. When natural or manmade cover and concealment is not available, Rangers should employ obscurants to conceal their approach. There are times when Rangers will want to employ obscurants to enhance existing cover and concealment. Members of the breach / entry team should be numbered for identification, communication, and control purposes.

(1) The number one man should always be the most experienced / mature member of the team, next to the team leader. The number one man is responsible for frontal and entry / breach point security.

(2) The number two man is directly behind the number one man in the order of movement and is normally responsible as an entry or clearing team member.

(3) The number three man is normally the team leader and is responsible for initiating all voice and physical commands. The team leader must exercise situational awareness at all time with respect to the task, friendly force, and enemy activity. One technique would be to use the number three man as the breach man. The breach man may employ one of the three breaching techniques, which are:
- Ballistic (Shotgun, Rifle, etc...)
- Mechanical (Hooligan Tool, Prybar, Sledge Hammer, etc...)
- Explosive (Door Knob Charge, Chain-link Ladder Charge, E-Silhouette Charge, etc...)

(4) The number four man is normally the automatic rifleman and is usually equipped with an M249 Squad Automatic Weapon. He is responsible for rear security and is normally the last man into the room and can respond with a tremendous amount of firepower, should the team leader require him to do so. Another technique is to utilize the number four man as the breach man.

e. Actions Outside the Point of Entry. Entry point position and individual weapon positions are important. The clearing team members should stand as close to the entry point as possible, ready to enter. Weapons are oriented in such a manner that the team provides itself with 360 degree security at all times. Team members must signal to one another that they are ready at the point of entry. This is best accomplished by sending up a "squeeze". If a tap method is used, an inadvertent bump may be misunderstood as a tap.

f. Actions Upon Entry. Non-lethal grenades can be used prior to entering any type of structure. If an enemy force is known to occupy a room, fragmentation grenades can be used if the walls and foundations are suitable. A fragmentation grenade has tremendous overpressure and missile hazard and may severely damage lightly constructed buildings. Team members must exercise fire control and discriminate between enemy and noncombatant targets. Rooms are never entered with less than two men. The #1 or #2 man may shout "Short Room" if the room is too small for the whole team.

g. Clearing the Entry Point. Team members must clear the point of entry to eliminate the enemy threat and allow remaining team members to move into the room. An entry point acts as a fatal funnel since it is the focal point for enemy weapon acquisition.

h. Clear the Room. Team members move away from the entry point and assume positions within the room where the threat can be best eliminated. Any threat is eliminated or neutralized as individual team members move to their points of domination, not once you get there. Never move faster than you can accurately engage targets.

(i) Four-Man Stack: example (Figures 14-5-1 through 14-5-9). To be effective, team members are numbered #1 through #4. The #1 man must act the quickest and make immediate decisions. The #1 Man enters the room eliminating the immediate threat and has the option of moving left or right, moving to one of two corners. His ability to move to a corner will be determined by obstacles, size of the room, and the enemy situation. As he enters through the entry point, he can visually check one of the corners and determine if there is an immediate threat. If there is a threat he moves to the threat, eliminating it as he moves to the corner. If no immediate threat exists in the first corner, he should consider "button-hooking" to the other corner to avoid being shot in the back. The #2 Man moves along the wall in the opposite direction of the #1 Man. Both the #1 and #2 Man clear the breach point, their immediate threat areas all while moving to their dominating corner in the room. The #3 Man goes the opposite direction of the #2 Man inside the room and at least one meter from the door. The #4 Man moves in the opposite direction of the #3 Man. All team members stop when they have cleared the door and have reached their point of domination within the room. NOTE: All team members must be prepared to perform the duties of all positions (#1-4) after initial room is cleared. All team members must be cross trained in each position.

NOTE: Room clearing procedures are techniques or SOPs and not doctrine. Rangers are encouraged to establish SOPs when they get to their units. However, SOPs for the urban environment need to be well thought out, and may not fit all conditions that the force may encounter. For example, ROE will impact the munitions employed and techniques utilized during urban clearing operations.

(j) Sectors of Fire. The number one man enters and goes left or right based on immediate threat location. The number two man goes the opposite direction of the number one man and engages all targets of opportunity in his sector. These actions normally result in the room being "divided" in half and 100% of the room being scanned except for the upper levels. The number three man enters, clears the fatal funnel to the left or the right, and primarily scans overhead areas. The number four man enters and goes opposite the number three man and continues to provide rear security as the situation dictates.

(k) Locking Down the Room.
   (1) Control the situation within the room.
   (2) Use clear, concise arm and had signals. Voice commands should be kept to a minimum to reduce the amount of confusion and to prevent the enemy (which may be in the next room) from discerning what is going on. This enhances the opportunity for surprise and allows the assault force the opportunity to detect any approaching force.
   (3) Physically and psychologically dominate.
   (4) Establish security / report status.
   (5) Cursory search of the room to include the ceiling (3 Dimensional Fight).

(6) Identify the dead using reflexive response techniques (Eye thump method).
(7) Search the room for PIR, precious cargo as per the mission and time available.
(8) Evacuate personnel.
(9) Mark room clear (chemlights, engineer tape, chalk, paint, VS-17 panels, etc.).

This space intentionally left blank for notes.

SINGLE TEAM CENTER-FED ROOM
Figures 14-5-1a - d

Figure 14-5-1a, #1 Man

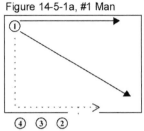

STEP 1: Visually clear immediate threat, if no threat, buttonhook.
STEP 2: Visually clear far corner before arriving at corner.
Note: The #1 man makes a decision on which way to go based on enemy, obstacles, and his intuition.

Figure 14-5-1b, #2 Man

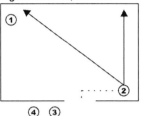

STEP 1: #2 man goes opposite #1 man.
STEP 2: Visually clear near corner, clearing to the left. Clear far corner before arriving at near corner. (Point of Domination)
STEP 3: Move to point of domination, clearing to the left. Sector is one meter off the #1 man.

Figure 14-5-1c, #3 Man

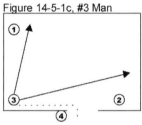

STEP 1: #3 man clears the immediate threat, moves opposite #2 man, clears doorway, and stops at his point of domination.

Figure 14-5-1d, #4 Man

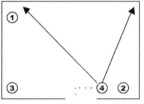

STEP 1: #4 man clears immediate threat, moves opposite #3 man, stops at his point of Domination.

SINGLE TEAM CORNER-FED ROOM
Figures 14-5-2a-d

Figure 14-5-2a, #1 Man

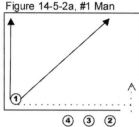

STEP 1: Visually clear immediate threat and right corner, no threat, buttonhook.

STEP 2: Visually clear left corner.

Visually clear far corner before arriving at corner.
Note: The #1 man makes a decision on which way to go based on enemy, obstacles, and his intuition.

Figure 14-5-2b, #2 Man

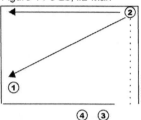

STEP 1: #2 man goes opposite #1 man.

STEP 2: Visually clears near corner, clearing to the left. Clears far corner before arriving at near corner. (Point of Domination)

STEP 3: Move to Point of Domination, clearing to the left. Sector is one meter off the #1 man.

Figure 14-5-2c, #3 Man

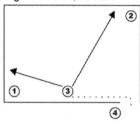

STEP 1: #3 man clears the immediate threat, moves opposite #2 man, clears doorway, and stops at his point of domination.

Figure 14-5-2d, #4 Man

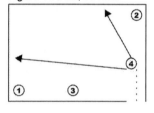

STEP 1: #4 man clears immediate threat, moves opposite #3 man, stops at his point of Domination.

14-11

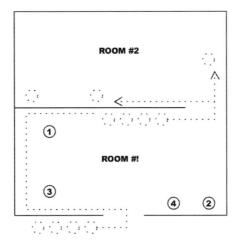

Figure 14-5-3

STEP 1: First team enters and clears Room #1.
STEP 2: Squad Leader determines direction the second clearing team must enter Room #1 based on location of Room #2 entry point.
STEP 3: First team collapses inward to allow the second team to move into the room.
STEP 4: Second team "stacks left" and prepares to enter Room #2.

OPEN STAIRWELL

Open Stairwell: Gap between flights of stairs that allows a person to visibly look up / down between flights of stairs. Figure 14-5-4 depicts an open stairwell.

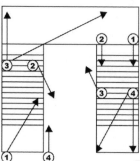 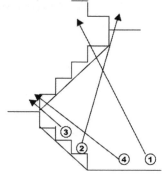

Figure 14-5-4

STEP 1: The #1 man pulls security on the highest point he can see / engage.

STEP 2: The #2 man moves up the stairs on the inside with the #3 man to a point that he can see / engage the next landing, where he turns around and continues to move up to the next landing.

STEP 3: The #3 man moves up the stairs with the #2 man on the outside and engages the threat on the immediate landing.

STEP 4: The #4 man moves up the stairs with the #1 man, on the squeeze, the #2 man turns around to engage the next landing.

STEP 5: The flow continues with the #2 man picking up the sector of the #1 man had. The #3 man picks up where the #2 man was. The #4 man picks up where the #3 man was. The #1 man picks up where the #4 man was.

NOTE: Most stairwells will require a second team.

CLOSED STAIRWELL

Closed Stairwell: Any Stairwell separated by walls between flights of stairs.
Figure 14-5-5 depicts a closed stairwell.

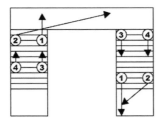

Figure 14-5-5

STEP 1: The #1 man checks high to insure there is no opening on the landing or between the stairs.
STEP 2: The #2 man pulls long security to the next bend or landing.
STEP 3: The #1 man or #3 man with the #2 man move up the steps. As they approach the corner the #2 man will tap the #1 man on the shoulder signaling that he is with him.
STEP 4: Keying off the #1 man's movement, they will both simultaneously break around the corner.
STEP 5: If no fire is received #2 man will move to the opposite wall and continue to move up until they reach their objective.
STEP 6: The #3 and #4 men will continue to move 3 to 4 steps behind.
NOTE: Do not get locked into security position. (e.g. Inside stairwell)
Do not get spread out thin or separated by more than one floor of stairs.

HALLWAY MOVEMENT

Hallway Movement: Clearing team(s) move down the hallway utilizing the frontal security (cross cover technique). See Figure 14-5-6.

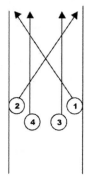
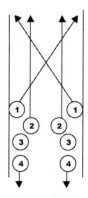

Single Team Hallway Movement   Multiple Team Hallway Movement

Figure 14-5-6

T-Shape Intersection

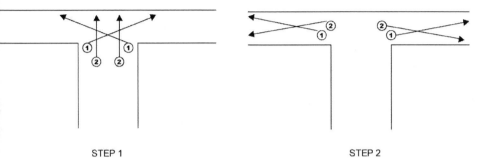

STEP 1   STEP 2

Figure 14-5-7

STEP 1: Each #1 man goes to a knee covering his sector.
STEP 2: On a predetermined signal each two man team
will break the corner picking up their sectors of fire.
NOTE: This technique can incorporate the Dynamic Corner Clear.

14-16

Dynamic Corner

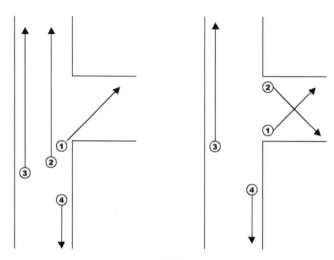

Figure 14-5-8

STEP 1: The #1 and #2 man as they approach the corner they have to clear do not slow down.
STEP 2: The #2 man will tap the #1 man on the shoulder about 2 - 3 meters away from the corner letting the #1 man know the #2 man is with him.
STEP 3: Keying off the #1 man's movement they both break the corner simultaneously.
STEP 4: The #1 man goes to low to a knee, the #2 man stays high.
STEP 5: If the Rangers are not receiving fire the #2 man rabbits / moves to the far side.
STEP 5: The #1 and #2 man take up sectors of fire.
STEP 6: The #3 and #4 man take long security in the direction of movement.

Three Way Intersection

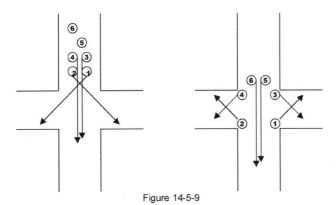

Figure 14-5-9

STEP 1: The #1- 4 men will use one of the corner clearing techniques to clear the corner that they have.
STEP 2: The #5 and #6 man move through the intersection and enter the room as the #1 and #2 man or
 pick cross coverage if they are entering more hallway.
STEP 3: The #3 and #4 man will then follow into the stack as a four man team, or they will become the rear
flank security if entering more hallway.
STEP 4: The #1 and #2 man will provide security where needed unless they are needed in the room.
 If entering more hallway the #1 man will become center ling security and the #2 man will become rear or floater.

14-6. GENERAL. Understanding how to employ and incorporate breaching as part of a leader's planning process is an important part of urban operations. It is imperative that elements of your patrol be skilled in the art of breaching. Whether infiltrating or exfiltrating from an objective, leaders must plan for either option. One constant disadvantage with the employment of explosives is that placement requires soldiers to expose themselves to possible enemy fires. Breach teams need to be supported by fires or obscurants and breaching operations should be performed during hours of limited visibility whenever possible.

14-7. CLASSIFICATIONS OF BREACHING

a. Mechanical. Mechanical Breaching should be an important part of a leader's breaching training program because it is almost always an option. Mechanical Breaching is best described as gaining access by the use of tools or saws. Although most tools and saws used are recognizable and self explanatory to the individual Ranger, one must practice on various techniques to increase speed an effectiveness. This reduces fatigue and expedites the actual assault.
   (1) Mechanical Breaching Tools.
      (a) Hooligan Tools (Doors/windows of all types).
      (b) Sledge Hammer (Heavy Duty Doors, Locks, and Window Frames).
      (c) Picket Pounder (Doors of all types, Light Walls).
      (d) Bolt Cutters (Chain Link Fence, Locks, and Wire Obstacles).
      (e) Pick Ax (Lightweight Doors and Locks).
      (f) Saws (Fences, Light Doors, Locks).

b. Ballistic. Ballistic Breaching is defined as a forced entry or exit by the use of weapons. Whether using shotguns, M16A2/M4, M249 SAW, specific considerations must be addressed.
   (1) Ballistic Breaching Considerations.
      (a) Type of round and ricochet factor.
      (b) Composition of the breaching point.
      (c) Composition of the floor beyond the door.
      (d) Personnel behind the door (Friendly/Enemy).
      (e) Always shoot at a 45 degree angle.

c. Explosive. Explosive Breaching is the most viable because it is the most effective. When employing explosives during breaching operations, leaders must consider three major factors.

   (1) Overpressure. The amount of PSI released from the concussion of the blast.

   (2) Missile Hazard. Fragmentation or projectiles sent at tremendous speed from the explosion area. This occurs from either the charge or target being breached.

   (3) Minimum safe distance requirements (MSDs). Use of explosives in the urban environment must consider the presence of noncombatants and friendly forces. Additionally, the are many hazardous materials located in the urban environment, these may include chemicals as well as construction materials. There is always a risk of secondary explosions and fires, when employing explosive breaching techniques.

   (4) Charges. Various charges can be utilized for explosive breaching. Leaders must conduct extensive training on the use of the charges to get proper target feedback. Listed are examples of charges used for explosive breaching.

      (a) Water Impulse (Steel/Wood Doors).

      (b) Flexible Linear (Wood Doors).

      (c) Ranger Wall Breach (Masonry/Brick Walls)

      (d) Chain Link Ladder (Chain Link Fence)

      (e) E-Type Silhouette (Wood Doors)

      (f) Brashier Breacher (Concertina Wire)

Charge	Obstacle	Explosives Needed	Advantages	Disadvantages
Flexible Linear Charge	Wooden Doors, cuts door lengthwise	Detonation Cord	- Small, lightweight - Quick to place on target - Several can be carried by one man - Will defeat most doors regardless of locking system	
Charge	Obstacle	Explosives Needed	Advantages	Disadvantages

Chain-link ladder charge	Rapidly creates hole in chain-link fence large enough to run through	C-4; Detaprime Booster; Detonation Cord	- Quick - Effective	
Wall Breach Charge	Breaches through wood, Masonry, or Brick Walls	C-4; Detaprime Booster; Detonation Cord	- Easy and quick to make - Quick to place on target	- Will cause shrapnel - Does not destroy rebar - High over-pressure
Brashier Breech Charge	Creates hole in triple-standard concertina wire and chain-link fence large enough to drive a vehicle through	C-4; Detaprime Booster; Detonation Cord	- Easy to make - Easy to emplace	- Only 50% chance of completely cutting reinforced triple strand wire
Water Impulse Charge	Opens light metal doors and wooden doors	Detaprime Booster; Detonation Cord	- Easily constructed - Low fragmentation if prop stick is Not used	- Missile hazard if prop stick is used - Attachment method is to be carefully considered - Likely that liquids could spill or leak during transportation

Made in the USA
Middletown, DE
06 August 2020